ACCLAIM FOR SHANE READ'S TEXTBOOKS

Shane Read has tried over 100 trials to verdict and also teaches highly acclaimed litigation courses throughout the United States. *Turning Points at Trial* is an award-winning and bestselling textbook, and the bestselling *Winning at Deposition* won the highest award from the Association of Continuing Legal Education for a legal textbook. He is the only author to win this prestigious award twice.

In Read's latest textbook, *Winning at Persuasion*, he brings you innovative strategies and skills to use at your next hearing or trial.

WINNING AT PERSUASION

"Shane Read got it right with this book. I love the combination of legal theory and the psychology of trial. If you follow Shane's advice, he can turn you into a great trial lawyer. Shane does a masterful job analyzing what Mark Lanier does in his trials to get such astounding verdicts. This book is loaded with great ideas that will help you improve your presentation before a jury."

—Lisa Blue, Past President, The National Trial Lawyers and American Association of Justice, and National Trial Lawyer Hall of Fame Inductee (2015).

"The late Jacob Fuchsberg, one of our greatest trial lawyers, agreed that only the few may be born orators, but he also believed that the many can become artisans of the craft if they think of Carnegie Hall and practice, practice, practice. Shane Read's masterful art and science of public speaking, whatever your age and experience, will change your practice and your life. We can all be excellent closing argument trial lawyers if we follow his wonderful scholarship, discipline and insights. We can become and continue to be our own Aristotle, Lincoln, Churchill, Mark Lanier, and Allyson Ho. When preparing your argument, listen to Dolly Parton sing "Mama's Coat of Many Colors" (or something else equally inspiring), review your notes from Shane, and get to work. So guided, fear or no fear, writer's cramp or free flow, it will come."

—Edward J. Nevin, Past President, American Board of Trial Advocates

"My search for a single book that distills and synthesizes the very best wisdom on persuasion is finally over. Shane Read loads up *Winning at Persuasion* with invaluable insights and guidance. Here in one volume is a clear, concise set of principles and examples that will enable and empower any lawyer to become a master at persuasion."

—Quentin Brogdon, President, Texas Trial Lawyers Association

"In this highly accessible book, Read masterfully explains everything you need to know about how to persuade at hearings and trials. What a great compilation of the research, distilled to a concise step by step guide. We have all struggled in court, and this great read provides the key to success. Everything is covered. In addition, Read interviews the best trial and appellate lawyers to get their insights and share with you analyses of their greatest wins."

—Tracy Walters McCormack, Director of Advocacy at
The University of Texas School of Law

"Shane Read focuses not only on the external, physical mechanics of persuasion, but also on the psychological, inner game of persuasion—reminding us to take the time to be creative and yet focus on the end game as we capture the audience through compelling stories. *Winning At Persuasion* should be a staple in the library of every trial lawyer— novice and experienced alike."

—Jennifer H. Doan, President, The Texas Chapters of the
American Board of Trial Advocates (2022)

WINNING AT CROSS-EXAMINATION

"As Shakespeare said, 'If you can't run with the big dogs, stay on the porch.' Not only does Read's *Winning at Cross-Examination* give you the tips you need to run with the pack, he gives you real life examples of cross-examinations by the big dogs."

—Dicky Grigg, Past President, International Academy of Trial Lawyers

"Shane Read has done it again. Building on his model of teaching through great examples, he as has assembled the perfect 'how to' guide."

—Tracy W. McCormack, Director of Advocacy,
The University of Texas School of Law

"*Winning at Cross-Examination* is so full of so many wonderful things that it is almost impossible to do justice to it with simple descriptions. It should be an indispensable resource for young, aspiring trial lawyers, but trial lawyers of any age or experience would do well to refer to it regularly to achieve more focused and meaningful cross-examinations."

—Lewis Sifford, Past President, American Board of Trial Advocates

TURNING POINTS AT TRIAL

"Required reading for trial lawyers, but also exceptionally informative for anyone interested in legal proceedings."

—*Kirkus Reviews*

"*Turning Points at Trial* showcases the work of outstanding trial attorneys using a combination of description, commentary, and transcripts. Through this layered approach, the author has created a superb modeling exemplar and how-to resource for trial and appellate attorneys of all experience levels."

—*The Colorado Lawyer*

"In *Turning Points at Trial*, a chamber of trial advocacy secrets and strategies is revealed. Read's mastery of writing in the narrative softens the edges to these academic and complex topics through storytelling, illustrative cases, and transcript excerpts. Great trial attorneys are masterful oral storytellers. Read does the same here, just on paper."

—*The Texas Bar Journal*

"*Turning Points at Trial* is a keeper. . . . This book is like going to an advanced seminar on litigation and listening to a prominent lawyer giving a presentation on a particular subject."

—*The Wisconsin Lawyer*

WINNING AT DEPOSITION

Winner of the Association of Continuing Legal Education's highest honor for a legal textbook.

"The book is a triumph.... [I]t makes for gripping reading, made all the better by Read's focus on the missteps of the famous lawyers and litigants he studies."

— *The Vermont Bar Journal*

"No matter how many depositions you have taken or defended, or how good you think you are, Shane Read's *Winning at Deposition* is a must read. It is the most informative and entertaining 'how to do it' book for trial lawyers I can ever remember reading."

— Robert G. Begam, Past President,
Association of Trial Lawyers of America (ATLA)

"*Winning at Deposition* is a cutting-edge litigation masterpiece."

— Jean Hoefer Toal, Chief Justice, Supreme Court of South Carolina

ACCLAIM FOR SHANE READ'S
UNIQUE TRAINING COURSES FOR LITIGATORS

"Shane Read's *Winning at Deposition: Skills and Strategy* seminar is one of UT Law's top-rated CLE programs. It sold out three weeks before the program date and attracted both beginning and experienced lawyers. Many of them told me afterwards how impressed they were with Read's passion for teaching and willingness to share his innovative deposition strategies. He is an extraordinary speaker."

— Gregory J. Smith, Assistant Dean for CLE,
The University of Texas School of Law

"Shane Read is always our keynote speaker. He is dynamic, well-organized and thought provoking."

—Paul Enriquez, Program Director, NITA Southern Region Trial Skills Program

"Shane Read is an immensely skilled teacher and storyteller. With visual examples, he takes an everyday action, such as swinging a bat, and turns it into a common-sense lesson for achieving success in the courtroom. He has studied hours of video from famous trials and has pulled from them valuable 'do's and don'ts' that help his audiences perfect their own personal strategies during trial."

—Stacey Thomas, Program Manager, Pennsylvania Bar Institute

"Shane is one of the highest-rated presenters in our seminar evaluation forms—ever—and we were surprised that attendees continued to offer their feedback even months after the program."

—Barbara Moddes, Program Planner, State Bar of Wisconsin

STAY CONNECTED

SIGN UP FOR SHANE READ'S FREE LITIGATION TIPS E-NEWSLETTER

Would you like to get invaluable tips on discovery, depositions and trials? Sign up for Shane Read's *Litigation Tips* Email newsletter at www.shaneread.com. Twice a month, you will receive practical insights that you can use to immediately improve your practice.

SUBMIT A REVIEW ON AMAZON.COM

Your praise of *Winning at Persuasion* will help other lawyers discover this book. It only takes a minute to write two to three sentences about why you like this book. You can find the link to write a review at the bottom of the book's product page on Amazon.

Customer Reviews

★★★★★ 38
4.8 out of 5 stars ▾

5 star		87%
4 star		10%
3 star		3%
2 star		0%
1 star		0%

See all 38 customer reviews ›

Share your thoughts with other customers

Write a customer review

WINNING AT PERSUASION FOR LAWYERS

The Art and Science of Public Speaking at Hearings and Trials

SHANE READ

This book is sold with the understanding that neither the author nor the publisher is engaged in rendering legal advice. Every effort has been made to make this book as accurate as possible. However, there may be mistakes, both typographical and in content. Therefore, this text should be used only as a general guide and not as the ultimate source of public speaking in court. Readers are responsible for obtaining such advice from their own legal counsel.

The purpose of this book is to educate and entertain. Any forms and agreements herein are intended for educational and informational purposes only. The author and publisher shall have neither liability nor responsibility to any person or entity with respect to any loss or damage caused, or alleged to have been caused, directly or indirectly, by the information contained in this book.

The views expressed in this book are solely those of the author and do not necessarily reflect the views of the Department of Justice.

Cover design by George Foster
Interior design by Kevin Mellen

Library of Congress Cataloging-in-Publication Data

Read, Shane
   Winning at Persuasion for Lawyers: The Art and Science of Public Speaking at Hearings and Trials / Shane Read
      p. cm.
   ISBN: 978-0-9850271-6-2

   1. Trials— United States. 1. Read, Shane. II. Title

KF8900.R44 2022

Discounts are available for bulk orders.
   Westway Publishing
   4516 Lovers Lane, Suite 182
   Dallas, TX 75225
   support@westwaypublishing.com
   (888) 992-9782

Shane Read is available for one-on-one consultation, training and continuing legal education programs for organizations and law firms. For more information, go to www.shaneread.com or contact him at shane@shaneread.com.

For Linda

CONTENTS

PART TWO
How to Deliver Your Presentation

PART THREE

How the Masters Persuade

FOREWORD

For 45 years, I have sought to learn how to persuade and argue effectively. Beginning in high school forensics, continuing through college debate, preaching in pulpits, participating in law school moot court, and trying hundreds of cases, I have always been captivated with studying the science, the art, and even the craft of persuasion. My studying took me into the logical fields of communication studies, but I also mined the fields of art, marketing, neuroscience and memory, behavioral psychology, sales, and more. I wanted (and still seek) to know all I could to aid me in communication.

I had no one place to turn, and there was no one integrating the disciplines for me. Then one day, I was met during the break of one of my cases by this fellow who introduced himself as Shane Read. He told me he was a lawyer with a passion for writing books educating others about trying cases. He wanted to talk about some things I was doing in court, why I was doing them, and how I came about the process.

Shane was an intent listener, but an even more focused observant. He had seen things I was doing, things I thought were too subtle for anyone to pick up on, and he had latched onto them. His curiosity made that of the proverbial cat seem mild in comparison. Over time, which is a rare commodity in the throes of a trial, Shane and I had many dialogues. At some point, I recommended that he attend one of my training seminars. It was in those that I explained in much greater detail the whys and hows of my work.

Over the years, Shane has produced works of art on his own. He has taken things he picked up from a number of lawyers, studied them, and put them into very readable, concise, and logical books, digestible for anyone. This book can be added to that list.

Whether he is taking on the implications that the last few decades brought us into the thinking process and mental shortcuts (a lá Thaler and Sunstein's *Nudge* and Kahneman's *Thinking Fast and Slow*) or delving into the ancient contributions of Aristotle's Rhetoric, Shane has put together a veritable compendium of proven ideas and concepts to aid the pursuit of persuasion.

These ideas work for persuasion in any field, not only law. I use them in the pulpit to preach. I use them in schools to teach. I even use them at home to learn! "Science" rightly belongs in the subtitle of Shane's latest book. He is bringing science into the world of persuasion in a form that is easy for all to grasp.

So read this book, put it to use, and let's make the world a better place!

—*Mark Lanier*

INTRODUCTION

The genesis of this book started with a book club I was leading that was studying books on persuasion and public speaking. As we were a half year into the meetings, two of the lawyers said that they wished there was just one book that contained all they needed to know. I empathized. The problem is that there are many different components to public speaking—from storytelling to gestures to effective PowerPoint slides—and I have not found one book that covers them all effectively. Also, the books on these individual topics have so many different viewpoints that it becomes frustrating trying to figure out a set of principles to follow.

With this book, I hope to solve the problem for you that I could not solve for my book club. If you have read my other books, you know that I believe in the Rule of Three, the idea that you will have the most success if you try to persuade your judge or jury with only three points. Consequently, this book is divided into three parts. Part I, "How to Persuade," teaches the principles of public speaking, how to tell a story, and explains insights from brain science that you can use in your next presentation to be your best. But most important, Part I starts with what most textbooks fail to candidly address: how to overcome the fear of public speaking.

Part II teaches how to deliver your presentation. You will learn tips from memory experts so that you will never have to use notes again when you speak. You will also learn through examples how to gesture persuasively and naturally. Finally, you'll learn how to practice your presentation efficiently and effectively.

Part III examines how the masters, both old and new, have used public speaking skills to achieve greatness in trials, oral argument, and beyond. By examining the masters, you will realize that the principles set forth in this book worked for them and that they will immediately work for you.

I also hope that I can provide a unique perspective. The two most important lessons from this book are that you need to be true to yourself and speak from the heart to persuade. To do that, you have to face your fear of public speaking, learn how to overcome it, then show your sincerity to your audience and persuade them. My unique perspective comes not only from trying over a hundred cases and teaching trial advocacy for 20 years, but also from a love of tennis that I played at the collegiate level and a love of singing and playing instruments. What I have learned from these interests is that to succeed, you have to overcome your fear of failure and connect emotionally with your audience. Obviously, tennis did not require me to connect with an audience, but it sure taught me lessons about fear and failure.

You will find that I emphasize throughout the book that you cannot become a great communicator if you try to mimic someone else, because your lack of authenticity will lead to a lack of sincerity and a failure to communicate with and persuade the audience. You have to find your own voice from within, not by copying someone else. Through the principles, suggestions, and examples that follow, you will be able to tap the greatness that is already within you and reach your fullest potential.

I believe in less is more, so, I am not going to write a needlessly long introduction. Let's get started with the first step on our journey together in chapter 1, overcoming your fear of public speaking.

PART I

How to Persuade

In this section, you will learn the principles of public speaking, how to tell a story, and gain insights into the brain science behind how an audience makes decisions about what you say. But most importantly, this section starts with what most textbooks fail to candidly address: how to overcome the fear of public speaking.

CHAPTER ONE

Overcoming the Fear of Public Speaking

"There are two types of speakers in the world: those that are nervous and those that are liars." —*Mark Twain*

1.1 MY PUBLIC SPEAKING FEARS

The quote above by Mark Twain should give great comfort to everyone, and truer words have never been spoken. However, very few public speakers will admit they are true. As a result, when we get nervous before we speak—rather than calm and confident, like everyone else appears to be—we think of it as a personal failing. Whatever your fears are, I feel it is essential that I start this book by confronting the elephant in the room head on, because I believe you cannot fix a problem unless you admit that it exists, and many people won't. One of the most popular college textbooks for public speaking courses does not even list the word fear in its index and pays only a passing reference to being nervous in its 500-page text.

My belief is based not only on my feelings and experience teaching others, but also on what national polling reveals. Gallup regularly polls Americans to list their top fears. Consistently, people's number one fear is public speaking. That fear is often listed ahead of snakes, cancer, and even death. When you think about it, there is no reason it should be listed above death. But maybe the rationale is that while death cannot be avoided, public speaking can. When the comedian Jerry Seinfeld heard about the poll's results, he quipped, "This means to the average person, if you go to a funeral, you're better off in the casket than doing the eulogy."

I want to share with you the fears I had before my first trial, for two reasons. First, if you are scared of your first hearing or trial, I want you to know that those feelings are normal. Second, by following the tips in this book, you can

> **CHAPTER ROAD MAP**
> - You are not alone. Realize that almost everyone is scared of public speaking.
> - Focus on the process of how to win your trial or hearing, not the end result of winning.
> - Learn 10 steps to conquer your fear of public speaking and failure.

avoid the very tortured path I went through to become a calm and confident public speaker.

Before my first trial, my emotions swung like a pendulum between "I've got this" and "I'm going to completely fail." Unfortunately, the pendulum spent almost the entire time on the negative side. While it was there, my confidence got sabotaged by both my mind and my body. On the day of the trial, this assault revved into full gear as soon as I walked into the courtroom. I am not sure why, but something about opening the heavy doors of the courtroom and stepping inside such a formal place triggered an involuntary physical and psychological reaction within me. I felt like I was entering a place of no return, where jurors' expectations of me as a lawyer were high and my performance would be scrutinized.

First, I felt my leg muscles tighten as I walked into the courtroom. Then, I felt my chest constrict just a little as I walked up to the courtroom deputy, introduced myself, and asked her the order of the cases being called that day. I had hoped that mine wouldn't be first so that I would have more time to collect my thoughts.

After my case was called, I sat at the counsel table and tried to casually look over my shoulders to sneak a peek at who was in the courtroom that might be watching my trial. I'd rather succeed or fail when no one was watching. My breathing got shallower, my stomach tightened a little, my mouth got dry, and it was much harder to listen as the judge spoke because I'd become anxious. I forced myself to listen better, but it was no use. I started to slouch a little in my chair, hoping that the anxiety would all go away, but then I forced myself to have good posture, which, unfortunately, only stiffened my muscles even more. I would have really liked to have been able to get up and walk around to release this nervous energy, but that was not allowed.

Oh, and worst of all, I had a fear that I would forget what I had prepared to say. I went to a dark place in my mind, one which is filled with panic and that I don't like visiting. I hated realizing that this weakness existed in me. I literally feared to hear the sound of my own name, "Mr. Read," because that meant the judge had spoken it and was expecting me to stand up and be persuasive.

That trial was a long time ago, and fortunately, through a lot of research and trial and error that culminated in the writing of this book, I no longer have those overwhelmingly intense experiences and actually love being in a courtroom. That said, the honest truth is that after 30 years of being in a courtroom, I still get nervous before a hearing or trial. Unfortunately, as Mark Twain remarked above, unless you are an outlier, you can't be a public speaker and not be nervous. However, there is a very big difference now. The pendulum of emotions that I mentioned earlier spends most of the time on the side of "I've got this!" I have a deep confidence that I will push through the door of nerves and get to the other side where I can really enjoy giving my presentation. So, when I get a dry mouth and my breathing becomes shallow, and I'm afraid that I will forget what I want to say, I have full confidence that the fears will pass. Frankly, I would be worried if I did not get nervous because it would mean that I didn't care.

Now, I know that as soon as I stand up, the nerves will quickly dissipate, as if they never existed. On the occasions when they don't, I realize that they are manageable. In either situation, when I speak I am confident and very excited that I get to present what I have prepared and connect emotionally with a judge or jury in a setting that few have the privilege to be in.

One final thing I want to confess to here is that I am an introvert and I hate—absolutely hate—being the center of attention. This contrasts sharply with my burning desire to be a trial lawyer because I love the battle of persuasion and pursuit of justice that takes place in a courtroom. I desperately want to be a part of the competition. The reward of a jury verdict after a hard fought trial or a court's ruling after an intense hearing gives me an exhilarating feeling that is hard to duplicate. The point is, being an introvert, I have had some unique challenges to overcome when being a public speaker.

You may have less anxiety or more anxiety than I have, but the truth is, we are part of the majority that Mark Twain spoke about in the quote that started this chapter. For those of you who are blessed with an ability to enjoy hearing yourselves talk and do not get nervous when speaking in public, you get a pass on this chapter. You have our envy. For the rest of you, keep reading. There is peace ahead.

1.2 WHY LAWYERS ARE AFRAID OF PUBLIC SPEAKING

The Fight-or-Flight Response

The driving force behind our fear of public speaking is the "fight-or-flight" response. It is a survival mechanism of the human brain and body that can be very useful, but it is also horrible for public speaking. It developed early in human existence as a means for people to react very quickly when they found themselves in dangerous situations, such as during an attack from animals or other humans. It triggers an almost instantaneous reaction—both physiological and psychological—to overcome these dangers by either fighting or fleeing, depending on the circumstances. This response is rarely needed in the present day now that physical dangers are much less common. However, it can still help you get out of the way of a suddenly fast-approaching car when you are crossing a street.

Without going into all the scientific details, here is generally how the fight-or-flight response works. When someone perceives a dangerous situation, the brain sends out a distress signal. The sympathetic nervous system takes over and adrenaline is produced, which increases the heart rate and blood pressure, and prioritizes blood flow and energy for the big muscles at the expense of the extremities and deliberative thinking. There is now a near instantaneous burst of energy available throughout the body to respond to the danger. When an oncoming car is barreling towards you, your brain will automatically make the decision for you to get out of the way, and your body uses adrenaline (a hormone produced by the adrenal gland, which is located on the top of each of your kidneys) to help you immediately get out of the way.

As it relates to public speaking, this fight-or-flight response can also be triggered by being in a stressful situation or being in a situation where people focus their eyes on you, both of which occur in public speaking. This trigger was very helpful in our early evolution, such as when a stranger's or animal's unwelcome gaze signaled an impending physical attack, but it is not helpful when you are a public speaker in a courtroom. In addition, the fight-or-flight response can be triggered just by thinking about a stressful situation, whether it be a job interview or an upcoming court appearance. Since we cannot fight or run away, we need to control the physiological response (see sections below). This chapter will explain how to overcome your fears of public speaking and the stress and anxiety associated with it.

> *Fear paralyses you—fear of flying, fear of the future, fear of leaving a rubbish marriage, fear of public speaking, or whatever it is.*
> —Annie Lennox

The Fear of Failure

There are two additional reasons for why lawyers are scared of public speaking. The first is the fear of failure. Lawyers, in particular, are expected to be eloquent in the courtroom. We went to law school so that we could argue before judges and juries, but now that the moment has arrived, we are scared that we won't live up to the expectations—be they the judge's, the jury's, our client's, or our own. The second reason is the fear that we don't have the skills to succeed, and it is a fear that stems from either the makeup of our personality or a lack of public speaking skills. In addition, the courtroom is a very formal place. Next to a place of worship, it is the most formal setting that we have probably ever been in. Who wants to mess up there?

1.3 FOCUS ON THE PROCESS OF WINNING, NOT THE END RESULT OF WINNING

The first step to overcoming your fear of public speaking is to spend your time on what you can control and accept the things you cannot control, such as whether the judge or jury will rule in your favor or if they will like you. Consequently, your mindset prior to and during your presentation is the key to being successful. There are also physical exercises you can do to help overcome stress, which are discussed below. But first, let's figure out what the right goal is because that will provide the framework to have the right mindset and become confident.

I played college tennis and found that the stress and the fear of failure on the tennis court is identical to the stress and fear of public speaking. Indeed, the fears you face are the same for any sport. Your ego is on the line, you want to succeed, and you are afraid to fail. Let's look at two approaches to succeeding at sports that you can learn from and apply when giving your next presentation. The conventional wisdom when entering a competition, whether it is in the sports arena or the courtroom, is embodied by the famous quote, "Winning isn't everything; it's the only thing." This saying is most often attributed to Vince Lombardi, who was the legendary Green Bay Packers football coach of the 1960s. However, the quote was actually originated by UCLA football coach Henry Russell "Red" Sanders in the 1950s. I will call this the Lombardi Rule. (Interestingly, although Lombardi said this quote several times, he backed off it and later claimed that he was misquoted and that he meant to say, "Winning isn't everything. The will to win is the only thing.")

In contrast to the conventional wisdom, consider having a different philosophy, one that is followed by many successful coaches and players, but is much less popularized by the media. It is what I call the Rice Rule. It puts the emphasis of competition not on the result, but on the *process* of winning. Grantland Rice was a legendary sportswriter from the early 1900s. He was so revered that his name was on the trophy given to the best college football team as voted on by the Football Writers Association from 1954 to 2013. In a poem titled "Alumnus Football," Rice wrote, "For when the One Great Scorer comes to mark against your name, He writes—not that you won or lost—but how you played the Game." This poem certainly emphasizes courage and sportsmanship, but it also speaks to not getting caught up in the end result of competition.

I suggest that you follow the Rice Rule. Why? Because by doing so you can really have your cake and eat it too. The Rice Rule does not ask you to forgo winning in the hopes of achieving some alternate form of satisfaction, such as displaying better sportsmanship than your opponent. Indeed, attorneys could not even choose a goal other than winning because most states' professional responsibility rules require attorneys to "zealously assert the client's position under the rules of the adversary system."

The Rice Rule assumes that any athlete is going to want to win because that is the purpose of the competition. But the Rice Rule is better than the Lombardi Rule because it focuses on the *process* of winning; that is, how you play the game, and not the outcome. The problem with focusing on the end result is that you make the situation more stressful than it needs to be because of your preoccupation with the hope of winning and overcoming the fear of losing. As we will see below, when you become emotional in a stressful situation, the mind and body work against your efforts to accomplish your task.

John Wooden, perhaps the greatest college basketball coach in history, said, "If there is anything you could point out where I was a little different, it was the fact that I never mentioned winning." Tom Landry, one of the most successful NFL coaches, was also focused on the process and not the result. He said, "The secret to winning is constant, consistent management."

In addition, the Lombardi Rule is open to the interpretation that the end justifies the means. However, while cheating can certainly affect outcomes in sports, cutting corners or being less than completely honest will lead to failure in court because judges and jurors will eventually find out if a lawyer is being dishonest and make him or her suffer the consequences through their decisions.

Moreover, the Rice Rule gives you the power to concentrate on the steps you can take to give yourself the best *chance* of winning, because it accepts that there are many things you cannot control. Those factors include the skill of your opponent, the undisputed facts of the case, the temperament and viewpoint of the judge, and the biases of the jurors. Just knowing that there are some factors that will influence the outcome that you cannot change should immediately relax you.

Now, focus on what you can control. Perhaps you've decided that the process for you to win includes emphasizing your three best points. Or, maybe it is to listen better than you ever have to the opposing side and respond directly to their best point. Or, maybe you decide that at all costs, you are going to have a conversation with the judge instead of an argument. Your strategies will be different for each hearing, depending on the challenges of the case and what you feel you need to do to improve on your last performance. In short, focus on what you need to do to succeed, not the end result. (See the chart on page 11 that shows the benefits of the Rice Rule over the Lombardi Rule.)

1.4 HOW PROFESSIONAL ATHLETES OVERCOME THE FEAR OF FAILURE

Now that we have seen what your proper mindset should be, let's look at some techniques you can learn to ensure success. I want to share with you some

HOW THE LOMBARDI AND RICE RULES AFFECT ATTITUDE	
Focus on Result (Lombardi Rule)	Focus on Process (Rice Rule)
You experience a roller coaster of emotions of happiness and fear, depending on whether you seem to be winning or losing.	You are calm because you are focused on a game plan and not the outcome.
When thinking ahead, your fear of losing often overwhelms the confidence you need to win.	Your thoughts stay in the moment because you are not thinking of the outcome.
You lose focus when you try to control the uncontrollable, such as focusing on what your opponent is doing.	You maintain your focus because you accept that many things are out of your control, such as your opponent's skill level.
Your strong desire to beat your opponent makes the battle too personal, increases your emotions, and distracts you from the task at hand.	You don't take anything personally. You are focused on what you can do to succeed.
Overthinking how to win increases your stress and makes the process of winning more complicated and difficult.	You focus on your simple strategies and let the winning take care of itself.

wonderful insights from the world of professional tennis that will help you in your next presentation in court.

Phil Farmer has coached 20 world-touring tennis professionals, including the #1 doubles team in the world, Mike and Bob Bryan, who are better known as the Bryan brothers. The Bryan brothers are the most successful doubles team of all time. Here are a few of their many accomplishments: (1) only team to win every Grand Slam plus an Olympic Gold Medal; (2) only team to win at least one Grand Slam title for 10 consecutive years (2005–2014); and (3) all-time doubles team record holders and most prize money ever won by a doubles team ($32,699,083).

Focus on the Process, Not the Result

Farmer preaches, "Don't get caught up in the result." He explains that obviously you set goals such as trying to win a tournament or achieve a certain ranking, but then "you've got to follow the process and figure out what it's going to take to get there. That may be fitness. That may be a certain weapon such as a forehand or a serve. It may be a better strategy, hitting more cross-court shots instead of down the line, getting to the net more, or finishing off points. Once you're focused on the process and what you need to do, the winning becomes a result that you don't get too emotional about."

When I spoke with Farmer, I mentioned the Lombardi quote to him. Farmer agreed with me that you should not focus on winning too much. "If the goal upfront is, 'I've got to win. I've got to get this money,' even though you already know that, then it creates, in my opinion, a lot of emotion, which leads to stress. In tennis, emotion that leads to stress leads to not being your authentic self on the court, and causing more mistakes than success."

I asked him what he meant by being "authentic." Farmer replied, "It means asking yourself, 'What do I need to do to give myself the best chance to perform?' Which, if you perform consistently on a high level, then you're going to achieve the result, eventually. You're going to have better chances to achieve that success."

Farmer gave a specific example from the Bryan brothers. "For example, with Bob and Mike, if their best chance of winning a match with their six-foot-four frames is getting to the net before the other team, having a higher first-serve percentage, looking to lob, getting the other team off the net because they're really close to the net, you start to implement strategies that give you the best chance to win." Farmer freely admits that no one wants to lose, and everyone wants to win, including the Bryan brothers. "But if you start thinking about the result and that's your whole focus during the competition, then in my opinion you're playing with too much emotion. Again, when you're not able to play authentically—meaning with less emotion, less stress, playing with more freedom—then emotion leads to errors."

I pressed Farmer on this idea of focusing on the process to win rather than on the end result of winning, as embodied in the Lombardi Rule. He explained his coaching philosophy further. The great athletes, whether they are Michael Jordan, Roger Federer, or the Bryan brothers, would admit that winning is everything. But what makes them great is that they were able to perform with a freedom that is not constricted by focusing on the outcome, which includes a fear of losing. "It is their ability to go out and perform under that pressure and play with their freedom to let go, knowing that they may not succeed."

The Equal Sign

Farmer then explained his idea of the equal sign as a tool to help frame what your focus should be on in a tennis match. (I will explain below how we can use it in public speaking.) For example, he will draw an equal sign on a whiteboard

SUCCESS = ?

Figure 1. Use an equal sign to focus on the right goal.

and write "success" to the left of the equal sign, then ask his tennis students to fill in the right side of the equation, where the question mark is (see figure 1). Most students will fill in the right side with goals such as "I want to win the point." Such goals are not helpful because they focus on the result of winning, rather than on the *process* of winning. When you get caught up in the result, you will become too emotional as you win and lose points throughout a match.

Most important, the goal of "I want to win the point"—although it sounds reasonable—is not realistic. The right side of the equation (where the question mark is) should have realistic and attainable goals. For example, Farmer relates that a recent study analyzed the career winning percentage of points played by three of the greatest tennis players of all time: Roger Federer, Rafael Nadal, and Novak Djokovic. It is surprising that those all-time greats lost 45 percent of all the points they have played in their careers. As a result, even for those three champions, it would be a mistake to put "I want to win the point" on the side of the equation with the question mark because there is a 45 percent chance they will lose it. Consequently, the question mark should be replaced with reachable goals such as hit to your opponent's weaker shot, watch the ball, or try to get to net to hit volleys.

After hearing his students' new answers, Farmer then creates a cheat sheet that incorporates what his players' equal sign should be to ensure his players focus on the process and not the result. For the Bryan brothers, a cheat sheet would include strategy information, such as the following:

If both opponents are near the end or back of the tennis court, who's the weaker player from the baseline? If we catch them when they're both at the net, who's the weaker player at the net? Who's going to break down and produce more mistakes on crucial points? What's our strategy for big points?

Farmer added that you do not want to overcomplicate the cheat sheet. "You want to have themes, maybe four or five. If you're overcrowding the mind with thoughts, then to me it's creating more stress and more emotion, which equals more mistakes, which equals less execution, and probably not winning."

You might wonder, "What if a player replaced the question mark with 'Win the match'?" Again, not only does that goal focus on the end result and not the process, but it also does not allow for your development as a tennis player. You can lose to a better player or lose a close match because of a bad call by the umpire, but if your goals are process-based instead of result-based then you still were successful. Accomplishing realistic and attainable goals is the best way to develop your skills so that you can set new goals for the next match.

We will examine more of my interview with Farmer later in this chapter, but for now, let's apply what we have just learned to our own situation.

1.5 HOW LAWYERS CAN OVERCOME THE STRESS AND FEAR OF FAILURE ASSOCIATED WITH PUBLIC SPEAKING

1. Create a Lawyer's Cheat Sheet

Farmer's idea of a cheat sheet is perfect for what a lawyer needs before entering the courtroom. Your cheat sheet might contain the exact words for when you begin to speak, reminders of the story you want to tell, such as its three most important points (see chapter 3), and the weakness in your case that you want to concede in order to maintain credibility. It might also list a couple of short positive reminders to help you overcome your fears, such as "have a conversation with the judge," "breathe deeply," and "I've got this." All of those ideas are great replacements for the question mark in the success equation (see fig. 1.)

2. Know That Jurors and Judges Want You to Succeed

Keep in mind that jurors and judges want you to do well. Even if a judge doesn't like your position based on the written briefs, they will be respectful while listening to you argue your points. Do you doubt this? Have you ever been in the audience when a lecturer or a preacher has forgotten their place? How about when someone struggles when making an important toast? I'm sure you were sympathetic to the speaker and not judgmental, because that is the reaction almost everyone has. Consequently, one of the keys to overcoming the fear of failure is to realize that your audience wants you to do well and will forgive you immediately for mistakes that are related to nervousness. Judges and jurors are no different than any other audience.

In a trial, you have the added benefit that the jurors know that they need your help to understand your side of the case. As a result, they are pulling for you to recover from your "mistake." Indeed, they are on your side. When you are talking to a jury, look for the friendly faces in the jury box. There will be several that you can tell are encouraging you with their facial expressions. Feed off of their positive reinforcement.

As for judges, even though they have read your briefs, they want to make sure they understand your position. Also, remember, they were once young lawyers standing in your shoes. If judges are not nice to you, don't worry. It simply means that they have already made up their minds and you never had a chance.

Also, take comfort in knowing that you are not alone in being afraid before a performance. Phil Farmer has seen fear in the eyes of the greatest tennis players on earth. He relates that they all have a desire to win so badly that it creates a fear that they will fail to do so. In professional competition, there is the added awareness that a stadium full of people will see your failure. To counteract this, Farmer will put a bullet point on the cheat sheet to remind his player that the spectators "are there in awe of what [the players] are about to do. They're taking it in."

3. Allow Yourself to Make Mistakes

The idea that you should achieve perfection in your presentation is the enemy of a successful performance. The perfect closing argument has never been given since American jurisprudence began. How do I know that? Because there is always a mistake in a live performance. Mistakes and live performances go hand in hand. All singers, actors, preachers, and great trial lawyers, to name a few, know this.

The solution to the problem is to realize that those mistakes are bound to happen. When you realize that perfection is impossible, you will relax. You are certain to forget something to say in your presentation, phrase an important point imperfectly, speak too quickly, or forget the perfect gesture. The Spanish painter Salvador Dali once said, "Have no fear of perfection—you'll never reach it." And if you need more evidence, Stephen Hawking, the English theoretical physicist, said something similar: "One of the basic rules of the universe is that nothing is perfect. Perfection simply doesn't exist."

Here is a trick that almost always works. When things are not going smoothly during your presentation, you may feel like you are driving an old car and the wheels are about to come off. Everything feels shaky and there is no comfort that things will get better. However, if you forget to say something, lose your place, or get scared you don't know what to say next, don't show a thing. There is a reason the old adage "Don't let them see you sweat" has survived the test of time. Your audience has no idea what you are going to say, so, if you forget what's next, they won't even notice. Do everything you can to keep the wheels on. Just move on. Whatever urge you have to start over needs to be stamped out. If you start over, it just means that you have given into the fear. Once you do that, it is impossible to recover.

If you don't know what to move on to, take a moment, take a sip of water from a water bottle you have handy, and calmly think of what you intend to say. Almost every time, the idea you forgot about will come to you.

One trick I use which always calms me down is that I have my outline next to a cup of water at counsel table. If I forget what to say, I walk to the table to get a sip of water, look at my outline, and no one knows that I ever lost my place.

> *There are always three speeches, for every one you actually gave. The one you practiced, the one you gave, and the one you wish you gave.*
> —Dale Carnegie

It bears repeating, never start over. When you have lost your place, you'll experience a strong urge to get a fresh start and begin again. Your thinking is that once you get in the flow again, you won't lose your place and you will just roll on through. While a jury and judge will have sympathy for you losing your place, that kindness will quickly turn to impatience if you start over. Your audience has a limited attention span. Don't test it by saying the same thing twice.

Finally, Dale Carnegie's observation in the text box was meant to encourage you. Carnegie was pointing out that perfection cannot be achieved in a live performance, despite our mistaken belief that it can be. So, accept that fact and relax when you perform by knowing that you are doing the best that you can.

4. Overcome the Spotlight Effect

A study was done in the 1990s. The author of the study concluded that the most unhip singer at that time was Barry Manilow. For the study, a participant put on a T-shirt with a large picture of Manilow on it and walked into a conference room where others were answering a questionnaire. By wearing the T-shirt of the famous but uncool singer (fans of the singer were made fun of by the public), the participant would naturally feel self-conscious believing that others in the conference room would likely notice such a T-shirt. After a couple of minutes, the participant was told he was in the wrong room by the author of the study and was asked to leave. This exercise was repeated several times with different participants and groups of people. Afterwards, the author of the study would ask each participant who had been asked to leave what he thought was the percentage of people in the room who remembered who was pictured on his shirt. The average answer they gave was 46 percent. In contrast, the average percentage of people in the room who actually remembered who was on the T-shirt was only 21 percent.

The point of this study is that we all are more self-conscious than we should be. We magnify mistakes that we make when others minimize them or don't even notice them. While it is true that as a lawyer in the courtroom you are truly in the spotlight, the analogy of the study still holds true because you emphasize your importance more than your audience does. If you make a mistake—which you are bound to do—others won't notice it, or, even if they do, they will have forgotten about it long after you are still remembering it.

I love this next quote because it speaks to two truths that initially appear some-what contradictory, but that I think are really not. One of the greatest violinists of all time was Jascha Heifetz. He said, "If I don't practice one day, I know it; two days, the critics know it; three days, the public knows it." This quote ties into the spotlight effect and the section above about making mistakes. That is, if you make a mistake, it is very likely that you'll be the only one who will notice. So, relax. But it also ties into the importance of being prepared (see below), which I think was the real intent of the quote. Strive to be the best you can be. Practice so much that you are never in a position where you will notice that you are not as sharp as you could be. The reason is that the failure to practice leads you down a slippery slope where eventually your audience will notice.

5. Be Prepared

A discussion about nerves would not be realistic without facing the fact that a significant reason people are nervous and don't speak well in public is that they simply have not practiced enough. This topic will be discussed in detail in chapter 8, but it merits an initial overview here.

The simple truth is that if you have not practiced more than you think is necessary, then what do you really have to be confident about? Daniel Webster, a senator and one of America's greatest orators, said, "I would as soon appear before an audience half-clothed as half-prepared." You have a choice to make. One is to not practice enough and have a feeling of insecurity when you are about to speak, knowing that you could have done more to get ready. When you are insecure, it is much more difficult to overcome the fight-or-flight response.

But you could choose another path. Practice until you reach a point of complete satisfaction. Get to a point where you know your material so well that you have a really good feeling about it in the practice setting. Then, when you are about to speak in court and the fear of public speaking tries to create doubt in you, you can reason through that fear and overcome it by knowing that you could not be better prepared for the moment. Muhammad Ali said, "The fight is won or lost far away from witnesses—behind the lines, in the gym, and out there on the road, long before I dance under those lights."

I love Ali's words "long before." If your trial starts on a Monday, don't wait until the weekend before to practice an opening statement like most attorneys do—if they practice it at all. Have your final rehearsal on the Friday before the trial. Nothing will give you more confidence than knowing that you are ready days *before* you have to stand up in court.

In addition, look for chances to practice public speaking. Those opportunities are everywhere. You can offer a short valuable

> *Amateurs practice until they can get it right; professionals practice until they can't get it wrong.*
> —Harold Craxton, former professor at the Royal Academy of Music

point at the next meeting at your firm. At the next lecture that offers a question-and-answer session, stand up and say something intelligent.

Another obvious opportunity is to join Toastmasters. There are some wonderful speakers there and you can learn a lot. However, I found that for my situation, the large time commitment involved did not pay off for the limited opportunities to give presentations. But you ought to investigate your local club. You might find it to be just what you need.

However you get practice, the more you speak in public, the more confidence you will gain. That confidence will help you with each subsequent presentation that you give.

Let's return for a moment to the Bryan brothers. One reason they are so successful is their practice is very focused. Farmer reveals that more than other doubles teams, "they would practice their serves and return of serves a very high percentage of their practice time. They knew those first two shots, especially in doubles, were very important." Farmer believes that the other important thing in practice is to put something on the line. Just don't hit balls, but keep score during drills. If you are nervous in front of crowds, play more tournaments to get used to them. Not only should you seek out opportunities to speak in public, but you should practice your presentation in front of family, friends, and colleagues to "put something on the line," as Farmer recommends.

6. Visualize Success

Here is a neglected tip that will help you immensely. It is a trick that athletes, actors, and musicians use, so you should too: visualize success. Think about it. In preparing for your presentation, you have constantly struggled to overcome the fear of failure. This negative voice in your head and its accompanying image needs to be replaced by a positive one. Spend some time picturing in your mind the successful presentation you are going to give. Really fill in the details of the picture. Imagine the courtroom, the judge, and the jury, if there is one. Silently go through your presentation as you picture yourself delivering it in court. See yourself as confident, well dressed, having good posture, relaxed, and making natural gestures. See the judge or jury smiling back at you and being receptive to your ideas. Do you want to be calm and confident? Then, picture it.

Similarly, Farmer coached the Bryan brothers to "visualize how you're going to handle tough situations, maybe even what you do if you lose the first set. It is also important to visualize holding the trophy up, winning that last point, and being successful with certain patterns that you've been practicing. If you visualize it, then when you get out there, you've already seen it."

Farmer told me that how much a professional tennis player should visualize depends on the player. Some players visualize as early as the week before a match.

However, all players should definitely visualize the night before and repeat the visualization in a smaller amount about an hour before the match.

The same advice applies to lawyers. Find out what works best for you.

7. Visit the Courtroom

In addition to visualizing, you need to actually visit the courtroom before you present. Bryan Stevenson, one of the greatest civil rights lawyers, has had innumerable hearings and oral arguments before appellate courts and the U.S. Supreme Court. He makes it a practice to visit the court the day before his oral argument. Why? He wants to get comfortable with his surroundings—even if he has argued in that courtroom before. He wants to get a feel for the judges and their questioning of other lawyers—even if he has been before those judges before. Likewise, you should go visit the court where you will be speaking and just soak it all in. You will see that the vast majority of lawyers are not master communicators and that you are actually better prepared than they are.

Also, arrange a time when you can be in the court when it is not in session. Contact the bailiff or the courtroom deputy and explain that you need just a few minutes to practice your presentation, and find out if arrangements can be made for you to gain access to the courtroom. Usually this can be arranged. When you practice your presentation in the court, you will immediately gain confidence for when you deliver in front of a judge and jury. If this cannot be arranged, go to the court first thing when it opens in the morning. Walk around it when no one is there but the court personnel. Get comfortable with the surroundings. It will make a world of difference.

Consequently, when it is showtime, you will have the confidence of at least seeing the court in action the day before and hopefully the added benefit of actually rehearsing your presentation in the courtroom itself. As a result, many of the unknowns of a live performance will become known: (1) Will you need to adjust the microphone?; (2) What are the acoustics like?; (3) How does it feel to speak from the podium?; and (4) Will your visual aids show up with the lighting?

Before your hearing, you can also create a mock courtroom in your office or home. Depending on the type of hearing you have, set up some chairs as props for the jury box or a chair for the judge's bench as best you can. Practice projecting your voice and making eye contact with your imaginary audience.

Similarly, Farmer likes his players to visit the stadium court before a tournament, just to get the feel for it. He also relates a story that Brad Gilbert told him about the time he coached Andy Roddick to his first and only Grand Slam title. Gilbert and Roddick were

> *It usually takes me more than three weeks to prepare for a good impromptu speech.*
>
> —Mark Twain

driving through New York City to a warm-up tournament about three weeks before the U.S. Open in 2003. Gilbert took a detour to Arthur Ashe stadium. Roddick was surprised and asked what they were doing. Gilbert responded, "I just want to go in there and sit for a moment and let you visually see the court, and get ready for what you're about to accomplish." When they got there, they took it in, and he said, "Now, Andy, this is where you're about to win your first Grand Slam."

8. Own Your Excellence

When you are young or new to the courtroom, you think everyone else is better than you, and that adds to your fear of public speaking. While it is true that it may be your first time in court, believe it or not, you are the expert on the issue in dispute. No one knows your client's needs better than you. No one, not even the judge, has read the cases as thoroughly as you have prior to the hearing. No one should be more familiar with your brief and your opponent's brief than you are. In essence, you should have all the confidence in the world. Don't wait for someone to tell you how good you are. Like a lot of things in life, you need to recognize and value your own expertise and talents before someone else affirms them for you.

> *Whether you think you can or you think you can't—you're right.*
> —Henry Ford

9. Overcome Adrenaline Before and During Your Presentation

As discussed above, adrenaline is wonderful if you need to fight or sprint away from danger, but it is devastating to a public speaker who does not have those two options. It can not only affect you during your presentation, but before it as well. Let's look at how to overcome it in both situations.

Before they perform, professional athletes, actors, and singers take deep breaths to relax. There is no reason why you shouldn't also. Taking 10 deep breaths before you speak can do wonders to cure two effects of adrenaline: shallow breathing and speaking too quickly once you start. You should breathe in slowly, using your diaphragm until you feel like you have an inner tube around your stomach filled with air (discussed further in section 7.4). When you get this feeling, you have actually used your diaphragm to create a vacuum that helps fill your lungs with air. Then, slowly exhale through your mouth and feel the tension leave your body.

Sometimes, when an actor sees a fellow actor who is nervous before taking the stage, he will smile reassuringly at them and say, "Don't forget to breathe." This wise advice is not only an attempt to break the tension with some humor, but also an attempt to provide some sound guidance. If you focus your mind on your breathing, three things happen: (1) you become focused on something you can easily do, instead of thinking about how nervous you are; (2) you counteract shortness of breath and an increased heart rate, which are symptoms caused by an adrenaline rush; and (3) you become focused on the present and you don't worry about the future.

Find a few moments before your presentation to focus exclusively on your breathing. Do it as you walk inside the courthouse and once again when you are at counsel table. I have found that the moments before my opening statement, when the judge is reading preliminary instructions to the jury, are the perfect time to focus on my breathing and make sure that I am relaxed. Those instructions give me the perfect prep time to get in a relaxed state.

Drink water. That advice assumes you have water with you. Most courtrooms provide it but make sure you have water one way or the other. Nothing calms the fear of having dry mouth, or actually having it, better than drinking some water. It will also calm you during your presentation if you know that a sip of water is nearby.

I have never tried this, but research has proven that if you imagine being in a soothing place, such as a beach, the peaceful visualization will help relax you.

I also have never tried a beta blocker pill. Its use is controversial, and I mention it only because some performers have used it to help reduce some of the symptoms of an adrenaline rush, such as sweaty hands and tremors. The beta blocker will not get rid of the feeling of anxiety, but it will lessen the symptoms. However, there are possible side effects, such as fatigue and feeling as if you are in a fog. Also, be careful of caffeine. As much as I like caffeinated beverages, I am conscious to avoid them before I speak because caffeine can stimulate the fight-or-flight response and increase anxiety.

Once the moment has arrived for you to speak, walk confidently to the podium or where you will be speaking. One school of thought is to be very deliberate, move slower than you normally would, and take another deep breath to calm yourself and counteract the adrenaline. Doing so helps you reassert control. Instead, I like to have a spring in my step and bring energy to the podium, because doing so helps to get rid of my fear. Being energetic also helps me start strong. Experiment with both ways to see which is best for you.

Feel confident about your stance. When your feet are grounded, you will gain confidence. (For a more detailed discussion on this topic, see chapter 7.)

Start confidently. The first 30 seconds are very crucial, but since you have practiced so many times, all that negative energy that you have been feeling will suddenly turn into positive feelings as soon as you get started. You will enjoy getting to finally present what you have practiced so hard on.

Once you start speaking, if you still feel the adrenaline, you will probably speak too quickly. Obviously, if people cannot understand what you are saying or if it takes them too much effort, you will not be able to persuade them. I always have to fight the urge to talk too fast. One tip that helps me is to take a sticky note and write "SPEAK SLOWLY" on it in big letters. I also put a smiley face on it as a visual cue to help me relax. I will bring that with me to the podium, or, if I am speaking first, I put it there before the hearing begins.

10. Accept That Some Fear Will Always Be Present

Although we have learned a lot of skills necessary to succeed, there is no getting around the fact that we can never completely overcome our fear of public speaking. The good news is that by accepting that it is normal to feel nervous, we can rationally decide how to deal with it instead of seeing it as a shortcoming. We are nervous for a lot of reasons, but perhaps the main reason is simply that we care about what we are doing. Tiger Woods was asked after the third round of the Masters in 2019 if he was nervous going into the final round. He is arguably the greatest golfer of all time, and at age 43, he was 11 years removed from his last major championship. He responded, "The day I don't feel pressure is the day I quit. . . . If you care about something, obviously you're going to feel pressure."

SUGGESTED ADDITIONAL READING

1. *Feel the Fear and Do It Anyway*, Susan Jeffers, Ph.D. (Jeffers Press, 2007). A national bestseller that examines how to overcome the negative self-talk that prevents you from reaching your potential. Chapters 1 through 5 are particularly relevant. If you don't have time to read those chapters, just use the title of the book as one of your mantras.

2. *Quiet: The Power of Introverts in a World That Can't Stop Talking*, Susan Cain (Random House, 2013). This highly acclaimed book shines a light on introverts, and chapter 5 specifically addresses the fear of speaking in public.

3. *Inner Game of Stress: Outsmart Life's Challenges and Fulfill Your Potential*, W. Timothy Gallwey, (Random House, 2009). Chapter 4 explains how to overcome the fight-or-flight syndrome, and other chapters examine causes of fear and stress and how to overcome them.

CHAPTER CHECKLIST

1. Relax in the knowledge of Mark Twain's observation: "There are two types of speakers in the world: those that are nervous and those that are liars."

2. Confront the elephant in the room and admit that almost everyone gets nervous speaking. That is the first step to overcoming the fear of public speaking.

3. Lawyers are particularly afraid of public speaking because of the judge's, jury's, client's, or their own high expectations.

4. The "fight-or-flight" response is another cause of public speaking fear.

5. Change your mindset about your goal. Winning is not everything. Instead, focus on the process of practicing and performing (the Rice Rule).

6. If you focus on the process, and not the result, the following will occur: (a) You will be calm because you are focused on a game plan and not the outcome; (b) Your thoughts stay in the moment because you are not thinking of the outcome, (c) You maintain your focus because you accept that many things are out of your control, such as your opponent's skill level or the facts of the case; (d) You don't take anything personally; you are focused on what you can do to succeed; and (e) You focus on your simple strategies and let the winning take care of itself.

7. Determine what your "equal sign" is to have success. Is it to have a conversation with the judge, make your three best points, or something else?

8. Create a cheat sheet that might have your best points on it and/or encouraging advice, such as "breathe deeply" or "I've got this."

9. Relax with the knowledge that judges and jurors want you to succeed.

10. Permit yourself to make mistakes. As Salvador Dali said, "Have no fear of perfection—you'll never reach it."

11. Be aware of the spotlight effect, which makes you think more people are paying attention to you than really are, causing you to become nervous.

12. Be prepared. As Daniel Webster said, "I would as soon appear before an audience half-clothed as half-prepared."

13. You have a choice to make. One is to not practice enough and have a feeling of insecurity that you are about to speak and that you could have done more to get ready. Or you could choose the other path: Practice until you reach a point of complete satisfaction.

14. Find opportunities to speak in public with organizations you belong to or join Toastmasters.

15. Do what successful athletes and actors do: visualize success.

16. Visit the courtroom before your hearing in order to get comfortable with your surroundings.

17. When your presentation begins, you are the expert for that moment. Own your excellence.

18. Overcome adrenaline rushes by breathing deeply and slowly 10 times before you speak.

19. Start confidently. The first 30 seconds are crucial, but, since you have practiced so many times, once you start, all that negative energy that you have been feeling will suddenly turn into positive feelings.

20. Accept the fact that some fear will always be present. As Tiger Woods said, "The day I don't feel pressure is the day I quit. . . . If you care about something, obviously you're going to feel pressure."

CHAPTER TWO

The Seven Principles of Public Speaking

"Be yourself; everyone else is already taken."

—Oscar Wilde

Now that you have learned what tools and skills you need to have to overcome your fear of public speaking, let's learn about a very important item you need to acquire on your journey to becoming a great public speaker. Then, we'll examine the seven principles of public speaking.

2.1 KEEP A JOURNAL

The most important tool you can have is a journal to capture all the creative ideas that will eventually become your presentation. Get one that you will look forward to writing in. I suggest one that is 7 x 10 inches with a soft cover and blank, not ruled, paper. The soft cover has a good feel, and the blank pages encourage you to get creative with drawings and different size writing. Ruled paper feels too rigid and boxes you in. A favorite of mine is the Moleskine Classic Notebook size XL (7.5 x 9.5 in.) with plain paper and a soft cover (www.moleskine.com).

Tom Gauld is an illustrator and cartoonist who has been regularly published in the *New Yorker*. He explained why he prefers paper over a computer for his writing. When he is on a computer, "things are on an inevitable path to being finished. Whereas in my sketchbook the possibilities are endless." Mark Lanier, one of the titans of the plaintiff's bar, always has his journal at counsel table during trial and wherever he goes. Follow the lead of these experts. Use a journal to collect ideas and use your computer to finalize them.

In addition to using the journal to help you prepare for your next presentation, use it to keep track of important inspirations for your career and life. For example, my journal includes sections for public speaking tips I come across, trial themes for my most important cases, interesting analogies, quotations that I like, and anything else that I

> **CHAPTER ROAD MAP**
>
> • Get a journal before you begin your journey.
> • Learn the seven principles of public speaking.
> • Analyze what makes a great public speaker.

find important. Don't filter the ideas you put in the journal too much. Just collect your ideas and worry about how you are going to use them later. Finally, one of my sections is for daily entries where I list three things that I am grateful for that day and one thing that I am looking forward to. It is a nice way for me to keep grounded.

You will also find that putting ink to paper spawns creativity in a way that using a computer cannot replicate. It is often hard to get inspired by staring at an electronic screen. I believe you will find that inspiration is easier to come by when you have your journal and you are sitting in your yard, the balcony of your apartment, a coffee shop, or a park. When you are in these places, let your mind wander. You will be surprised what happens when you slow down, let your mind bounce from one idea to another, and then write what comes to you on a piece of paper. There is a growing body of research to support the success of this creative process. Of course, you could dictate your ideas into your phone, but I promise you it won't be as creative as when you write with a pen. While we are on the subject, get a good pen. My favorite is the Pilot G-2 07 ink pen. But you may like writing with a felt-tip pen or a pencil or all of the above. The point is, get something you look forward to putting in your hand.

Finally, there is something empowering about carrying around a notebook that has all your brainstorming in it and is ready at a moment's notice to be filled with inspiration, and that will stimulate you with what you have already written. Make the journal something that you care about and look forward to adding to each day. Also, be smart and copy it every so often so that if you lose it, you'll have a backup. Similarly, put your name and phone number with an offer of a reward on the front page.

Now that you know what tools you'll need, let's talk about the seven principles of public speaking.

2.2. THE SEVEN PRINCIPLES OF PUBLIC SPEAKING

There are seven principles of public speaking: (1) be true to yourself; (2) speak from the heart to persuade; (3) know the needs of your audience; (4) think of conversations and visual presentations, not arguments; (5) make the complicated simple; (6) always strive to get better; and (7) tell a story. Let's give each one a closer look.

2.3 BE TRUE TO YOURSELF

Oscar Wilde's quote at the beginning of this chapter. "Be yourself; everyone else is already taken," is a universal wisdom that has been articulated by many others. Michael Jordan's son once asked his father how he could be like him. Jordan responded, "There's only one Michael Jordan." Jordan's response was not arrogant, but kind. It was meant to take the pressure off his son and point out that we are all unique.

Similarly, Carlos Santana, a 10-time Grammy-winning guitarist, said, "We tend to look for greatness always in somebody else rather than yourself. Go inside and get your sound." This book is all about getting the most out of your own sound.

Being true to yourself is the starting and ending point of this book. What I mean by that is that if you are true to yourself, each consecutive idea will successfully build on this foundation. For example, you cannot execute the second principle, speak from your heart to persuade, if you aren't true to yourself. Similarly, if you read this chapter and the rest of the book and create a speaking style that is not true to yourself, you won't be sincere, and as a result, you won't succeed.

Being true to ourselves, whether in life or public speaking, should be easy, but it is made difficult by others' expectations, expectations that may be inconsistent with our own beliefs and hopes. For example, in life, we know that we should resist and overcome pressure from people who are close to us who might want us to become something we are not.

> *Let us paint, and, with all our faults and qualities, be ourselves.*
> —Vincent van Gogh
> (his response to the vicious criticism of *The Potato Eaters*, which would become known after his death as one of his masterpieces)

Don't sacrifice who you are in order to try to imitate someone else. If you do, you will most certainly fail, and if you succeed, you won't be sincere. For example, if you are not folksy, don't try to be. If you are not a master of details, don't try to become one. If you do, you will spend all your time worrying about whether you can remember all the facts instead of what is important about your presentation. Nonetheless, everyone can improve their skills without losing their integrity.

Steal Like an Artist

Pablo Picasso said, "Good artists copy. Great artists steal." What he meant was that great artists pick and choose what they like from other artists, and then they add to it and improve by making it their own. Steve Jobs proclaimed a similar idea, saying "It comes down to exposing yourself to the best things humans have done and then try to bring those things into what you are doing. I have been shameless about stealing great ideas."

A profound book you should read is *Steal Like an Artist: 10 Things Nobody Told You About Being Creative*, Austin Kleon (Workman, 2012). Kleon has wonderful insights on how you can become your best. He relates the following story:

Conan O'Brien has talked about how comedians try to emulate their heroes, fall short, and end up doing their own thing. Johnny Carson tried to be

Jack Benny but ended up Johnny Carson. David Letterman tried to copy Johnny Carson but ended up David Letterman. And Conan O'Brien tried to be David Letterman but ended up Conan O'Brien. In O'Brien's words, "It is our failure to become our perceived ideal that ultimately defines us and makes us unique."

Kleon advises, "Copy your heroes. Examine where you fall short. What's in there that makes you different? That's what you should amplify and transform into your own work." I wholeheartedly agree with Kleon. As you continue reading, find what works and what doesn't for you, and through your experiences create a public speaking style that is true to who you are and uniquely your own.

2.4 SPEAK FROM THE HEART TO PERSUADE

The second principle of public speaking is to speak from your heart to persuade. One daunting aspect of public speaking for lawyers is the reality that you are not only talking to a judge or jury in a very formal setting—which is intimidating in and of itself—but you are also trying to connect with them in order to win for your client. The stakes are very high. Given this environment, it is very tempting to read from your notes to get every word just right and to talk about the many strengths of your case but none of its weaknesses. You want to be in control and never go off your script because it gives you a sense of strength. However, this perception of strength is misguided.

As we will learn throughout this book and particularly in chapter 4, you cannot persuade someone with logical reasoning if you don't connect with them emotionally. You have to make them care about what you are saying. If you read your argument, are not candid, and don't engage your audience, you will lose your chance to persuade them. Consequently, whatever the venue for public speaking, you need to speak from your heart to persuade and that requires being vulnerable. It is a little intimidating at first, but once you do it, you will find it gives you tremendous peace and confidence. The key is to let the audience into your world, into what you are really thinking. If you let them into your world, they will let you into theirs, and then you have a chance to emotionally connect with them and win them over. It is a trade-off that few speakers are willing to make because it is easier and feels safer to read from your notes than to have a real conversation.

Lawyers are reluctant to make the trade-off because if you have a conversation, you risk getting asked hard questions that get to the heart of the problem, which will probably lead you to having to admit a weakness in your case. But your willingness to be vulnerable is really a strength, and the courage to have a sincere conversation will gain you immense credibility with a judge. Indeed, the judge or jury already knows about the weakness, has questions about it, and will get very frustrated when you don't address it in a straightforward way. Anyway, the other side is going to point out your weakness, so why avoid it?

When you are speaking from your heart and really getting to the bottom of the issue before the court, you might say the following things, depending on the case: (1) "Your honor, I have really struggled with this issue as I am sure the court has, but here is why the law supports my position;" or (2) "I can certainly see why the court is troubled by this fact, but let me try to shed some light on it." To a jury, even though they are unable to talk back to you, you are still having a conversation with them, because you need to address their unspoken questions. You might say the following: (1) "Let me talk about the elephant in the room " or (2) "Let me candidly answer the three questions that I bet are on everyone's mind."

Bryan Stevenson, a civil rights lawyer who Desmond Tutu has said is "America's Nelson Mandela" and whose life story was the basis of the movie *Just Mercy*, has appeared countless times before appellate courts, including the U.S. Supreme Court. The key to his success is that he does not use notes and he speaks from his heart to persuade others. He has to execute this second principle of public speaking at its highest form because he almost always takes up the cause of the underdog—such as death row inmates asking for a delay or relief before their execution—and is trying to convince others who hold a very different viewpoint, onc that is widely accepted but not the one he is advocating. In an interview for my book *Turning Points at Trial*, he said:

> If you just make the substance point first, the people who came in hostile are going to be fighting you the whole time you're talking. But if you can get people to think about something that calms everything down and neutralizes the instinct to be oppositional, all of a sudden they'll hear whatever substance argument you are making and the fact that you are presenting it in a very different way.

As we discuss this principle further, let's frame it by using an idea I learned from Lisa Blatt, who holds the record for the most oral arguments before the U.S. Supreme Court for a woman (33 and counting). She declares that the key to success is that you must "channel your client." That is a wonderful way to visualize how to speak from your heart to persuade. In order to do this successfully, you have to be so sincere that your audience trusts you without a doubt and connects with your client, who is not even speaking.

Unfortunately, instead of speaking from the heart, lawyers not only read aloud their arguments, but they also let their brains do all the talking. They spend all their time sharing the voluminous facts, case law, and multiple arguments they have put together. In addition, they try to spin their arguments to persuade their audience. That is, they use disingenuous tactics such as exaggeration, inaccurate statements, and overly emotional appeals. This practice of spinning is so widespread that it is carried out not only in courtrooms, but also in workplaces,

> *And mind you, emotions are among the toughest things in the world to create out of whole cloth; it is easier to manufacture seven facts than one emotion.*
>
> —Mark Twain

politics, schools, and other institutions. How refreshing and rare it is for someone to get to the heart of the matter and speak the truth, which includes admitting the bad facts at issue that go against your argument. This doesn't mean you highlight your weaknesses, but when you are candid, you gain credibility and are more persuasive.

Gerry Spence is one of America's greatest trial lawyers. He tells the story of a lawyer who was struggling with how to speak from his heart. The lawyer explained that when he was younger and did not know much technique, he won all of his cases. But now that he was older and had learned all the tricks of trying a case, he could not seem to win anymore. Spence explained why this lawyer was now failing where he once succeeded: "Technique has little to do with credibility and therefore little to do with winning." How do you become credible? Spence explains that you must argue from "that rare, rich place, that nucleus of our being. That is the magical place where credibility dwells."

This idea of connecting with others from your heart is so universal that it is true not only with regard to public speaking but with regard to any art form, whether it is painting, music, or writing. As mentioned in the above section, Carlos Santana is a legendary musician that *Rolling Stone* magazine listed as the twentieth greatest guitarist of all time. Santana relates that people ask him all the time what kind of equipment he used to create his unique sound. For example, was it the type of guitar, strings, or amp. He replies, "No, it was soul, heart, mind and your vitals." He adds, "You can only go into the heart by you being vulnerable yourself. Only then can your music bring light into the darkness."

Similarly, Brené Brown, a qualitative researcher, in a TEDx Talk that has been viewed over 46 million times, discussed her research on vulnerability that we can learn from to improve our public speaking. Her studies found that humans are hardwired to be connected emotionally with other people. But as children become adults, many adults lose their ability to connect with others because they feel vulnerable. However, Brown found that vulnerability could be a strength, not a weakness. In her research, she found that those people who were connected with others embraced their vulnerability and were not afraid to show it. Her conclusion is very similar to Spence's advice. Embrace your vulnerabilities as a person and as a public speaker, and embrace the vulnerabilities in your case, too. It will help you connect with a judge or jury, make you more trustworthy, sincere, and credible when you speak.

Connecting with others when you speak in public is an ability that is built on a lifetime of experiences that you've had before you walk into the courtroom. You cannot be an uncaring person who does not connect with people outside the courtroom and then magically turn on another persona once you are inside and start arguing. You must be authentic. Depending on your age and family circumstances, the capacity to connect with others starts by caring about your parents, siblings, and children. Then you need to expand that to work, colleagues, friends, and strangers who need help. Put yourself in a wide variety of circumstances so that when you meet a president of a company or a homeless person, you can treat both with compassion and respect, and truly care about them. As Brown suggests, you will find out that they are struggling just like you, and that is how you can connect with them.

> *What the people really want to hear is the truth—it is the exciting thing— to speak the truth.*
> —Winston Churchill

Example from Fred Rogers

Let's tie everything together by examining a video that best shows the difference it can make when you speak from your heart to persuade. Fred Rogers created the children's television program *Mister Rogers' Neighborhood,* which ran for 33 years from 1968–2001 on PBS (Public Broadcasting Service). He won the Lifetime Achievement Award from the National Academy of Television Arts and Sciences and the Presidential Medal of Freedom. Rogers was an ordained preacher, had a degree in music composition, and his children's show was known for its deep concern for children and for discussing the problems they faced, something that other shows did not do.

In 1969, PBS was in its infancy, as was the show. President Nixon wanted to cut funding for the network, and Congressional hearings, headed by Senator John Pastore, were held to determine if the funding should be cut. Senator Pastore was not a friend of PBS and had never seen *Mister Rogers' Neighborhood.* On May 1, 1969, on the second day of hearings, Rogers appeared before the gruff and opinionated Pastore, who complained that he was tired of hearing everyone reading their remarks. It appeared that PBS had no chance to keep its funding. Rogers had intended to read his speech that would take about 10 minutes. He had put countless hours into writing his speech that expressed in detail the philosophy of his show.

After hearing Pastore's complaint, Rogers pushed back a little and explained to the Senator what was in his prepared speech and how he hoped the Senator would read it. The Senator quipped, "Would it make you happy to read it?" Rogers had to make a quick decision. Rogers replied that he would rather just talk about it. Rogers' choice changed the course of history for his show and PBS.

Watch the video on this book's website at www.winningatpersuasion.com to see how powerful it can be when you speak from your heart. Rogers does not try to spin an argument or overwhelm the Senator with facts. Instead, he exudes sincerity, authenticity, and gets to the bottom of the issue at the hearing: whether PBS deserved funding. Rogers is nervous, but he doesn't try to hide it. He knows that it is OK to be vulnerable. His priority is to connect with Senator Pastore. At the beginning, Senator Pastore is very skeptical of Rogers. You can see it in Pastore's facial expressions and tone of voice. But Rogers overcomes this attitude through his eye contact, body language, calm tone of voice, and the words he chose. He used words that invited the Senator into Rogers' thinking and sought a common ground with the Senator's emotions. For example, Rogers said that he cared about children and knew the Senator also cared about what children were seeing on television. You will see in the video that the Senator's initial expression of skepticism changes to one of deep interest in what Rogers is saying.

Rogers pointed out that the current budget for his 30-minute show would only pay for the equivalent of two minutes of a television cartoon, and added that cartoons are a bombardment on children's sensibilities. In contrast to cartoons, Rogers said his show was concerned about the inner drama of childhood, from something as simple as getting a haircut to the anger that occurs in simple family situations, and that his show spoke about it constructively. Rogers continued:

> I give an expression of care every day to each child, to help him realize that he is unique. I end the program by saying, "You've made this day a special day, by just your being you. There's no person in the whole world like you, and I like you, just the way you are." And I feel that if we in public television can only make it clear that feelings are mentionable and manageable, we will have done a great service for mental health.

The Senator—who had never seen Rogers' show—was captivated and said, "I'm supposed to be a pretty tough guy, but this is the first time that I have had goose bumps in the past two days. . . . Looks like you just earned the $20 million."

> *Words mean more than what is set down on paper. It takes the human voice to infuse them with deeper meaning.*
>
> —Maya Angelou

Finally, I hope it goes without saying, but in case it doesn't, an overly emotional plea is no way to win, just as a dry recitation of the facts will court disaster. You must find the proper balance, just as Rogers did.

2.5 WIN

The third principle of public speaking is to find out the answer to this question: What Is the Need of your audience (WIN)? The idea behind this question builds on the previous section, but its meaning is counterintuitive: your hearing or trial is not about the needs of your client or yourself. Let that thought sink in for a moment. How could that be possible? The truth is that your next appearance in court is about the needs of the judge or jury that you are trying to persuade. Figuring out those desires first, not your client's or your own, is the key to success. You have to put your ego aside and find out how you can best persuade your audience.

Almost every lawyer in a jury trial makes the mistake of assuming that the jury begins the trial with the same knowledge base of the case as the lawyer does. Why? It is not an intentional assumption, but rather one that comes from lawyers having lived with the case so long that the facts are ingrained in their bones, and it is difficult for them to take a step back and explain their case as if someone is hearing about it for the first time—which it most likely is for the trial jury.

Similarly, when most lawyers are arguing before a judge, they don't tailor their argument to their specific needs, but instead they rehash their written briefs, because that is what they have prepared and feel comfortable arguing.

For example, assume that you represent someone who is about to be sentenced for the federal crime of unlawful possession of a firearm by a previously convicted felon. You are getting ready for the hearing. You have pointed out to the court in your sentencing brief that your client has been on release in the community since his arrest one and a half years ago. He has gotten a job as a truck driver and stopped drinking completely because he had been an alcoholic at the time of his arrest. In your brief, you have pointed out that although he has had many serious arrests and convictions, they were from 15 years ago, when he was in a gang that he has now renounced. You have hired a gang expert who has written a lengthy report declaring that studies show that once someone renounces ties with a gang, his likelihood of recidivism decreases dramatically.

The day of the sentencing hearing has arrived. You have flown in your expert from several states away. You have prepared several hours to put on the expert's testimony and argue to the court. But, when the judge takes the bench, she seems impatient, a little bothered to be in court on a Monday morning, and she declares succinctly, "Mr. Jones [defense counsel], I have *carefully* read your voluminous brief and the expert's lengthy report, please take that into account. What would you like to tell the court?"

Would you put on your expert witness anyway because of the expense and time involved in bringing her in from another state? Would you summarize what you had written in the brief because that is what you had prepared to do? Most attorneys don't adapt to the circumstances because they are not listening to a judge's cues or flat out ignore them because they think they know better than the judge what the judge wants. Why, I do not know. But I have seen this happen countless times in the courtroom. The judge tells the lawyer what question needs to be answered, and the lawyer answers something else.

The correct response in the above scenario is to pivot from your original plan to put on expert testimony in support of your argument. Instead, give a short presentation that provides information in a new way to the impatient judge. For example, you might say, "Thank you, your honor. Let me then just *briefly* mention something that I want to highlight for you that cuts to the chase." In one sentence, you have indicated to the judge three important things: (1) you heard her comments about how the hearing should go; (2) you will be brief; and (3) you will talk about the most important point.

> *You never really understand a person until you consider things from his point of view.*
>
> —Harper Lee

You could then ask the court if she had any questions for you or the expert that you had flown in from out of state—reminding the court of an important witness who is available—and go from there depending on the court's response.

This idea of seeing all of your presentations through the eyes of the recipient (i.e., the judge and the jury) will change everything about how you approach your next hearing. It will convince you that you should not use notes, and it will help you decide how to use visual aids, structure your argument, and much more (discussed in later chapters).

WIN will also prevent you from ever speaking even just a second longer than your time allotment. Everyone's time is valuable, and when you are given 15 minutes for an opening statement and you go over that time limit, not only will the judge cut you off, but even if they don't, the jury will stop listening. Better yet, bring a smile to your audience's faces by using less time than you are allowed. If a judge gives each side five minutes at a hearing, tell the judge you only need four. They will listen to you even more closely knowing that you have given them the gift of time.

Try this the next time you are at a hearing with no time limits. Instead of making 10 points or four very long ones, start by saying, "Your honor, I will be very brief. This case boils down to. . . ." Then powerfully and succinctly make your point. You will be a hero in the judge's eyes.

Incorporate WIN into your strategy and you will stand head and shoulders above the rest.

Listen

An important key to WIN is that you need to listen. You need to listen to your clients so that you understand what they want, and you need to listen to the judge so you can answer his or her questions. When Bryan Stevenson argues before the United States Supreme Court, he takes a legal pad to the podium. The legal pad does not have his notes on it, but he takes it so he can write down questions from a justice to make sure he answers them, because he is afraid he won't be able to remember them. In addition, you need to listen to the other side's argument so that you can respond effectively. The problem is that we are not very good listeners.

> *When people talk, listen completely. Most people never listen.*
> —Ernest Hemingway

It might seem strange to discuss listening in a book devoted to public speaking, but listening is a more important skill than speaking. If you are listening, you are observing. And through observation, you can assess the situation and make an effective presentation. For example, perhaps the greatest quality a poet or writer has is the ability to observe. Writers cannot convey ideas if they are not first able to observe and understand the subject matter they are writing about. Likewise, a lawyer needs to be an astute observer and listener to be a persuasive speaker.

Listening is a behavior and requires a lot of concentration. Unfortunately, we have formed bad listening habits, because everyday listening, like everyday seeing, is very passive and requires very little effort. Watching and listening to television, having a conversation on a phone, and listening to a friend tell us about their day are all very passive activities. The fact that it is so easy reflects on how poorly we are engaged and truly observe or understand what is being said.

At first glance, the following distinct listening skills may seem obvious. But by reviewing them, we can identify what type of listening works in different situations.

Informative listening is what you did during lectures at law school. Your goal was simply to understand the lecture. A necessary ingredient to your understanding was to comprehend the vocabulary being used and the ideas being presented.

Relationship listening is another listening skill. Unlike during a lecture in a law school (informative listening) when you probably could have cared less if the professor felt that you were hanging onto their every word, in court, relationship listening is very important. Another term for relationship listening is *empathy*.

Understanding the emotions that are underpinning a judge's questions is the key to answering those questions effectively. Your goal is to make the judge feel that their message is being understood, but also that you under-stand why they believe as they do.

Critical listening is needed to determine a speaker's believability. Determine if opposing counsel is knowledgeable in the area they are talking about and listen to how the judge reacts to their arguments.

The last listening skill discussed here is called discrimination. Discrimination helps one determine a word's meaning by the change in pitch, volume, or pace of a speaker's voice. Listen for these subtle changes in both the judge's questions and opposing counsel's argument. For example, a Judge might ask you, "You mean to say that there is only one answer to this problem?" By listening to the judge's tone of voice, you can discern whether the judge is skeptical (pitch of voice is higher at the end of the question and the judge emphasizes the word "one") of your position or agrees with it (there is very little change in pitch throughout question).

In sum, the point is to be an observant listener to what others in the court-room are saying and understand their point of view so that you can tailor your presentation accordingly.

2.6 THINK OF CONVERSATIONS AND VISUAL PRESENTATIONS, NOT ARGUMENTS

The fourth principle is to never have an argument but instead have a conversa-tion with the judge and deliver a visual presentation to the jury. For context, I have used the word argument in the above paragraphs because that is the term lawyers are familiar with. But from now on, you should hit the reset button for all of your "arguments." Never again should you think of making an argument to the judge. Instead, you should have a conversation with them. Webster's Dictio-nary defines conversation as an "oral exchange of sentiments, observations, opinions, or ideas." On the other hand, Webster's defines argument as the act of arguing, or "to contend or disagree with words." Ask yourself, in everyday life, are you more likely to be persuaded if there is an exchange of ideas and opinions or if a person is using words to disagree and argue with you? There is a reason that the saying "You catch more flies with honey than you do with vinegar" has survived the test of time.

The same principle is true in the courtroom. Bryan Stevenson explained further his philosophy for when he appears before a judge at a hearing or the U.S. Supreme Court. "I want to have a conversation with the court. I really don't want it to be an argument. I want them to feel like they can ask me anything and that they're going to get an honest answer." He further points out that "I think an appellate judge is going to be really frustrated if people come in only prepared to say the things that they've prepared to say. That's really frustrating for a judge who has real questions, because then you have to hope that you could anticipate what his questions are so perfectly that every question is answered in what you prepared. That's just not likely—particularly in the Supreme Court, where you've got nine very distinct perspectives and divergent views about the Constitution and about the issues. There is no way."

If you are before a jury, the same truths apply. The only difference is that you cannot have a two-way verbal conversation with the jury because they cannot talk to you during the trial. Consequently, think of making a *presentation* with visual aids that invites them into your thinking and answers their questions, not an *argument* that gets them defensive if they disagree with you. In addition, by focusing on making a presentation, you will always be thinking of your role as a teacher in the courtroom, someone who is passionate about the subject and who anticipates all the questions that need to be answered, instead of someone who is argumentative, with little care for any disagreements or for answering the hard, unspoken questions. In short, a successful presentation invites the jury to see the case from your point of view.

2.7 MAKE THE COMPLICATED SIMPLE

Albert Einstein said it best, "If you cannot explain it simply, you don't understand it well enough." Once you master this fifth principle, you are practicing the art of persuasive public speaking at the highest level. Lawyers, among others, usually are dealing with complicated legal arguments and an overwhelming number of facts. It can be daunting to distill that information into a clear and persuasive presentation. Not only is it daunting, but it takes a lot of work.

> *Our life is frittered away by detail. Simplify, simplify.*
> —Henry David Thoreau

A good example of someone who took the time to make the complicated simple comes from David Christian's TED Talk (see chapter 12). In 18 minutes, he told the history of 13 billion years, from the beginning of the universe to the present. To do this he had a clear message, his thoughts were organized, and he had powerful visual aids. If he can take on such a large topic successfully, we can certainly make our complicated legal and factual arguments simple and persuasive. This principle and how to implement it will be discussed more in chapter 3 and also in chapter 10 when we analyze Mark Lanier's opening statement. But this principle cannot be done at the expense of accuracy. As Einstein cautions, "Everything should be made as simple as possible, but no simpler."

2.8 ALWAYS STRIVE TO GET BETTER

The sixth principle of public speaking is to always strive to get better. It is amazing how low the bar has been set in courtrooms across the country for what is considered good advocacy. If you walk into any courtroom today and watch a hearing or trial, you will probably become bored after five minutes—and definitely after 10. I have thought about this problem for a long time and discussed it with many lawyers and judges. Here is my best answer to the question of why this is so.

The first reason is that we were taught in law school, and graded accordingly, that the student who could spot the most legal issues in an exam and give the most reasons and facts to support their answer would get the highest grade. You would get an even higher grade if you could pile on alternative arguments to your main arguments. In short, those students who provided the most complicated answer would succeed because the professor graded from an extremely detailed checklist of what a student needed to meet in order to get a perfect score.

However, in the real world, when the decision-maker is a judge or jury and not a professor, the goals should be completely different. If the judge's or juror's brain were a computer that made an unemotional decision based on which lawyer had the most facts and arguments, our law school training would be perfect. But brain science research proves that our training is wrong and sheds light on how the human brain makes *emotional* and imperfect decisions—not perfect decisions based on facts and reasons. This science shows that a story format that is interesting, memorable, and persuasive is the best way to present information. This will be discussed further in chapters 3 and 4.

But there is another reason, and that is the "OK plateau." This phrase was coined by the science writer Joshua Foer and explained in his books *Maximize Your Potential* and *Moonwalking with Einstein*, among others. He came up with this phrase after researching how people learn a new skill. In the 1960s, Paul Fitts and Michael Posner studied how humans learned, and they concluded there were three phases of learning. The first phase is the "cognitive stage," where we are simply learning how to do the new skill. You don't know anything, you are making a lot of mistakes, but you are getting better.

The second stage is called the "associative stage." You are getting more comfortable with your skill, making fewer errors, and becoming more efficient. The third stage is the "autonomous stage," where you have learned the skill well enough that a lot less thought goes into what you are doing, and you can accomplish the skill naturally without a lot of thought. Foer explains that functional magnetic resonance imaging (fMRI) scans of brains show that when people reach this third stage, the part of the brain involved with conscious reasoning disengages and allows other parts of the brain to take over to accomplish other tasks. In short, Foer describes this accomplishment as the "OK plateau," the point at which you decide you're OK with how good you are at something, turn on autopilot, and stop improving.

Foer gives two examples of this OK plateau: typing and driving a car. We get good enough to be successful and then we stop getting better. Foer then cites the research of Anders Ericcson, an internationally recognized expert in human performance, to show how we can be better than just good enough. Ericcson has found that with "deliberate practice" you can separate yourself from the rest of the field. The key to becoming an expert at something is to avoid getting stuck in the OK plateau, where everything you do with a skill is autonomous. Ericcson explains that there are three things that experts do that average people don't: (1) they stay focused on their technique; (2) they keep focused on their goals; and (3) they seek lots of feedback about their performance. In short, to become an expert, you need to avoid stage three, the autonomous stage, and always stay in stage two, the associative stage.

You can probably think of many examples from your own life. For me, it is piano practice. I would practice a piece from beginning to end over and over until I got it ready for the recital. The result was always that overall it sounded good enough, but it was certainly stronger in the easy sections and weaker in the hard sections. But to excel, I should have deliberately practiced the hard parts of the piece much more than the easy parts. In short, the better piano players get so comfortable with the hardest parts of the piece that they actually become easy.

Foer points out that "When you want to get good at something, how you spend your time practicing is far more important than the amount of time you spend. In fact, in every domain of expertise that's been rigorously examined, from chess to violin to basketball, studies have found that the number of years one has been doing something correlates only weakly with level of performance. . . . To improve, we must watch ourselves fail, and learn from our mistakes."

However, it is hard for lawyers to get this feedback. Are we seriously going to show weakness and ask our clients how we did after a hearing? Are we going to ask the partner or senior associate who is with us at counsel table how the direct examination went? It would be nice, but the reality is that we don't want to show weakness by asking for help.

One answer is to have the motto "I am always trying to get better." If you start your conversation with your client or colleague with this request for help, you can get immediate feedback without showing any weakness, and you are likely to get some candid advice. Also, a great source of feedback is the courtroom staff, and even the judge. The staff is almost always willing to give you some advice. They see lots of lawyers and rarely get asked for their opinions. They love to help. In addition, look for an opportunity to get some feedback from the judge.

The significance of the OK plateau for lawyers is really two-fold. First, we are fighting against human nature, which makes it easy for us to just get good enough to succeed. Second, for a myriad of reasons, lawyers, like people in other

> *Every man I meet is my superior in some way. In that, I learn of him.*
> —Ralph Waldo Emerson

occupations, have certainly seen someone excel in the courtroom, but they have failed to recognize why someone excelled and to adapt what they have seen to their own practice. They don't take Emerson's advice in the callout box at left to heart.

Inspiration From Jonathan Livingston Seagull

The late Kobe Bryant was speaking to the Los Angeles Chargers football team before their first season in Los Angeles after moving from San Diego. He was explaining to them the challenges of being a professional athlete in LA. One player asked him what was his favorite book? Instead of naming a book on sports, he surprised the entire group by saying *Jonathan Livingston Seagull,* by Richard Bach. He was pointing out that on average most football players careers last only three years and that most players were unrecognizable to the public. Like the main character in the book, he challenged them to have an exceptional life and to get the most out of it in football and beyond.

I am going to second that idea for you and also recommend that book. The book is a fable about a seagull named Jonathan Livingston Seagull. While other seagulls in his flock were satisfied with being average and would never consider exploring how well they could fly, Jonathan did not accept the limitations of his seagull wings and found a greater peace and fulfillment by seeing how low he could glide, how high he could fly, and how fast he could dive. The message of the book is that we all have a lot more potential than we realize, and we will be more complete when we strive to use it.

> *Sameness is the mother of our disgust, variety the surest cure.*
> —Petrarch (Francesco Petrarch), Italian scholar and poet, and the Father of Humanism (1304-1374)

Take Kobe's advice and learn from Jonathan Livingston Seagull. Let's excel. The only way to do that is to be yourself and be the best you can be. I love the quote in the textbox from Petrarch. Judges will have seen hundreds of lawyers before first seeing you, and they will see hundreds of lawyers after you. Be different. Be creative. Be memorable.

2.9 TELL A COMPELLING STORY

This seventh principle of public speaking needs its own chapter (see chapter 3) because it is so important. Now that we have learned how to overcome our fear of public speaking and learned the foundation for how to speak in public, let's go to the next chapter and learn how to tell a compelling story, so that people will be persuaded by what we say.

SUGGESTED ADDITIONAL READING

1. *Steal Like an Artist: 10 Things Nobody Told You About Being Creative*, Austin Kleon (Workman, 2012). This book will inspire you to become more creative and give you concrete ideas on how to accomplish that. A very quick but powerful read.

2. *Jonathan Livingston Seagull*, Richard Bach (Scribner, 1970). Summarized in this chapter. The book inspires you to be your best.

3. *The Quick & Easy Way to Effective Speaking*, Dale Carnegie (Pocket Books, 1962). A great resource from one of the most successful teachers of public speaking in the twentieth century.

4. If you want a further example to learn from Fred Rogers, watch his acceptance speech to the TV Hall of Fame at https://youtu.be/TcNxY4TudXo.

CHAPTER CHECKLIST

1. Use a journal to keep track of your creative ideas. As the illustrator Tom Gauld said, when he is on a computer, "things are on an inevitable path to being finished. Whereas in my sketchbook the possibilities are endless."

The Seven Principles of Public Speaking

1. <u>Be true to yourself</u>. Like great artists, pick and choose what you like from other lawyers, and then add to and improve it by making it your own. As Oscar Wilde said, "Be yourself; everyone else is already taken."

2. <u>Speak from the heart to persuade</u>. Instead of speaking from the heart, lawyers let their brains do all the talking. You must become vulnerable, let your audience in, and connect with their emotions. When you do, your words will impact them. As Maya Angelou said, "Words mean more than what is set down on paper. It takes the human voice to infuse them with deeper meaning."

3. <u>WIN</u>. Your hearing or trial is not about the needs of your client or yourself. The acronym WIN stands for What Is the Need of your audience? You have to put your ego aside and find out how you can best persuade your audience. An important key to WIN is that you need to actively listen.

4. <u>Think of conversations and visual presentations, not arguments</u>. As Bryan Stevenson, the acclaimed civil rights lawyer said, "I want to have a conversation with the court. I really don't want it to be an argument. I want them to feel like they can ask me anything and that they're going to get an honest answer." If you are before a jury, the same truths apply. The only difference

is that you cannot have a two-way verbal conversation with the jury because they cannot talk to you during the trial. Consequently, think of making a visual presentation, not an argument. Make a presentation that tries to anticipate their questions and answers them convincingly.

5. Make the complicated simple. Albert Einstein said it best, "If you cannot explain it simply, you don't understand it well enough." Once you master this principle, you are practicing the art of persuasive public speaking at the highest level.

6. Always strive to get better. Avoid the OK plateau. After you have achieved some success, don't turn on the autopilot and stop improving. With "deliberate practice," you can separate yourself from the rest of the field. There are three things that experts do that average people don't: (1) they stay focused on their technique; (2) they keep focused on their goals; and (3) they seek lots of feedback about their performance.

7. Tell a compelling story. It is the most persuasive way to communicate your ideas.

CHAPTER THREE

How to Tell a Compelling Story

"Stories are just data with a soul."—*Brené Brown*

3.1 STORYTELLING AT HEARINGS AND AT TRIALS

As you read this chapter, keep in mind that there are two significant differences between telling a story at a hearing and telling a story at a jury trial. Obviously, you will have less time at a hearing. Second, for a hearing, you and opposing counsel will have already submitted written briefs that lay out the factual and legal arguments, so the court is already focused on the problem and possible remedies. Nonetheless, don't abandon storytelling. Most lawyers just recite the facts and legal arguments from their briefs. Instead, you need to answer the judge's unspoken question, "Why should I care?" The best way to persuade them is with a compelling short story.

In chapter 2, under the section "Speak from the Heart to Persuade," we looked at lawyers who weren't speaking to jurors at trial but rather to the most sophisticated judges at the highest court in our country. When Lisa Blatt, who holds the record for the most oral arguments before the U.S. Supreme Court for a woman, declares that the key to success is that you must "channel your client," she means that you must tell a short story about your client and their case to explain to the justices why they should care.

Later in this chapter, and then in much more detail in chapter 10, we will take a close look at trial lawyer Mark Lanier's persuasive speaking techniques, but I want to share in this section his thoughts on the differences between hearings and trials that I wholeheartedly agree with. Lanier believes that how you tailor your presentation is incredibly dependent on the situation. He likes to think of it as "GPS [global positioning system] lawyering." You have to not only know where you are going but also where your starting point is with the judge. Unlike jurors, who want you to start at the beginning of your journey, judges are not blank slates

> **CHAPTER ROAD MAP**
>
> - Understand why stories are so persuasive.
> - Learn the seven elements of a compelling story.
> - Overcome writer's block anytime.

with few or no preconceived notions of you or your case. Some judges will have read the briefs, some won't. Some will have already looked at other similar cases, some won't. As Lanier says, "Some will have an ideological bent that moves them one way, some don't. Some like to be entertained, some don't. So, for some, the route is very short, and you just take three side streets and you're there. For others, you've got to get on the freeway. For others, it just all depends."

Lanier elaborates, "For some judges, if I stand up there and start giving a story, it's very patronizing, like, 'I'm a judge. I'm not a juror. Don't treat me like a juror. I went to law school. I passed the bar exam. I've got clerks that work for me. I've read the briefs.' So, for some of them, it's just, 'Your Honor, I have three points to make in three minutes. Point one, they're wrong on this because. . . . Point two, they're wrong on this because. . . . Point three, they're wrong on this because. . . . Thank you, Your Honor. Have a good day.'" In those situations, Lanier uses a list to tell a story (discussed below), and lists can be an effective alternative storytelling method.

But no matter what judge you are before, remember that you have to tell them why it matters, not just what happened. And when you tell them why it matters, a story—at whatever appropriate length—is the best format. Let's now look more closely at why and how you should do this.

3.2 WHY TELL A STORY?

The conventional wisdom is that the formal setting of a courtroom does not lend itself to storytelling, and that there is a premium for getting straight to the facts and legal arguments.

> *Storytelling is the essential human activity. The harder the situation, the more essential it is.*
> —Tim O'Brien

But common sense and sound science prove that the conventional wisdom is wrong and back up the principle that storytelling is your best form of persuasion. As for common sense, we have all been at a meeting, a lecture, or in a place of worship when the speaker begins talking by saying something to the effect, "Let me tell you a story." What is our response? We immediately become interested. Humans have an irresistible desire to listen to stories. Since childhood, when our parents first read or told them to us, stories have been the primary way we have learned about the world around us.

There is something about just hearing the word "story" that grabs our attention and connects us with the person speaking. Not only do we want to hear a story, but we have a natural desire to connect with other people, and listening to their stories helps us do this.

Brain Science Studies

Even when we don't hear a story but just hear facts, we have a desire to make sense of them, and the way we do that is through a story. Not only does common sense tell you that we tend to create stories when presented with facts, but studies have confirmed that if you give people random facts, they will create a story from them. To demonstrate this, psychologists Fritz Heider and Marianne Simmel conducted an experiment. They created a short animated film (a recreation of it can be found on YouTube here: https://youtu.be/sx7lBzHH7c8 or by searching "Heider & Simmel animation 1944"). Please view it now, and then read the following paragraph.

As you saw the big triangle interact with the smaller triangle and the circle, you undoubtedly created a story. Perhaps you saw the small triangle as a hero who was saving the circle from the larger triangle who was the villain. If you did, you were in the vast majority. Only three of the 114 subjects in the study correctly answered that what they saw were geometric shapes moving around.

In another study, Uri Hasson, a professor of psychology and neuroscience at Princeton University, found that when a person listens to a story, their brain waves actually start to synchronize with those of the storyteller. The more the storyteller captivated the listener, the more that the listener's brainwaves matched the storyteller's. What happens is that the areas of the listener's brain that process complex information become active and mimic the storyteller's brain activity as they draw that person into the meaning and context of the story they are telling.

There is also evidence that the brain produces chemicals that can persuade a listener when stories are told. Paul Zak is a professor of economics and psychology at Claremont Graduate School. His studies have found that an effective story occurs when it captures and holds the audience's attention and transports the audience into the narrator's world. When this happens, oxytocin (Zak calls it the "moral molecule") is produced in the brain, which makes the listener more trusting and compassionate. Those are exactly the kinds of traits and reactions that you want from the judge or jury you are speaking to.

> *You're never going to kill storytelling, because it's built into the human plan. We come with it.*
> —Margaret Atwood

3.3 DEFINITION OF A BORING STORY

Before we learn how to tell a story, let's do an exercise. Could you tell someone what the definition of a story is? Spend at least a minute and really try.

The reason I begin with this exercise is that one of the biggest and most legitimate criticisms of lawyers is that they get lost in the facts of the case and miss the importance of just telling a "story." But creating a story is not easy, unless you know how to do it and spend the time on it. Even most "how to" books on story-telling assume the reader knows what a story is and then go full steam ahead on how to write or tell one. In truth, it is very hard to define, and if you start to examine it too much, you will get lost in the weeds. The good news is that this chapter will give you all you need to know about how to tell a *compelling* story without overwhelming you.

The most basic definition of a story can be found in the dictionary, but it is not that helpful because it really just defines what a boring story is. Webster's dictionary defines a story as "an account of incidents or events." It is fair to say that all lawyers are meeting this definition in the courtroom. But the justified criticism directed towards lawyers is meant to point out that their "account of incidents" does not move the emotions of the judge or jury and is therefore not persuasive.

At the beginning of this chapter, there is a wonderful quote, "Stories are just data with a soul." This chapter will teach you how to get out of the rut of giving a boring and unpersuasive "account of events" and instead tell a compelling story with soul that touches peoples' hearts and wins them over.

3.4 DEFINITION OF A COMPELLING STORY

A compelling story: (1) delivers a bottom-line message you want your audience to understand above all else; (2) has a soul, by emphasizing at least one human truth about why the story matters; (3) uses a captivating structure that starts strong; (4) uses descriptive language; (5) tells the good, the bad, and the ugly about your case; (6) creates an emotional connection between your client and the audience (i.e., the jury); and (7) is based on the law that governs your case.

With all that in mind, let's examine each of the seven elements.

3.5 DELIVER A BOTTOM-LINE MESSAGE WITHIN YOUR STORY (1ST ELEMENT)

Too many lawyers get lost in the details and never simply convey in a persuasive manner the main reason why they should win. The solution is to create a bottom-line message. I did not create this idea: I found it when I was researching the life of President Dwight D. Eisenhower. The concept is perfect for trial lawyers. Dwight D. Eisenhower was not only the president of the United States (1953–1961), but he was also the Supreme Commander of the Allied Expeditionary Force in Europe during World War II. He obviously knew how to get a large number of armed forces from point A to point B. His laser-like focus was also evident in his speeches. He once told a speechwriter in the Oval Office that before you ever start to write a speech, "You ought to be able to put your bottom-line message on the inside of a matchbook." (see fig. 1).

Think of what that simple maxim teaches us. Eisenhower knew that before writing a draft of a speech, contemplating its beginning and ending, or deciding on its order of topics, you must first decide what the speech's message is. And then, not only must you decide on a message, but that message should be so clear and concise that you can write it on the inside flap of a matchbook cover. If you look at figure 1, you will see that you can only write a few words in this limited space. If President Eisenhower thought a bottom-line message was important enough to create in order to persuade the country with his speeches, we should not be hesitant to try using one to persuade in a courtroom.

Figure 1. Inside flap of matchbook cover.

How to Develop Facts for a Bottom-Line Message

On your computer, or preferably in your journal mentioned in chapter 2, make a list of all the important facts in your case. Put them in three columns: good facts, neutral facts, and bad facts. Analyze the bad facts and see if you can offer a legitimate explanation that could move them into the neutral category or the good category. Similarly, try to move the neutral facts into the good category.

> **Practice Tip**
> Ask yourself, "What is the most dramatic statement I can make about my case?"

Mark Lanier explained to me how he changes bad facts into good facts. Lanier tried several cases against the pharmaceutical drug company Merck for selling the drug Vioxx, a drug that helped people with pain but could also cause heart failure if it were taken for too long. In the first Vioxx trial, Lanier won a national record-setting verdict representing plaintiff Bob Ernst, who was in excellent health when he died from taking Vioxx. But in another trial, Lanier represented John McDarby, who, Lanier told me, was "one pork chop away from a heart attack. He had every risk factor there was. He was very old, he was obese, he was diabetic, he had a family history, and he had high cholesterol." People asked Lanier how he could win the case with all those negatives. He replied, "I'm just going to turn them into positives."

He then demonstrated to me what he had explained to the jury at McDarby's trial:

> Look, we all live on a table or on flat land, but there's a table's edge or cliff, and that's the heart attack [Lanier points to the edge of a table in front of

us]. It's the leading cause of death in America. Some of us live real close to the edge, and other people live far away. If you are a 17-year-old kid, you're far away from the edge, but as you get to be 75, you're closer. Male, closer. Diabetic, closer. Smoker, closer. And all of these things move you closer to the edge of the cliff. [As Lanier is mentioning all of these risk factors (75, male, diabetic, smoker, etc.), he moves a Styrofoam cup, which represents the 17-year-old, from the center of the table closer and closer to its edge.]

Now let me tell you about Vioxx. Vioxx is a shove toward the cliff. [Lanier pushes the cup that is now at the edge of the table and knocks it off.] If you're a 17-year-old guy—girl, it doesn't matter—you probably could take all the Vioxx you wanted. It's not going to bother you: You can take that stuff, you can take that shove, but you take someone who's right up against the edge of the cliff, and Vioxx is the last thing in the world that person needs to be taking. I'll prove that to you, and I'll prove that Mr. McDarby was right up at the edge of the cliff, and he had no business being on that drug.

Lanier's use of the cup and the table as a visual aid perfectly demonstrates how to turn bad facts into good facts. As hard as Merck argued that McDarby's heart attack was caused by his other risk factors, Merck could not overcome the powerful image of McDarby as the last person in the world who should have taken Vioxx, given how close to the edge he was.

After you have created your three columns, you are ready to create a bottom-line message that best explains what your case is all about. Let's now look at why it is so important.

Why Create a Bottom-Line Message?

When lawyers tell me that they do not have enough time to focus on a bottom-line message because of other pressing matters, I simply respond, "You cannot afford not to." Whether you represent a plaintiff or defendant, it is the single most important task to accomplish. Let me repeat: there is nothing more important you can do to affect the outcome of the case. You need to be able to concisely state in one sentence why you should win and why it matters. If you don't, you run the real risk that the opposing lawyer will accomplish this task and win the battle of persuasion.

Given its significance, you should develop your bottom-line message as soon as you get your case so that you can perfect it by the time you need to tell your story at trial. Also, as you work on your bottom-line message, it will guide you toward what facts you need to develop for the story you will eventually tell at trial.

All right, I already sense some resistance from you. Who has the time to spend brainstorming and developing a bottom-line message when you are over-whelmed with gathering all the information at the beginning of a case or trying to make sense of it for an upcoming hearing or trial? Let me give you a couple of examples at the outset to convince you to make the time, because it will affect the outcome of your case.

The first example comes from U.S. history, and the second one comes from a trial. President Johnson's failure to develop a bottom-line message for the Vietnam War doomed him to failure. Every Tuesday, LBJ would have lunch with leaders of his cabinet and national security advisors to plan the next steps for the Vietnam War. LBJ thought these meetings were his best tool for winning the war. But his attendees knew that LBJ wanted the meetings to focus on the operational rather than on strategic questions, and on logistics instead of structural consid-erations. In short, the focus was on the details and not the big goal of winning.

For example, the meetings would discuss bombing targets, food rations, and new equipment that was available, but never once the nature of the war or its importance to national security. One of LBJ's most respected biographers wrote, "Someone once said as he watched Dean Rusk [Secretary of State] hurrying to the White House for a meeting of the Tuesday lunch, 'If you told him right now of a sure-fire way to defeat the Vietcong and to get out of Vietnam, he would groan that he was too busy to worry about that now; he had to discuss next week's bombing targets.'"

In contrast to LBJ, let's see how Mark Lanier developed a winning bottom-line message for the opening statement of his two-month trial against DePuy Orthopaedics, Inc., in which he represented plaintiffs who had defective hip replacement implants. He cut to the chase and told the jury, "This is a case about six people who trusted a product, trusted a doctor, and got terrible results." Lanier then candidly told the jury, "I would be a fool to tell you these things if I couldn't prove them."

What makes Lanier's bottom-line message so powerful? First, it is succinct. Brevity speaks loudly. Second, it is memorable not only for the emotional ideas it conveys, but also for its use of alliteration through the words "trusted" and "terrible." Alliteration is where two or more adjacent or closely connected words in a sentence start with the same consonant or sound, which gives those words a certain ring and makes them easier to remember. Finally, Lanier uses the "Rule of Three," which will be discussed in more detail later. For the trial lawyer, the bottom-line message ties your whole trial together. It can form the topics for your direct examinations. For example, if you were Lanier's co-counsel, you could introduce a witness to the jury by telling them, "Now, I'd like to ask you some questions about why you trusted Dr. Smith."

The Bottom-Line Message Cannot Be Bland

Many new lawyers will start their openings by saying, "This is a case about broken promises," or something to that effect. While such a tactic certainly frames the subject matter of the opening statement, it is not very creative. It would be similar to reading a headline on a website that said, "This is an article about the Yankees winning with their hitting." Instead, put some drama into it by writing something like, "Clutch Hit Shows Yankees' Grit."

> **Practice Tip**
>
> Win the jury's attention. Instead of saying, "This is a case about broken promises," declare that "The defendant promised gold and delivered mold."

The great jazz pianist Thelonious Monk once said that you should make your mistakes loud—don't hide them. The reason is that if you are cautious, you can never become great. Similarly, Steven Dietz, a playwright, said the most important thing he teaches students is "boldness. This is different from being 'interesting.' Boldness is action with purpose. I'd rather my students and their plays were strong and wrong than slight and right. Plays die of caution." Likewise, trials die from caution. Don't be boring. Juries will never reward you.

The Rule of Three

The "Rule of Three" is a perfect tool to craft a bottom-line message. The Rule of Three is a tried-and-true technique that is widely used in literature, movies, music, and advertising, because it provides a powerful way for conveying information. The reason for this is that the human brain is very receptive and easily remembers information that is presented in groups of three. For example, stories have a beginning, a middle, and an end. Songs are built around a three-chord progression. Painters and photographers create their compositions using the Rule of Thirds. Without realizing it, we organize our entire day using the Rule of Three as we plan breakfast, lunch, and dinner. The Christian religion is grounded in the Holy Trinity and many other religions use the Rule of Three. Our country was founded on three inalienable rights: "Life, liberty, and the pursuit of happiness." The examples go on and on.

The point is that groups of three have a familiar rhythm and pattern to them that are easy for audiences to understand and remember. Abraham Lincoln knew this and used the rule of three in his Gettysburg Address. Lincoln crafted his address on the past, present, and future. As his address crescendos to its powerful climax, Lincoln urges the audience to not let the soldiers' deaths be in vain but to resolve that the nation will "have a new birth of freedom—and that the government *of the people, by the people, for the people* shall not perish from the earth." This definition of democracy, using a list of three qualities, is one of Lincoln's—and for that matter, that of any other president's—most memorable phrases. Lincoln's economic word choice is so much more memorable than if he would have just listed 10 qualities of democracy or droned on and on as Edward Everett did in his two-hour speech before Lincoln's powerful address.

Alliteration, Assonance, and Anaphora

As stated earlier, alliteration is where two or more adjacent or closely connected words in a sentence start with the same consonant or sound, which gives those words a certain ring and makes them easier to remember. An example would be, "Peter Piper picked a peck of pickled peppers." Assonance is the repetition of the sound of a vowel in words, as in "Try to light the fire," for example. Rhyming is similar to assonance, but it is where the consonants and the vowels in two words are the same. It is also good to use. Anaphora is where the same word or phrase is used at the beginning of successive phrases, as illustrated in the Gettysburg address where Lincoln says "*We cannot* dedicate, *we cannot* consecrate, *we cannot* hallow this ground."

As a starting point, I always try to find three words that have alliteration that will be the anchor of my bottom-line message. It does not work all the time, but it usually does. For example, a simple bottom-line message for a criminal case could be: He committed a crime, covered it up, and got caught.

Using alliteration becomes easy with just a little practice. I suggest you do it as often as you can to describe people or situations so that you get good at it. It can be a fun game.

I always find that my bottom-line message gets finalized in my brain after I have exercised, walked my dog, or taken a shower. You need to think about your bottom-line message, let it go, and then you will be amazed at how it will come back to you fully formed.

3.6 GIVE YOUR STORY A SOUL BY EMPHASIZING AT LEAST ONE HUMAN TRUTH (2ND ELEMENT)

For your story to have any persuasive value, it has to stir the judge's or jurors' emotions. As Brené Brown advised at the beginning of this chapter, a story must have a "soul." To do that, it must convey a core human truth or value that helps explain why your story matters, which is the second element of a compelling story. This human truth or value must be contained in your bottom-line message and highlighted throughout your story. Let's look at some resources to help you articulate a human truth or value in your story.

> *Think less about what you are doing and more about why you are doing it.*
> —Pharrell Williams

A great place to start is *The Book of Virtues* by William J. Bennett. Bennett's book is a collection of stories from the Bible, Greek mythology, American history, English poetry, and other sources that exemplify important character traits. Better yet, Bennett divides the stories in his book into 10 traits that are essential to good character. Those traits are self-discipline, compassion, responsibility, friendship, work, courage, perseverance, honesty, loyalty, and faith. Any of those traits are wonderful human values for you to use in your story.

For example, do you have a breach of contract case that would be more interesting to the jury if you framed it around the human values of responsibility and honesty? If so, go to the specific chapter in Bennett's book and find a story that exemplifies that value, create a bottom-line message, and then expand on it for your opening statement and closing argument.

On the other hand, you might want to characterize your opponent with the opposite of these good character traits. For example, your opponent in a breach of contract case may be irresponsible and dishonest. You can also frame your story around your opponent's bad behavior using the seven deadly sins: wrath, greed, sloth, pride, lust, envy, and gluttony. Greed is an ugly trait that can describe many opponents' behavior.

Let's look at an example from a recent lawsuit involving a record $1.8 billion settlement agreement for insider trading. One of the top hedge fund companies in the country, SAC Capital Advisors (led by Steven Cohen, who is worth over $9 billion), settled criminal and civil charges of insider trading and agreed to unwind its business as an investment adviser. The FBI's special agent in charge, April Brooks, said, "Principles are just as important as profit. How your employees make their money is just as important as how much they make."

The special agent succinctly summarized her case with a perfect moral. She boiled down what she represented (principles) with what the defendant represented (illegal profits). Her bottom-line message is also effective because so few words are used. Her moral also resonates because "principles" and "profits" is an alliteration, so there is a memorable ring to her word choice. While any case can be boiled down to right versus wrong, this is more powerful because it explains why one side is right and the other side is not.

3.7 USE A CAPTIVATING STRUCTURE THAT STARTS STRONG (3RD ELEMENT)

The third element of a story is that it needs a captivating structure and a strong beginning. Let's look first at how to structure a story and then how to start it strong.

Freytag's Pyramid

Since Aristotle, there have been various descriptions of how to construct a dramatic story. The best one comes from Gustav Freytag, a German novelist and playwright who, in the 1800s, analyzed the dramatic story in what later became widely known

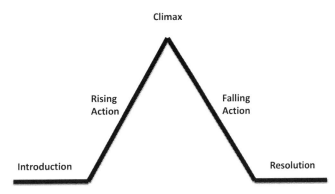

Figure 2. Freytag's Pyramid.

as Freytag's pyramid. It was based on viewing stories as a tension between a hero (protagonist) and an antagonist, which is exactly what plays out in a courtroom. Freytag's pyramid (see Fig. 2) is built on five parts of a story: (1) introduction; (2) rising action; (3) climax; (4) falling action; and (5) resolution.

This structure for storytelling is what you were taught in high school, but it probably was not associated with Freytag. Even though it is simple and obvious, it is a good starting place for giving you a foundation for how to structure your story. When you think about crafting your story, decide what the climax is going to be first, then think about the introduction; that is, how are you going to get your audience interested in your climax? The third thing to consider is how are you going to resolve or conclude your story. The other two parts—the rising action and falling action—just get you to and from the climax. They are the easiest parts.

> **Practice Tip**
>
> An effective structure is essential because there is a human desire to make sense of what one is hearing. Your job is to satisfy that longing by making sense.

Chronological Structure

Using the Freytag pyramid as a framework, the simplest way—but probably not the best way because it is so common—to structure your story is chronologically. Let's return to the DePuy hip implant case. If you were going to tell the plaintiff's story, you could start your story with a strong bottom-line message and then tell the jury a chronological story that begins with a plaintiff having hip pain (the introduction), then the search for a doctor and treatment for it (rising action). The climax would be the surgery where the DePuy metal-on-metal hip implant was put in the plaintiff. The falling action would be the complications from the surgery, and the resolution would be the current pain the plaintiff is in.

Conversely, if you represented DePuy, you could also tell a chronological story that begins with DePuy's development of a hip implant to help relieve people's pain and provide them with mobility; the rising action would be a doctor's decision to use the hip implant as a medically reasonable solution; the climax would be the surgery; and the falling action would focus on reasons for post-surgical complications other than the hip implant. One reason could be the patient's hip alignment that caused a more difficult recovery, compared to those of other successful surgeries. The resolution could be a showing of sympathy for the plaintiff and further explanation of why the product was safe.

However, depending on your case, the chronological structure may not be the most persuasive one to use. Do you remember Petrarch's quote mentioned earlier? He said, "Sameness is the mother of our disgust, variety the surest cure." The chronological structure is the default for so many stories that if you can add some variety, you will take the lead in getting and keeping your audience's attention.

Flashback

The simplest way to alter and bring variety to the chronological structure is to use a flashback. Instead of starting at the beginning of the story, start at the end. If you were the plaintiff's lawyer in the DePuy litigation, you could talk about the pain, anger, and frustration a client is currently suffering (the resolution part of Freytag's pyramid). Then, you could flashback to the beginning by saying, "Ladies and gentlemen of the jury, let me go to the beginning and tell you how we got here." If you were the defense attorney, you should not use the flashback structure because it would unduly emphasize the plaintiff's pain by highlighting it at the beginning of your story.

Mystery

Although mystery is a genre of storytelling, for our purposes, think of it as a way to structure your story. Everyone loves a mystery. Brain science proves that it holds people's attention. (See discussion of the Zeigarnik effect in chapter 4). Think about how you can structure your story so that you continually add more facts to hint at the answer or the key to solving the mystery without revealing it. Then, when you have the jury at its fullest attention, you can give the big reveal. In the hip implant case, if you were the defense attorney, you could take away the power of plaintiff's emotional opening by beginning your opening statement with, "There is a mystery we want your help in solving. Why is the plaintiff accusing us of something we did not do?" Then, you could lay out the facts that explain why the plaintiff is misguided and then give them the answer or key to solving the mystery. Perhaps your answer is that the plaintiff was misdiagnosed, or maybe their anger is misdirected, or their expert has misled them about the cause of his problem. By the way, did you notice the alliteration in the previous sentence (*misdiagnosed, misdirected, misled*)? It would make for a perfect bottom-line message.

The List

Another structural variation is to make a list. This would be a departure from Freytag's pyramid, but it is easy to use and can be very effective. In the above paragraph, let's assume you are the defense attorney for DePuy. Using the list structure, you could begin your opening statement with a powerful bottom-line message and tell the jury the following, "This is a case about a misdiagnosis, misdirected anger, and being misled by a hired expert." Then, using that bottom-line message as your list of three topics, tell the jury, "Let me first tell you about the misdiagnosis of the treating doctor who claimed our product was at fault. . . . Second, let's talk about the misdirected anger."

You can get really creative with lists. You could tell the jury that this case is about four days. Then, tell the jury what it is that is important about those four days. Perhaps Wednesday, Feb. __, 20__ was the day that the company got the patent that allowed it to produce the product in question. The second day was the day the medical community hailed the company's innovation. The third day was the day a report showed that thousands of doctors had chosen to use the product on their patients. The last day is today, the day that a jury can finally decide that what the company did was right.

Comparisons

You can also frame your story by using comparisons. For example, you could tell the jury what your client was doing and then compare it to what the opposing side was doing at the same time. In a breach of contract case, you could explain how your client was spending money and investing time and resources to fulfill their obligations under the contract. Then, you could contrast that with the other side's failure to do things they committed to do under the contract during the same time period. Then, you could transition to another time period and make another comparison.

> The most amazing thing for me is that every single person who sees a movie, not necessarily one of my movies, brings a whole set of unique experiences. Now, through careful manipulation and good storytelling, you can get everybody to clap at the same time, to hopefully laugh at the same time, and to be afraid at the same time.
>
> —Steven Spielberg

A Closer Look at How Lanier Structures Stories

Let's examine in more detail how Lanier structured his opening statements in his four trials in the DePuy Hip Implant litigation. Over 9,000 plaintiffs filed suit against DePuy Orthopedics, Inc., and its parent company, Johnson & Johnson, regarding the alleged defective design and deceptive advertising of the Pinnacle Acetabular Cup System hip implants. Lanier was chosen by a Plaintiffs Lawyers' Committee to try the bellwether cases to determine the merit of plaintiffs' claims. Lanier's success at the trials led to DePuy's decision to settle thousands of the lawsuits.

For additional context, here are some more facts about the case. The implant was used to help patients who had diseased hip joints. Patients were told that the implant would alleviate their pain and allow them to regain motion in their hips. In short, the plaintiffs argued that DePuy negligently designed and deceptively marketed the Pinnacle System metal-on-metal (MoM) hip implant to patients. The plaintiffs' major complaint was that the Pinnacle System was sold without testing it in humans first (they had used a variant in their tests on humans).

The plaintiffs claimed the complications from the hip implants were disastrous. As the metal on metal system moved with each motion of the leg, metal ions were released into the blood stream with potentially toxic results for the body. In addition, around the area of the implant, irreversible damage to the muscles and bone often occurred.

In the first trial in September 2014, Lanier structured his story around a puzzle. He showed the jury a PowerPoint slide with the image of a courthouse as a completed jigsaw puzzle. The courthouse symbolized justice. He explained that his grandfather taught him that to solve a puzzle, you first looked at the picture of the solved puzzle to see where you needed to go, then you looked through the pieces to first find the misfit pieces, those pieces that stood out from all the others because of their irregular shapes. With that introduction, Lanier talked about the misfit pieces and how they were analogous to DePuy's bad conduct and key to solving the puzzle.

In the second trial, held in January 2016, Lanier used the metaphor of a book to structure his story. He showed them a PowerPoint slide with a picture of a book and the title, "The Account of a Medical Experiment Gone Wrong." There were three chapters to the book. Chapter One was "The Seduction," Chapter Two was "The Truth," and Chapter Three was "Consequences." His story was tied together by his bottom-line message: the plaintiffs "trusted a product, trusted their doctors, and got terrible results."

In October 2017, during the third trial, he explained to the jury that the devastation from Hurricane Harvey in his hometown, Houston, caused him to think about home inspections. He told the jurors to consider themselves to be like home inspectors—that their job was to examine the house that Johnson & Johnson and DePuy had built—and that his job was to show them everything they needed to file a home inspection report. He then began his story by describing the bad foundation that Johnson & Johnson's house was built on, in terms of the design, marketing, and sale of its metal-on-metal hip implant.

In the fourth trial, held in January 2019, Lanier structured his opening statement by using a PowerPoint slide that pictured a road with four signs on it. He explained to the jury that there would be four stops. The first stop would be "Overview," where the jury would hear an overview of the case. The second stop would be "Seduction," where the jury would hear how Depuy seduced the medical community to use their device. The third stop would be "Truth." At that stop, Lanier would explain the truth that Depuy knew about the dangers of its product but continued to use it. The last stop would be "Consequences," where Lanier would discuss the results of Depuy's actions.

Lanier used the road map as a way to structure his story so the jury could see where he was in his story and where he was going. At the first stop, when Lanier gave an overview of the case, Lanier mentioned his bottom-line message, which he had used in the second trial: "This is a case about five people who trusted a product, trusted their doctor, and they got a terrible result."

3.8 START STRONG WITH A LIGHTNING BOLT

Whether you are at a hearing or a trial, you need to start the structure of your story strong. Ironically, at the beginning of a trial, a very common instruction that is given to jurors is that they should "keep an open mind throughout the presentation of the evidence." In an ideal world, such an instruction would make sense. But in reality, it is nonsense, because human beings cannot help but to quickly start forming opinions when they receive information.

Thank the Jury or Judge

Consequently, the one hard-and-fast rule for ordering the parts of your opening statement at trial is that you must start strong. To do that, thank the jury sincerely for their sacrifice of serving on the jury. If it is not heartfelt, it is a complete waste of time and prevents you from creating momentum. But if it is heartfelt, it creates an immediate connection between you and them. Then, start with your bottom-line message.

Take Advantage of Confirmation Bias, Limited Attention Spans, and Snap Decisions

As you will see in chapter 4 on brain science, studies have shown that humans make decisions based on confirmation bias. That is, the brain forms a belief and will sift through subsequently conflicting information to find only the evidence that supports the initial belief. Studies also show (discussed below) that judges and jurors also have limited attention spans and make snap decisions.

For these three reasons, the beginning of your story is the most important and the hardest part to get right. Think of this moment as if it were a lightning bolt. It grabs everyone's attention. After seeing a lightning bolt, everyone waits to hear the thunder. Likewise, you have this one moment to set the tone, get the judge or jury on your side, and never let them go.

Common sense confirms the importance of a strong beginning, but for some reason, lawyers rarely execute it. It is no accident that news articles always lead with the attention-grabbing detail in order to entice the reader. Trailers for movies always start with an exciting scene. Musicians start their shows with one of their best songs. Art exhibitions put the most popular work of art on the brochure's cover.

Your compelling story is no different. The reason you cannot delay is that if you are bland and boring, the audience (i.e., the jury) will quickly decide there are better ways to spend its time and will focus instead on something else.

Moreover, people can't help but make these snap judgments. There is a new field of psychology that studies the part of our brain that makes these very quick judgments—and often accurate ones—using only minimal information. It is the study of the adaptive unconscious.

One psychologist conducted a study to measure the accuracy of snap judgments made by students about a professor they did not know compared to the snap judgments of students who had taken a class with the professor for an entire semester. The study found that "a person watching a silent two-second video clip of a teacher he or she has never met will reach conclusions about how good that teacher is that are very similar to those of a student who has sat in the teacher's class for an entire semester." What is even more fascinating is that the students were watching a *silent* video clip. Other studies have shown that we start to make up our minds about other people within seven seconds of first meeting them.

After thanking the jury, deliver your bottom-line message. Your bottom-line message is your lightning bolt, but keep the momentum going for the first part of your story. Below are some suggestions.

Use a Quote from Anticipated Witness Testimony

You could follow your bottom-line message with an exact quote from your star witness's expected testimony. It needs to be dramatic, but you must be certain that the witness will testify exactly as you predict. You get this assurance from repeated witness preparation or knowing that the witness has made the statement previously in a deposition or a written document.

Likewise, you can capture the jury's attention by using a quote from a key witness for the opposing side that highlights the hypocrisy of their position at trial. When the devastating quote is from the opposing witness, you need to be certain that on cross-examination you can prove that the witness made the statement in the past. Although lawyers are often fearful of boldly predicting testimony in opening statement, there is nothing to fear about this, as long as the witness has made the statement prior to trial and you can prove it (i.e., through deposition testimony or a written document).

Use a Dramatic Exhibit

Consider displaying an eye-catching exhibit in the first 30 seconds of your presentation. Oftentimes, by the agreement of counsel, the exhibits will be pre-admitted before the trial even starts. Other times, you can argue to the judge that the exhibit will easily be admitted once the trial starts, so there is no harm in showing it (you are essentially asking for it to be pre-admitted).

Another tool to use is to create a persuasive visual aid such as a road map with signposts that have the opposing side's mistakes written on them. Another idea is to show a photo of a jigsaw puzzle and explain to the jury that you are going to put the pieces of the puzzle together for the jury so that the picture on the puzzle is crystal clear. This will be discussed in more detail in chapter 5.

> **Practice Tip**
>
> In your lightning bolt, you can gain credibility by connecting what you are saying to a famous person's quote. People are more likely to believe you if Abraham Lincoln said something similar. I often work Mark Twain into my presentations. Brainyquote.com is a great source for quotations from him and others.

Introduce Your Clients

A powerful technique to use when starting your story is to introduce your client to the jury. By doing this, you immediately create an emotional connection between your client and the jury. Sometimes, there is no better way to create sympathy for your client and your case than to start off by putting a human face on the story you are about to tell. As we saw above, jurors make snap decisions, and they can learn a lot just by you focusing their attention on your client through a simple introduction.

Examples of Lightning Bolts from Trials

Here are just a few famous (and not-so-famous) and effective (except where noted) lightning bolts.

HARTZLER: *Ladies and gentlemen of the jury, April 19th, 1995, was a beautiful day in Oklahoma City—at least it started out as a beautiful day. The sun was shining. Flowers were blooming. It was springtime in Oklahoma City. Sometime after six o'clock that morning, Tevin Garrett's mother woke him up to get him ready for the day. He was only sixteen months old. He was a toddler; and as some of you know that have experience with toddlers, he had a keen eye for mischief. He would often pull on the cord of her curling iron in the morning, pull it off the countertop until it fell down, often 'til it fell down on him.*

That morning, she picked him up and wrestled with him on her bed before she got him dressed. She remembers this morning because that was the last morning of his life.

—Joseph Hartzler, prosecutor in the Oklahoma City bombing trial

> **Practice Tip**
>
> Hone your skill to create a lightning bolt by collecting passages from books and articles that start strongly, or, for comparison's sake, very badly.

Compare this excellent beginning to the terrible beginning made in an opening statement in the O.J. Simpson trial. Christopher Darden was a prosecutor in the O.J. Simpson trial. He had so many resources available to him to make a compelling story. He had great facts, the vast resources of the government, and the technology to create visual aids. How would you capture the attention of the jury that was being sequestered for the trial, knowing that your words would be broadcast live on national television? This is what he said in his opening:

Darden: I think it's fair to say that I have the toughest job in town today except for the job that you have. Your job may just be a little bit tougher. It's your job—like my job, we both have a central focus, a single objective, and that objective is justice obviously.

Can you think of one good reason why he would begin this way? I hope not, because what he said is the last thing the jury wanted to hear. Are we supposed to feel sorry for Darden that he has a tough job? Why admit a weakness unnecessarily? On top of that, he cautions that the jurors that they have an even tougher job.

What if, instead, Darden had said the following:

Ladies and gentlemen, this is a straightforward case. All the evidence points toward O. J. Simpson's guilt. There is the defendant's glove and DNA evidence found at the murder scene. There is blood from the victims found in Mr. Simpson's car. There is blood from Nicole found on Mr. Simpson's socks. Your job will be easy.

Below are two examples from the Vioxx litigation mentioned earlier in the section on how to develop facts for a bottom-line message. These are the beginnings of the defendant's opening statements from two different trials. Remember, the plaintiffs alleged that when they took Vioxx for an extended period of time for their arthritis, the Vioxx caused their heart failure.

Defense Opening in First Vioxx Trial

May it please the Court. Good afternoon, ladies and gentlemen. My name is David Kiernan, and I'm pleased to speak with you this afternoon on behalf of Merck.

As you might imagine, we wouldn't be here today if there weren't two sides to this story. If it were an open-and-shut case, as plaintiffs have suggested, this case would have been over long ago. As Judge Hardin mentioned during jury selection, this will be a somewhat lengthy case, lots of evidence to be presented, documents, and witnesses, some live, and some who gave their sworn testimony before trial and videotape. You'll see both during this trial.

We appreciate the important job that each of you have ahead of you. It's a tough job to sort through and weigh all of the evidence, to tell the difference between allegations and proof; and we appreciate you undertaking that responsibility here.

*We believe that at the end of this case you will see that the scientists and leaders at Merck conducted themselves **prudently and responsibly**.*

Here, the attorney tells the jury that it will be a long trial, they have a tough job, and the best he can hope for is that they will conclude Merck acted prudently and responsibly. On the other hand, the plaintiffs' attorney, Mark Lanier, told the jurors he would make their job easy for them. He explained that they should see themselves as if they were detectives on the show CSI Angleton (Angleton is the town where the trial was being held). Lanier told the jurors that it was their calling to bring Merck to justice because no one else could.

Which side do you think won? Lanier won a record-setting verdict for the plaintiffs. To prove that your lightning bolt can make a difference, let's look at another Vioxx trial with similar facts. The plaintiff's attorney was not Mark Lanier, but there was also a different defense attorney, and he approached his opening statement much better.

Defense Opening Statement in Another Vioxx Trial

Thank you, your honor. Mr. Birchfield [plaintiff's counsel] talked for about 60 minutes. While he was talking, about 60 people across the United States died from exactly the same thing that caused Mr. Irvin's [plaintiff's] death and not a single one of them was taking Vioxx.

I'm going to talk for about 60 minutes, and while I'm talking another 60 people across the United States will die of the same thing that caused Mr. Irvin's death, and not a single one of them is taking Vioxx. The reason is that the thing that caused Mr. Irvin's death is the leading cause of death in the United States of America. That was true before Vioxx ever came on the market, and that's true today after Vioxx is no longer being sold. Several hundred thousand people a year die from having arteries that are clogged up with plaque, then having a rupture in the plaque, and then having a blood clot form in the artery so that not enough blood gets to the heart. It's the leading cause of death in the United States.

Merck would get a hung jury in this trial and then win on the retrial. Notice how well the defense attorney, David Beck, frames his argument. Unlike Kiernan's view in the first trial that it is going to be a long trial with a lot of evidence that presents a tough job for the jury, Beck says the case is simple: the plaintiff died from something that is very common in America; indeed, it is the leading cause of death and it has nothing to do with Vioxx. While Kiernan's approach was defensive and apologetic, Beck came out swinging. Finally, while Kiernan's content was bland, Beck provided the jury with a startling fact about how heart disease is the leading cause of death in the United States.

3.9 USE DESCRIPTIVE LANGUAGE (4TH ELEMENT)

The foundation of persuasive courtroom storytelling is to describe the issue and solution so vividly for your audience that what you say is interesting and memorable. Whether you are describing a simple car accident or a complicated business contract that was breached, you need to paint a picture using descriptive words and fresh images to make the event come to life. This is the fourth element of a compelling story. This idea that descriptive language is persuasive is not just based on common sense, but is backed up by brain science research. (See the discussion in chapter 4, the Primacy of Association: Words and Metaphors.)

One way to use descriptive language is to create an analogy (a comparison that is made between two things to provide an explanation). For example, in a patent infringement case, which can be often quite technical and complicated, you could declare, "Like a student who looks over another student's shoulder and cheats on a test, Samsung stole Apple's ideas for its latest phone."

But be careful. The right image is extremely powerful, but if the image does not connect with your audience, you will strike out and have little chance to recover. The power of metaphors and similes is that they can help deepen an audience's understanding of an idea. In the Apple and Samsung example, the image that Apple used could backfire if the facts do not support Apple. Samsung could respond, "Apple claims Samsung cheated. The exact opposite is true. Like the student taking the test, why would anyone try and get answers from someone who was failing the test. Samsung was the smartest one in the class. . . ."

Metaphors and similes are also persuasive. A metaphor makes comparisons by substituting one thing for another, while a simile makes specific use of the words "as" or "like." For example, a metaphor would be "Plaintiff's claim is a house of cards," and a simile would be "Plaintiff's claims are like a house of cards."

Lessons from *The Phantom Tollbooth*

One of the best ways to develop descriptive language skills is to read well-written articles and literature and pay close attention to how great authors use words to paint a memorable picture of what happened. One of the best starting places is to read *The Phantom Tollbooth* by Norton Jester. It is a classic children's book that follows a young boy named Milo (and his dog Tock) on his journey to a fantasy world when he goes through a phantom tollbooth that appears in his bedroom. You should read the book for two reasons. First, the book uses wonderful descriptive language that will inspire you to do the same in your storytelling. Second, it teaches a wealth of lessons that can be used by public speakers. As a bonus, the book teaches many life lessons for children and adults alike.

I won't summarize the whole book here, but here are two examples from that book that you can use without reading it. At the beginning of the book there is a drawing of a road map that depicts "The Land Beyond" that shows the many areas that Milo will visit. Use this drawing as a springboard to think of how you would map out your next presentation and the descriptive language you would use to describe it. This will be discussed in later chapters, but for now, write the name of the topics you want to cover in your next presentation and think of a picture that goes with it and draw it on your map. Having a picture associated with the area you will visit will help you remember it and give you ideas on how to describe it colorfully to your audience. If your picture is good, you could consider using it as a visual aid to help the jury follow along with your presentation when you are giving it.

One area that Milo visits is the Valley of Sound, which the author describes with beautiful language. But Milo and his friends soon realize that there is no sound at all, even when they try to speak. Milo learns that The Soundkeeper got mad that the citizens no longer appreciated sound, and so she abolished it. Milo visits The Soundkeeper, and she says, "It doesn't make me happy to hold back the sounds, for if we listen to them carefully, they can sometimes tell us things far better than words."

The author constantly reminds the reader to be more observant of their surroundings and he uses descriptive language to encourage the reader to do so. Let's test the Soundkeeper's observation. Set aside 15 minutes the next time you are out for a walk or driving your car with the windows down. Pay attention to all the different sounds you hear and then try to describe them. Two things will happen. First, you will be amazed at all the sounds that you have never heard unless you stop and listen for them. Then, when you try to describe them, you will learn how to use descriptive language to convey the noises you heard to others who did not hear them. That is exactly what you should do at trial. You need descriptive language so you can make what your client has seen, done, or experienced come alive through the use of vivid language.

Consequently, when you are developing your story, use all the tools great writers rely on, including metaphors, similes, descriptive words, and sensory images. Your goal is to awaken the senses of the jury, and the more senses that you can involve, the more connected the jury will be to the story—and to you. For example, as you develop the story, think of images that will cause the jurors to use each of their five senses: sight, hearing, smell, taste, and touch.

For example, don't say the plaintiff was taken to the hospital, but instead say that the plaintiff was "rushed to the emergency room. Strapped tightly to the gurney, the plaintiff could hear the wailing sirens outside and the life support monitors beeping inside." Similarly, if you represent a company as a defendant, make your characters three dimensional, not just two dimensional. The manager is more than just a name and a title. Describe the manager's personality. What was the manager's tone of voice? Did the manager have a common saying that people knew him or her by?

> *When poets write about a large topic, they use imagery as a point of entry.*
> —Billy Collins,
> former U.S. Poet Laureate

3.10 TELL THE GOOD, THE BAD, AND THE UGLY ABOUT YOUR CASE (5TH ELEMENT)

The fifth element of a compelling story is that you have got to tell the bad as well as the good to maintain your credibility with the audience. That process starts with being skeptical of your client's story.

Be Skeptical of Your Client's Story

When you create your story, avoid the big mistake of buying into your client's version hook, line, and sinker. It is not that clients lie, but it is certainly true that they are often mistaken about details and may exaggerate the wrong that the other side committed. More important, clients are often in denial to some extent about their own wrongdoing. Clients typically will claim that they have done nothing wrong when facts later prove otherwise. You need to learn every important fact about your case as soon as possible so you can develop a story that will ring true to the jury.

The reason your clients will mislead you is that they are human, like everyone else. Almost everyone has an agenda that affects how truthful they will be. For example, in an ideal world, the most respected judges in the country—those on the Supreme Court—would be counted on to be 100 percent forthcoming and honest. However, even these judges have been documented to be less than straightforward when it served their agenda. A recent study found that nominees to the Supreme Court answer only "between 60 and 70 percent of their questions [at their confirmation hearings] in a fully forthcoming manner."

Determine Your Opponent's Story

In addition to trying to learn the bad facts of your case from your client, you can discover your weaknesses by discerning what your opponent's bottom-line message and story are. It is very rare that an attorney takes the time to determine how their opponent is going to try to win their case. But the attorney who does so has a distinct advantage because that is what will be revealed at trial. You must be objective enough to see the weaknesses in your case; otherwise, your witnesses will be surprised at the deposition and then at the trial when asked about bad facts that you have not recognized. When you uncover your opponent's theory, you can prepare your story so that it addresses the hard questions raised in your opponent's presentation.

The best way to make sure your story is solid is to prepare a closing argument as if you were the opposing counsel. By assuming the role of your opponent, you will see facts in a whole new light. Some facts that you previously thought were helpful will become neutralized, and facts that hurt you case will become magnified. The reason for this is that when you start arguing the other side of your case, you will naturally give facts a different context and a different meaning. Once you draft your opponent's closing, you will see more clearly the weaknesses in your case and be able to take corrective action by finding evidence to bolster those weaknesses.

The hardest thing about this exercise is forcing yourself to do it early in your case. But doing so bears repeating because it is so important. Set aside a few hours of uninterrupted time one morning early in the case. Prepare a mock closing for the other side. It obviously does not have to be perfectly organized. Practice delivering it with emotion. Really get into it with some passion. Again, your delivery does not need to be perfect. After doing this exercise, I guarantee that you will see weaknesses in your case that you had not seen before.

Practice Tip

For every hour you spend preparing your case, spend 20 minutes looking for its weaknesses as if you represented your opponent.

3.11 CONNECT YOUR CLIENT WITH THE EMOTIONS OF THE AUDIENCE (6TH ELEMENT)

A compelling story connects the storyteller with the emotions of the audience by inviting the audience into your client's situation (the sixth element). If you represent a company, your audience needs to get to know the people that make up your company and why they should relate to them. In essence, you are inviting the audience into your client's world and connecting with them through a compelling story so that the audience will want to step in. Once the audience comes in, you can engage it. Remember Mark Twain's quote, "Emotions are among the toughest things in the world to create out of whole cloth; it is easier to manufacture seven facts than one emotion."

How do you do this? It is easier with individual plaintiffs, because you are trying to relate one human's experience, the plaintiff's, with another, the humans on the jury. We are hard-wired to care about other people, so you have an already built-in connection to build on.

But if you represent a company, you need to make your company human. Think of it this way. Instead of representing a company, you represent the people in the company. In a products liability case, when the injured plaintiff tries to paint the company as an uncaring organization that is only concerned about profits, you can connect with the jury by showing that the CEO, engineers, scientists, etc. are people who care deeply about the products the company makes because they want to help people (i.e., like the people on the jury).

3.12 BASE YOUR STORY ON THE LAW THAT GOVERNS YOUR CASE (7TH ELEMENT)

The final element of a compelling story is that its claim or defense must be supported by the law. People suffer wrongs every day, but that does not mean there is always a viable lawsuit.

Surprisingly, while many attorneys have a "pretty good" idea of what the law is that governs their claims or defenses, they do not know with certainty the details, and failure to have this knowledge can often prove devastating at a hearing or trial. For example, a plaintiff's attorney may file a lawsuit, take 10 depositions, and on the eve of a hearing find out that what he thought was a breach of contract by the defendant was not a "material breach" as defined by the case law, and that he cannot survive a defense motion for summary judgment at the hearing.

There are myriad reasons why lawyers don't know the law as well as they should when a case begins. One reason is procrastination; it is easier to start a case and worry about the details later. Another may be an eagerness to take a case, believe your client, and hope the law can be massaged to fit the facts of the case. Whatever the reason, the failure to know the precise law that governs a case is a common mistake lawyers make, whether the case is small or large.

Let's look at one of the most famous cases of this century, *State v. Zimmerman*, and see how important it is to know the law. The following are the important facts from the case.

On Sunday, February 26, 2012, seventeen-year-old Trayvon Martin and his father, Tracy Martin, were visiting Tracy Martin's girlfriend (Brandy Green) and her twelve-year-old son (Chad Joseph), who lived in a townhouse in a gated complex known as "The Retreat at Twin Lakes" in Sanford, Florida. Around 6:00 p.m., Trayvon left the home and walked to a 7-Eleven store to buy some Skittles candy and an Arizona brand fruit drink. On his way back to Green's home, George Zimmerman, a neighborhood watch captain at The Retreat, saw Trayvon and called the police non-emergency number to report that Trayvon looked suspicious.

Zimmerman explained to the operator that there had been several recent break-ins in his neighborhood and said "there's a real suspicious guy. . . . This guy looks like he's up to no good, or he's on drugs or something." The operator replied that the police were on the way. Zimmerman responded, "These assholes, they always get away." Later in the phone call, Zimmerman said under his breath, "Fucking punks." Meanwhile, Trayvon Martin was talking on his cell phone to his friend, Rachael Jentel.

What happened next that evening was hotly contested at trial. Both sides agreed that before the police arrived, Zimmerman had shot one bullet from his licensed handgun into Trayvon's chest. Trayvon was pronounced dead at the scene.

When police interviewed Zimmerman at the scene, he told them that he shot Trayvon because Trayvon had thrown him to the ground, gotten on top of him, and started hitting him in the face while he was flat on his back on the sidewalk. At trial, the prosecution argued that Zimmerman was a "wanna-be cop" who profiled Trayvon because he was Black, and then followed him and shot him because he was so frustrated with the numerous burglaries that had occurred in his neighborhood. The prosecution charged Zimmerman with second degree murder; Zimmerman claimed he acted in self-defense.

Given what we have learned so far, the prosecutors had to develop a bottom-line message that was supported by the law. We will see that the prosecutors—for whatever reason—did not know the law well enough.

At the beginning of a case, you should go to your jurisdiction's court website to find the "pattern jury instructions" (the model set of instructions) for your type of case. Most state and federal appellate courts have pattern jury instructions that apply to the most common civil and criminal trials. Trial courts routinely use these instructions to provide uniformity and because the appellate court has approved their use.

In deciding whether to prosecute Zimmerman and what crime to charge him with, the prosecutors chose second-degree murder. It has three requirements under Florida law: (1) a person is dead, (2) the death was caused by the criminal act of another, and (3) the unlawful killing was done by an act imminently dangerous to another and demonstrated a depraved mind without regard for human life. Unlike first degree murder, premeditation is not required.

Next, it would also be crucial for the prosecutors to know how the Florida court would define the third element of second degree murder: an act that is "imminently dangerous to another and demonstrating a depraved mind." That definition has several components, but the most relevant one is that the act "is done from ill will, hatred, spite or evil intent." So, the key for the prosecutors was to prove that Zimmerman killed out of ill will or hatred.

Finally, the prosecutors would need to know whether there could be any legal defense for Zimmerman's actions, even if they proved these elements of second degree murder. A possible defense to second degree murder includes self-defense. A person is justified in using deadly force "if he reasonably believes that such force is necessary to prevent imminent death or great bodily harm to himself."

Once you know the precise legal requirements that you will need to meet to win at trial, that knowledge will guide your investigation and preparation. Later, we will see that the prosecution made a critical error in charging Zimmerman with second degree murder. There were simply not enough facts for the prosecution to support the legal requirement of acting with ill will or hatred to prove that that Zimmerman committed second degree murder when he decided to kill Trayvon.

Tellingly, the prosecutor's first sentence in opening statement at the Zimmerman trial was, "Good morning, 'Fucking punks, these assholes, they always get away.'" This bottom-line message was built on the theory that Zimmerman said those words—as recorded on a call he made to a police dispatcher—a few minutes before the murder and that those words were evidence of Zimmerman's ill-will and hatred, which was necessary to prove second degree murder. The prosecutor's bottom-line message failed because he did not have enough evidence to back it up. He should get credit for taking the time to develop one, but he spent his time creating the wrong one.

The prosecutor mentioned this bottom-line message several times in his opening statement and closing argument. It was a refrain he would reuse repeatedly and each time follow up with different facts: "Those were the words in that man's chest when he got out of his car armed with a fully loaded semi-automatic pistol to follow on foot Trayvon Benjamin Martin, who was walking home from a 7-Eleven armed with 23 ounces of Arizona-brand fruit juice and a small bag of Skittles candies."

But as the *New York Times* observed, the prosecution had a difficult case that was "weak on evidence and long on outrage." While the outrage was very well founded, the problem was that the prosecution had very little evidence other than this one statement to prove ill will and hatred. The evidence at trial supported Zimmerman's self-defense claim that he was flat on his back on the sidewalk, getting repeatedly hit by Trayvon just before he pulled his gun. An officer who arrived on the scene said he believed Zimmerman's account, and a forensic expert testified that the gunshots were consistent with Martin straddling Zimmerman while Zimmerman was lying on his back as the shooting took place. There was additional evidence from a neighbor who saw Martin punching Zimmerman in a mixed martial arts style while he was straddling Zimmerman, and that Zimmerman was crying for help.

Also, in contrast to the prosecutor's bottom-line message, Zimmerman's recorded call to the police revealed that Zimmerman was very calm and not angry. Furthermore, there were photographs of Zimmerman's head showing abrasions and bumps on the back of his head and a bloody nose. Finally, the weakness in the prosecution's case was its own admission to the jury that the sad truth was that we all wanted to hear Trayvon's version but couldn't because of Zimmerman's actions.

3.13 OVERCOMING WRITER'S BLOCK

At some point when you create your story, you will encounter writer's block at least once, and likely many times. It affects everyone and can stop you dead in your tracks before you ever even begin to write a compelling story or at any point after you get started. One cause of writer's block is that we assume that creating an opening statement or a presentation for a hearing should come naturally, and when it doesn't, we wait for a moment of inspiration before we continue. Another cause is that we have very high expectations for our work, and when it doesn't meet them, we stop creating. While it is very tempting to procrastinate until the process becomes easy or the quality is high, that is not a viable solution because waiting does not move the process forward.

I have found that the fail-safe key to overcoming writer's block is to lower your expectations and to force yourself to set aside some time to either get started or keep writing, depending on when writer's block hits you. Once you have set aside the time, if you sit down and still can't write anything, lower your expectations some more. If you still cannot write anything, keep lowering your expectations.

At some point, your expectations may need to be so low that just by writing one word, you will exceed your expectations. And once you start writing—even one word—things will start to flow.

Taylor Swift said, "I have to write 100 songs before I write the first good one." Consequently, accept the fact that what you first write will be pretty bad, probably terrible. Take that first step. If writer's block hits you later in the creative process, recalibrate your expectations so that they are lower and you will get rid of it. Similarly, you can get inspiration from Margaret Atwood, who has been called the "Prophet of Dystopia" and one of our generation's best writers. She explained that when you are writing, "if you are struggling to get started, you are afraid of something. Remember, it is only you and the page. The wastepaper basket is your friend. It was invented for you by God. Any form of creativity is the process of doing it and getting better at it. You become a writer by writing. There is no other way. So do it. Do it more. Fail. Fail better."

Now that we have learned how to tell a compelling story, let's turn to the next chapter and learn the latest from brain science on how to turn your compelling story into a persuasive presentation.

SUGGESTED ADDITIONAL READING

1. *The New Book of Plots*, Loren Niemi (Parkhurst, 2012). This book explains how to structure a plot and gives examples from popular books and movies.

2. *From Plot to Narrative*, Elizabeth Ellis (Parkhurst, 2012). The author won the highest honor for a storyteller. "Putting It Altogether" and "Sharing It Aloud" are two outstanding chapters in this thoroughly excellent book.

3. *The Phantom Tollbooth*, Norton Jester (Yearling, 1961). The children's book uses wonderful descriptive language that will motivate you to do the same in your storytelling. Second, it teaches a wealth of lessons that can be used by public speakers, as discussed earlier in this chapter. As a bonus, the book teaches many life lessons for children and adults alike.

4. *On Writing: A Memoir of the Craft*, Stephen King (Scribner, 2010). One of the most critically acclaimed books on how to write a story.

CHAPTER CHECKLIST

1. Studies show that if you give people random facts, they will create stories from them.

2. When a person listens to a story, their brain waves actually start to synchronize with those of the storyteller. The more the storyteller captivated the listener, the more that the listener's brainwaves matched the storyteller's.

3. Even at a hearing before a judge who is familiar with the facts of your case, don't abandon the use of a story to persuade.

4. The judge or jury want to know three things at all costs: (1) What do you want?; (2) Why should I care?; and (3) Why should I side with you instead of your opponent?

5. A compelling story: (1) delivers a bottom-line message you want your audience to understand above all else; (2) has a soul by emphasizing at least one human truth about why your story matters; (3) uses a structure that starts strong and best relates what happened; (4) uses descriptive language to tell what happened; (5) tells the good, the bad, and the ugly about your case; (6) connects your client through the storyteller to the emotions of the audience; and (7) is based on the law that governs your case.

6. To create a bottom-line message, take the good, neutral, and bad facts of your case and find a way to make as many of the bad facts neutral or good ones as possible. Then, write a phrase or sentence that best explains your case and that fits on the inside flap of a matchbook cover.

7. A great example of a bottom-line message is the one Mark Lanier used in the hip implant case: "This is a case about six people who trusted a product, trusted a doctor, and got terrible results."

8. To create a memorable and persuasive bottom-line message, use the Rule of Three (three ideas) combined with alliteration, assonance, or anaphora.

9. For your story to have any persuasive value, it has to stir the judge's or jurors' emotions. To do that, it must convey a core human value that should be contained in your bottom-line message. Some examples of core human values are self-discipline, compassion, responsibility, friendship, work, courage, perseverance, honesty, loyalty, and faith.

10. Structure your story and start strong. A common structure is illustrated in Freytag's Pyramid, which describes the five parts of a story: (1) introduction; (2) rising action; (3) climax; (4) falling action; and (5) resolution.

11. For variety, don't use the chronological structure of the Freytag Pyramid. Instead, use a flashback, mystery, a list, or comparisons, or come up with your own structure.

12. Mark Lanier has used the following to structure his stories: putting together a jigsaw puzzle, reading a book with three chapters, filling out a home inspection list, and a journey on a highway with four stops.

13. Whatever structure you use, start strong. First, sincerely thank the jury, then deliver your bottom-line message. Next, present your best piece of evidence, which might be a quote from expected testimony, a dramatic exhibit, or a

comparison made between what your client was doing and the opposing party.

14. The foundation of effective storytelling is to use descriptive language.

15. One of the best ways to develop descriptive language skills is to read well-written articles and literature and pay close attention to how great authors use words to paint a memorable picture of what happened.

16. When you are developing your story, use all the tools great writers rely on: metaphors, similes, descriptive words, and sensory images. Your goal is to awaken the senses of the jury, and the more senses that you can involve, the more connected the jury will be to the story—and to you.

17. Tell the good, the bad, and the ugly about your case.

18. To make sure you are trustworthy, determine your opponent's story so that you don't fail to mention bad facts when you tell your story to the jury.

19. For every hour you spend preparing your case, spend 20 minutes looking for its weaknesses, as if you represented your opponent.

20. Base your story on the law that governs your case. Most lawyers make the mistake of only having a pretty good idea what the law is. Instead, get the jury instructions that will govern your case and make sure that you can make a claim or defend one based on the law.

21. The key to overcoming writer's block is to lower your expectations and to force yourself to set aside some time to either get started or keep writing. Keep lowering your expectations until you start writing something!

CHAPTER FOUR

Use Insights from Brain Science to Persuade

"Once a human intellect has adopted an opinion (either as something it likes or as something generally accepted), it draws everything else in to confirm and support it."
—*Francis Bacon*

Throughout the past several decades, advances in brain science research have shed enormous light on how people make decisions. Some of this research confirms what our life experiences have taught us, but much of it also gives new insights on how to be more persuasive. Use the brain science-based strategies and insights discussed in this chapter to guide you as you create your presentation.

4.1 CONFIRMATION BIAS

Confirmation bias is the decision-making process whereby the brain forms a belief and will sift through subsequently conflicting information to find only the evidence that supports the initial belief. That is why one of the key elements of storytelling discussed in chapter 3 mentioned the importance of starting your story with your bottom-line message. You want your audience to hear what your case is all about so that it will see and interpret the facts that follow through the lens and filter of your bottom-line message.

Although research by Peter Wason, who pioneered the Psychology of Reasoning, conclusively proved confirmation bias in the 1960s, the phenomenon has been observed throughout history. For example, in the 1600s, Francis Bacon was an English philosopher and the Lord Chancellor of England. He is also known as the "Father of Empiricism" for his development of the scientific method. The scientific method was a new way of scientific learning that

> **CHAPTER ROAD MAP**
>
> - Structure your presentation based on confirmation bias.
> - Learn the power of metaphors.
> - Know the psychological characteristics of your audience.

relied on careful observations and inductive reasoning and took pains to avoid cognitive assumptions that could improperly influence a scientist's conclusions.

Along these lines, Bacon highlighted the problem of cognitive assumptions. Expanding on the quote at the beginning of this chapter, he concluded that "Once a human intellect has adopted an opinion (either as something it likes or as something generally accepted), it draws everything else in to confirm and support it. Even if there are more and stronger instances against it than there are in its favor, the intellect either overlooks these or treats them as negligible or does some line-drawing that lets it shift them out of the way and reject them."

Although Bacon did not label this human tendency of searching for information that is consistent with one's beliefs as confirmation bias, the point is that he identified a problem that scientists had in how they acquired knowledge, and he argued that they could only overcome the problem by conducting rigorous experiments that lead to conclusions based only on data and observed facts.

As lawyers, we need to be aware of confirmation bias so that we choose the correct order in which we present information to a judge or jury. In short, what you present first to your audience affects how it views what you present next. Given the principle of confirmation bias, a chronological presentation (criticized in chapter 3) may be the worst structure for telling your story because it reveals that you've not given much thought to the order of your topics, and it makes your audience wait until the end of your opening statement—or wherever else you decide—to hear the most impactful ideas.

> ### Practice Tip
>
> You want to present a persuasive idea at the very beginning of a hearing or trial so that the judge or jury will use it as the filter and lens through which they view your entire presentation.

The following study illustrates the importance of the order in which you present information. University students were asked two questions: (1) How happy are you? and (2) How often are you dating? When the questions were asked in this order, the correlation of answers was low (11%). That is, the answers to the two questions were only related 11 percent of the time—in essence, barely related.

As an aside, to understand what correlation means, here are two examples that help explain it. First, you would be correct to expect no correlation between a question that asked what your favorite cereal is and a question that asked what your favorite color is. On the other hand, you would be correct to expect a high correlation between someone's caloric intake and their weight.

What was fascinating about the study was that when the questions were reversed and the students were asked (1) how often are you dating? and (2) how happy are you?, the correlation was high (62%), meaning that the answers had a strong relationship with each other. In the second example, when students were reminded by how few dates they were having, that anchored their response to the second question, and they decided they were really miserable.

However, it is not only the order of ideas that can take advantage of confirmation bias, but also how you frame the idea. A sample of Canadians was asked if they were unhappy or happy with their social lives. Notably, if they were asked simply if they were unhappy, they were 375 percent more likely describe their state of mind as unhappy.

In another study, researchers wanted to see if the way a proposition was worded (i.e., framed) could affect one's decision. Suppose you are in the hospital with a serious heart problem and the doctor suggests a difficult surgery. What would your decision be if he were to tell you that "of one hundred patients who have this operation, ninety are alive after five years"? Now, suppose the doctor framed the question much differently and stated, "Of one hundred patients who have this operation, ten are dead after five years." The researchers found that people react differently to these to statements even though the facts are the same in each.

If it makes you feel better, even surgeons succumb to this bias. When doctors were told that if a patient were to have the surgery that 10 out of a hundred would die after five years, they were less likely to recommend surgery than if they were told that 90 out of a hundred would be alive.

From what we have learned, how you phrase information is important, as is the order in which you present it. However, as we will see in the next section, it is also important to make it easy for your audience to formulate conclusions that are favorable to your case.

4.2 USE THE NUDGE THEORY TO YOUR ADVANTAGE (MAKE IT EASY FOR JURORS AND JUDGES)

Studies show that if you can increase the ease with which people retrieve certain information, then you can affect the outcome. This is known as the power of priming. Social scientists have found that when you ask people if they intend to do something, priming can actually affect their behavior. For example, candidates in an election often talk about their strengths or an opponent's weaknesses to inform people about the importance of voting and to encourage them to vote. However, studies show that if you ask people the day before an election if they intend to vote, you can increase voter participation by 25 percent. Another study showed that if you ask people if they intend to floss their teeth in the next week, they will floss more.

Moreover, research has shown that you can accentuate the effects of priming, or what brain scientists call a nudge, by asking people when and how they plan to do a certain task and by making it easier for them to accomplish that task. At your next hearing or trial, nudge jurors to the outcome you want by making the decision-making process easier for them. Here is a study that you can learn from. Yale seniors attended a presentation on the benefits of getting a tetanus shot and were told where on campus to get one. After the lecture, many of the students indicated that they planned to get the shot, but only three percent did. Another group of students heard the same lecture, but they were told to look at their schedules and commit to going to the health center by entering an appointment day and time on their calendars. They were also given a campus map that had the health center's location highlighted.

Further, the students were asked to look at the map and plan which route they would take to get to the health center. With this additional nudge, 28 percent of the students got the shot. What is surprising is that Yale is not a big campus and almost every senior would know where the health center is. But a little help by way of an appointment calendar and a map increased participation by nine times.

Likewise, the easier you can make it for the jury to assemble the evidence and exhibits in the case, the more certain you will be that they will reach the verdict you want. The idea that people, including judges and jurors, when nudged to make a decision take the path of least resistance to get there makes perfect sense to us, because we all do it.

4.3 PEER (SOCIAL) INFLUENCE BIAS

Social and brain sciences tell us that groups of people are influenced by two social influences: information and peer pressure. As to the former, people make decisions based on the information they have, but we all know from experience that those decisions can also be influenced by what others think we ought to do, which is peer pressure. In a study, federal judges who were on a three-judge panel were often influenced by the positions their colleagues took. For example, a Republican appointee showed more liberal voting patterns when that judge was sitting with two other Democratic appointees. Similarly, a lone Democratic appointee showed a pattern of voting more conservatively when he was on a panel with two Republican appointees.

Study after study proves the power of peer pressure. In one study, it was proven that the academic success of college students is affected by those who are close to them at college—particularly roommates. In addition, the chances of you becoming obese increase if those close to you become obese. And your friends not only influence your chances of becoming obese, but also of simply gaining weight. Those who eat with one other person will eat 35 percent more than when they eat by themselves. When that person eats with a group of four, they will eat 75 percent more than if they eat alone. Finally, if you eat with seven or more people, you will eat almost twice as much than if you were eating alone.

This peer influence bias, which stems from being influenced by others or following the herd, is something you need to keep in mind when trying a case to a jury. There are going to be leaders and followers on a jury during deliberations. The leaders are the most important because they will persuade the followers to reach the verdict the leaders want. To counteract peer influence bias, during jury selection, you could "nudge" jurors toward a commitment to resist peer pressure by asking, "If you were the only person who believed my client's innocence, could you withstand the pressure of the rest of the jury to change your mind?"

Let's look at one more study. Researchers wanted to see how much one could be influenced by the crowd. Imagine for a moment that you are in a study that has six people taking a test of visual perception. The questions are very easy. You are supposed to match a line printed on a card to one of three lines of different lengths that were displayed on a screen. During the first three questions, all six people in the group announce their answers simultaneously and everyone agrees on the easy answer. But in the fourth round, the other five people give their answers before you and their answers are wrong. What do you do?

While you are correct in thinking that you would show them the error of their ways and announce the obviously correct answer, you probably would not have done so. In the study, people followed the crowd's incorrect answer one-third of the time. In a series of twelve questions, almost three-quarters of the people went along with the group's incorrect answer at least once. What is troubling about this example of peer pressure is that the participants in the study were all strangers to one another. Consequently, there should have been no reason for anyone to feel any "peer" pressure to please others in the group.

4.4 THE IMPORTANCE OF COUNTERTHEMES

Let's assume you have an upcoming trial and are developing your opening statement. You need to push yourself to find counterthemes—or counterarguments—to use. That is, your opponent—if they are any good—will have themes for their opening that take advantage of confirmation bias. Make sure your bottom-line message not only incorporates the theme of your case in order to take advantage of confirmation bias but also acts as a countertheme to your opponent's so that you win the battle of competing themes. For example, remember that in the DePuy hip implant litigation, the plaintiff's attorney, Mark Lanier, used the bottom-line message "My clients trusted a doctor, trusted a product, and got terrible results." That bottom-line message is actually a countertheme as well because DePuy's entire case was built on the premise that patients could trust their product and get terrific results. Lanier's first piece of evidence was that DePuy's hip implant could not be trusted to work. As soon as the jury heard it, they were well on their way to punishing DePuy with a huge verdict.

Counterthemes are very powerful, because they go right to the heart of your opponent's case. If your countertheme is more persuasive than your opponent's theme, it has the added advantage of destroying the credibility of your opponent because the countertheme directly undermines their primary message. As a result, whatever your opponent presents to the jury after their failed theme won't be believed.

Here is an example from the world of advertising that shows the importance of counterthemes. In the late 1960s, Big Tobacco was surprised by a three-year slide in cigarette consumption, despite its very powerful advertising campaigns, which were consistent with previous years. Big Tobacco soon realized that the cause of the decline was the power of counterarguments. In 1967, the U.S. Federal Communications Commission (FCC) ruled that the "fairness doctrine" permitted opponents of tobacco use to have free and equal time on radio and television to counter Big Tobacco's advertising.

For example, if a tobacco ad featured a healthy and attractive person enjoying cigarettes, the opposing ad would show that tobacco use caused addiction and cancer. The counterarguments were so powerful that Big Tobacco learned that it could *increase* sales by not advertising on radio and TV so that consumers would not be exposed to the counterarguments of its opponents. Instead, Big Tobacco focused its advertising on print media and billboards, where the fairness doctrine did not apply and its opponents could not use free advertising to counter its arguments.

The lesson here is that you need to anticipate your opponent's themes and have a countertheme and counterargument that annihilates. Here's another example. Let's assume there is a products liability case. If you anticipate in an opening statement that the defense will brag about the company's emphasis on safety and the studies it conducted before marketing its product, use the counterthemes of "putting profits over safety" and "rigged tests" in your bottom-line message to discredit the story if you can prove it.

Practice Tip

Incorporate counterthemes into your bottom-line message and you will have greater success.

These principles apply to any presentation you are giving to the court. At a criminal sentencing hearing, anticipate what opposing counsel's theme is going to be and develop a countertheme. Perhaps you have a hearing on a motion for summary judgment or temporary restraining order. The same strategy applies.

4.5 THE PRIMACY OF ASSOCIATIONS: WORDS AND METAPHORS

As discussed in chapter 3, one of the elements of a compelling story is use of descriptive language. Let's examine further how and why to do this. The renowned psycholinguist Gun Semin said that the main purpose of speech is to direct listeners' attention to a selected sector of reality. Once that is accomplished, the listeners' existing associations to the now-spotlighted sector will take over to determine the reaction. In short, human understanding is based on metaphors. That is, we try to understand what we don't know by associating it with something we already know. As a result, the better the metaphors are that you use to explain your argument, the better the chances are that you have helped your audience understand your position and will ultimately persuade them.

The famous writer Joseph Campbell, who wrote *The Power of Myth* and is credited for inspiring the movie *Star Wars*, said, "If you want to change the world, change the metaphor." The novelist Joseph Conrad said, "He who wants to persuade should put his trust not in the right argument, but in the right word."

There was once a life insurance salesman, Ben Feldman, who single-handedly sold more policies in the 1980s than 1,500 *agencies* in the U.S. Obviously, he had tremendous drive, but he also had a way with words. Instead of talking about death with potential customers, he talked instead about how you would "walk out of life" and how there would then be a breach in your family responsibilities that would need to be filled. Feldman would pitch, "When you walk out, your insurance money walks in." This metaphoric lesson on moral responsibility would seal the deal. Other examples include companies that don't tell customers the "cost" or "price" of their offerings, words which imply a loss of resources, but instead use words like "purchase" or "investment"—terms that connote gain.

In addition, studies have shown that after watching a video of a car accident taking place, people's estimates of the speed of the cars involved was affected by the verb used to describe the crash. In one such study, a group of participants was asked how fast the cars were going when they "smashed" into each other. This group thought the cars were going faster than those in another group who were asked the same question using the verb "hit."

Consequently, the words that we use in our presentations can be outcome determinative. Assume you are a prosecutor in a typical case where the IRS has been defrauded through the submission of fake tax returns that resulted in erroneous refunds. The traditional and non-persuasive way to summarize your bottom-line message would be: "This is a case about a defendant who submitted false tax returns to the IRS and then got refunds that he was not entitled to and deposited those monies in bank accounts which he controlled." You would then build your direct and cross-examination questions around the technical words you used, such as "false tax returns," "deposited monies," and "control of bank accounts."

But there is a much better way to build your opening statement: use descriptive words, such as, "The defendant is an accountant who stole innocent people's identities in order to *steal* from the IRS and then *hid* the money in *falsified* bank accounts he *secretly controlled*." In this better version, you would frame your questions using "stolen identities," "falsified bank accounts," and "secretly controlled accounts," words that are much easier for the jurors to understand and relate to.

4.6 BUILDING TRUST PERSUADES YOUR AUDIENCE

As soon as you lose an ounce of trust with the judge or jury, you have lost the entire case. Even though this principle is obvious, there is a wonderful story I came across that I want to share about a fire alarm salesperson that reinforces this principle. A company's best salesperson succeeded on this simple principle: build trust to get the sale. He would knock on the door and ask to come inside. Once inside, and after the conversation had started, he would interrupt and pretend that he had forgotten his notebook, which he had purposefully left in his car. The potential customer would let him leave the room, walk to his car, and then return with the notebook. This process gained the trust of the potential customer who let him walk through the house unaccompanied to get the notebook and return without watching him.

The same is true for any presentation you make. You must build trust with the jurors or judge and never lose it. You must be the expert in the room and always back up your claims with proof. Remember when Mark Lanier told the jurors in his opening statement, "I would be a fool to tell you these things if I couldn't prove them."

In addition, you cannot be afraid of the weaknesses in your case. There is only one story for the trial, and you are going to tell all of it—the good, the bad, and the ugly.

4.7 COGNITIVE OVERLOAD (THE FALLACY OF MULTITASKING)

Never bore the judge or jury. You might think they are listening to your every word, but the secret is that they are constantly looking to multitask while they are listening to you. It is just human nature for people to start thinking of something else if they are not fully captivated. Research shows that when we pay attention to something, the cost is that we don't pay attention to something else. The same is true in court. If your audience is multitasking, you are losing.

This concept is called cognitive overload. Although it might seem that we are concentrating on more than one thing simultaneously, that's an illusion. We are just rapidly alternating our focus between two channels of information (e.g., talking to someone on the phone and reading an email). However, just as there is a price for paying attention, there is a charge for switching it. For about a half second during a shift of focus, we experience a mental dead spot, called an attentional blink, when we can't register the newly highlighted information consciously. Consequently, when we are rapidly alternating our focus between two channels of information, we are experiencing multiple mental dead spots that can cause a decline in processing and memory.

4.8 THE ZEIGARNIJK EFFECT (USE A MYSTERY TO HOLD ATTENTION)

Presenting a mystery is a great art form for holding people's attention. While we all know this to be true based on our life's experiences (hence the truism "Everyone loves a mystery"), brain science confirms it as well. Many studies have shown that people pay more attention when there is an unfinished task to complete. As a result, if you frame your story as a mystery for the jury to solve, you have given them an unfinished task, so they will pay more attention to you and what you have to say.

Studies conducted by Bluma Zeigarnik help to illustrate this point. Bluma Zeigarnik was the daughter of one of the founding fathers of modern social psychology, Kurt Lewin. Her studies gave rise to the Zeigarnik effect, which is used by psychologists to explain why people remember unfinished tasks better than finished ones. There have been hundreds of studies that have confirmed this effect, but it started when Zeigarnik was at dinner with her famous father and several others. She was impressed that the waiter could perfectly remember everyone's drink and food order without taking any notes. It came to her that he might not do as well once the food had been delivered. So, she and the other guests covered their drinks and plates after the food had been delivered and asked the waiter to tell them what they had ordered. He was very unsuccessful. Zeigarnik—as confirmed by many later studies—concluded that the unfinished task of delivering the correct order made the waiter's memory much better. But once the order was complete, his thoughts shifted away to other tasks, and he forgot what the orders were.

Mystery is such a good art form because the audience will pay attention to a mystery and remember it better because of their craving desire for resolution.

At your next hearing or trial, try using a mystery to structure your presentation. In many of Lanier's trials, he invites the jurors to become detectives to help him solve the mystery. One way to structure it would be as follows: (1) describe the mystery; (2) go into details about the mystery; (3) list the clues; and (4) provide the answer.

> *The most beautiful thing we can experience is the mysterious. It is the source of all true art and science.*
> —Albert Einstein

4.9 KNOW THE PSYCHOLOGICAL CHARACTERISTICS OF YOUR AUDIENCE

In chapter 2 we talked about the principle of WIN, or <u>W</u>hat <u>I</u>s the <u>N</u>eed of your audience. Those needs are influenced by your audience members' ages. You need to be aware of the different age groups of the people you are trying to influence and the environments that they have grown up in. Let's look at the different generations.

The oldest generation is the Silent Generation. They were born from 1928-1945. In 2021, its members ranged in age from 76 to 93. It is unlikely you would have them on your jury, but they are a starting point for us and provide context for the other generations. They were never a large group because birth rates were lower than normal during the Great Depression and World War II, events that dominated this period. This generation likely fought in the Korean War. McCarthyism and the threat of expanding communism from the Soviet Union were significant parts of their young adult lives.

Having grown up in the Great Depression, they tended to be frugal as adults. They were dubbed "the Silent Generation" by Time magazine, which described them as remaining silent on issues when compared to the Greatest Generation that preceded them. They found success by working within the system.

The Baby Boomers were born from 1946-1964. This generation got its name from the large increase in births that occurred after soldiers returned home from World War II, and its members generally participated in the rise in prosperity that followed World War II and the Great Depression. In 2021, its members ranged in age from 57 to 75. Many in this generation gave rise to the counterculture movement and protests in the 1960s, while others took part in the subsequent backlash to it. While some of the older ones in this group fought in the Vietnam War, the vast majority of the younger ones in this generation have never fought in a war.

Generation X is defined by people born from 1965-1980. As young children, they were known as the latchkey generation for their lack of parental supervision. In their teenage years, they were known as the MTV generation because of the popular music video channel MTV. In 2021, its members ranged in age from 41-56. As adults, they were known as the "Me" generation, and they made up a significant part of the growing number of women in the workforce. They also had higher divorce rates, and many of them fought in the Gulf War.

Millennials (occasionally referred to as Generation Y) are defined by people born from 1981-1994. They got their label because they were born after Generation X and before Generation Z. The oldest members in this group became adults at the beginning of the third millennium. Their parents are the Baby Boomers and Gen Xers. They are the parents of Generation Alpha (not discussed here because they are too young). This generation is associated with the internet, social media, and cell phones. One of their most dramatic life-shaping events was 9-11. In 2021, their members ranged in age from 27-40.

Finally, there is the iGeneration (occasionally referred to as Generation Z and Zoomers). Their birth year ranges from 1995 to 2012. They are intimately familiar with digital devices, have witnessed the wars in Iraq and Afghanistan, the election of the first Black president, and experienced the Covid-19 pandemic. In 2021, their ages ranged from 9-26.

What do you do with this quick overview of the possible demographic makeup of the people in your audience? If you are an older attorney, realize that since 25 percent of your jurors will be millennials or iGens, and that you will need to learn more about them and keep up your knowledge of the younger people who are entering the jury pool. One way to learn more about them is to read the suggested readings at the end of this chapter. Another source is the Marist Mindset List. It is evolving into something different, but in the past, including in 2019, it created a list each year of the experiences of a typical incoming college freshman. It found that those students starting in 2019 had the following in common: like Pearl Harbor for their grandparents and the Kennedy assassination for their parents, 9/11 has always been a historical event; the primary use of a phone has always been to take pictures or to text; the Tech Big Four (Apple, Amazon, Google, and Facebook) have always been to them what the Big Three Automakers were to their grandparents; and Oklahoma City has always had a memorial in the center of town.

The key is just to be aware of the different experiences of generations and don't make assumptions about what seems obvious to you, because it might not be obvious to them due to your different experiences. Baby Boomers had Cold War drills in school where they practiced hiding under desks in case a nuclear bomb from the Soviet Union was launched. On the other hand, millennials had school drills practicing how to hide if there were an active shooter. Baby Boomers prefer talking on the phone as a way to communicate, whereas millennials and iGens prefer to text. Baby Boomers like to read books, whereas the average iGen spends 439 minutes per month on Instagram.

It is also important to get to know as many different people as you can so that you can relate to them. You don't want to have to wait until you are in a courtroom to realize that you cannot connect with a jury because you can't find anything in common with them.

Now that you know some of what brain science has taught us about how we learn and make decisions, let's turn our attention in the next chapter to creating PowerPoint slides that are both memorable and persuasive.

SUGGESTED ADDITIONAL READING

1. .*Pre-Suasion: A Revolutionary Way to Influence and Persuade*, Robert Cialdini PhD (Simon and Schuster, 2018). The most accessible book on brain science. A very interesting read.

2. *Nudge: Improving Decisions About Health, and Happiness*, Richard Thaler and Cass Sunstein (Penguin, 2009). The second most accessible book on brain science. It has a wealth of studies and insights.

3. *iGen: Why Today's Super-Connected Kids Are Growing Up Less Rebellious, More Tolerant, Less Happy—and Completely Unprepared*, Jean M. Twenge PhD (Atria Books, 2018).

4. *Generation Me (Revised)—Why Today's Young Americans Are More Confident, Creative, Entitledand More Miserable Than Ever Before*, Jean M. Twenge PhD (Atria Books, 2018).

5. *The Millennial Promise: 40 Tips From the Mindset List*, Ron Nief, Charles Westerberg, and Tom McBride (2016).

CHAPTER CHECKLIST

1. Confirmation bias is the decision-making process in which the brain forms a belief and will sift through subsequently conflicting information to find only the evidence that supports the initial belief.

2. Francis Bacon said, "Once a human intellect has adopted an opinion (either as something it likes or as something generally accepted) it draws everything else in to confirm and support it. Even if there are more and stronger instances against it than there are in its favor, the intellect either overlooks these or treats them as negligible or does some line-drawing that lets it shift them out of the way and reject them."

3. Be aware of confirmation bias so that you correctly choose the order in which you present information to a judge or jury. In short, what you present first to your audience affects how it views what you present next. Given the principle of confirmation bias, a chronological presentation may be the worst structure to use, because it means you have given no thought to the order of your topics other than the path of least resistance: "I'll start at the beginning and finish at the end."

4. It is important how you phrase information and the order in which you present it.

5. Make it easy for your audience to follow your argument.

6. Groups of people are influenced by two social influences: information and peer pressure.

7. Counterarguments or counterthemes can be even more powerful than your bottom-line message because they strike at the heart of your opponent's credibility.

8. The novelist Joseph Conrad said, "He who wants to persuade should put his trust not in the right argument, but in the right word."

9. Build trust with your judge or jury. Once you lose their trust, there is no way to gain it back.

10. Be aware of multitasking. Humans are always doing it to some degree. If you lose the attention of your audience, it is very hard to get it back.

11. Mystery is a great way to hold your audience's attention. One way to structure it would be the following: (1) describe the mystery, (2) go into details about the mystery, (3) list the clues, and (4) provide the answer.

12. Know your audience so that you can connect with them.

13. The Silent Generation was born from 1928-1945. In 2021, its members ranged from 76 to 93. Members of this generation likely fought in the Korean War. McCarthyism and the threat of expanding communism from the Soviet Union were significant parts of their young adult life.

14. The Baby Boomers were born from 1946-1964. This generation got its name from the large increase in births that occurred after soldiers returned home from World War II, and it generally participated in the rise in prosperity that followed World War II and the Great Depression.

15. Generation X is defined by people born from 1965-1980. As young children, they were known as the latchkey generation for their lack of parental supervision.

16. Millennials (occasionally referred to as Generation Y) are defined by people born from 1981-1994. They got their label because the oldest in this group became adults at the beginning of the third millennium.

17. The iGeneration (occasionally referred to as Generation Z and Zoomers) was born from 1995 to 2012 and is intimately familiar with digital devices.

PART II

How to Deliver Your Presentation

Now that you know how to become a confident public speaker and develop the content to persuade effectively, let's turn to how to deliver your presentation.

CHAPTER FIVE

Use Creative and Memorable Visual Aids

"I can excuse everything but boredom. Boring people don't have to stay that way."—*Hedy Lamarr,* actor and inventor

5.1 PICTURES INCREASE MEMORY RETENTION

In chapter 3, we learned that a critical part of a compelling story is the use of descriptive words to create memorable images in the audience's mind. It is even better if you can display images that support the story you are telling about your client. There is enormous research that proves that we will retain more information if we both see an image and hear spoken words, as opposed to just listening to words. For example, one study found that three days after only hearing a lecture, a person can only remember 10 percent of it. The retention rate was increased to 65 percent simply by adding pictures. This principle is known as the Picture Superiority Effect (PSE). Other tests have shown that when people were shown 2,500 photographs for 10 seconds each, they could recall having seen them with 90 percent accuracy several days later. A year later, the accuracy rate was 63 percent.

Without getting into too much detail, the reason for the increased memory recall when pictures are used is that our brains are wired so that we process pictures differently than text or sounds. Pictures are processed in several brain channels instead of one, which allows them to be encoded far more deeply and meaningfully. These multiple channels also provide for easier recall.

Here is another way to think of it. The left side of the brain is where language is learned and expressed. The right side of the brain registers visual images. That

> **CHAPTER ROAD MAP**
> - Analyze how master trial lawyer Mark Lanier creates persuasive visual aids and PowerPoint slides.
> - Avoid the traps that result in "death by PowerPoint."
> - Take your presentation to the highest level by learning the seven principles of effective PowerPoint slides.

means that if you only rely on words, you will ignore the recipient's other half of the brain, which will likely set off a chain of events that includes that person becoming bored, deciding that they don't like you, and wondering if other people have the same feeling. Consequently, use visual aids whenever possible.

After a brief overview of the importance of the document camera and the best one to get for showing your visual aids, this chapter will analyze how Mark Lanier uses creative and memorable visual aids to win. Then, we will examine the worst mistakes that lead to death by PowerPoint. Finally, you will master the seven principles for creating effective PowerPoint slides, because PowerPoint, if used correctly, can be a very powerful tool for enhancing the story you are trying to tell on behalf of your client. If you need a refresher on PowerPoint skills, appendix A has a "how to" section on the basics of PowerPoint with lessons on how to create unique PowerPoint slides, including what style and size of font you should use.

5.2 THE RIGHT EQUIPMENT

All modern courtrooms have a document camera. The document camera is an update of the overhead projector that was prevalent in schools up until the late twentieth century. The document camera is a device that captures images of documents or other objects that are placed on a flat surface beneath it. It then projects those images onto a screen for a larger audience, such as a judge or a jury. However, even if you are in a modern courtroom, you may want to bring your own document camera because it will often be more versatile and user friendly than the one the court provides.

While there are many brands to choose from, and the most popular one is ELMO, I strongly recommend another one: the IPEVO VZ-R ($219) (see fig. 1). It has excellent image quality, is intuitive to use, and is light weight. IPEVO makes a more expensive wireless version (IPEVO VZ-X), but you do not need that feature. (The Wi-Fi version is intended for classrooms where a teacher might carry the IPEVO from their desk to a student's desk so the class could see a document on the student's desk—because the IPEVO would be wirelessly connected to the teacher's computer or the projection screen.)

Figure 1. The IPEVO VZ-R document camera.

With your IPEVO VZ-R in the courtroom, all you need to do is connect it to your laptop and then connect your laptop to the court's projector screen. Then, by projecting a document onto a screen from your IPEVO, it is easy to show it to the judge or jury. You could also use the IPEVO to display a timeline that you have created, a flow chart, or a list of an opponent's admissions. You can also zoom in to highlight important words of a document when necessary.

If you are going to use PowerPoint for your presentation—whether in conjunction with an IPEVO or by itself—you will need a remote control device to advance the PowerPoint slides. That is, you don't want to have to stand over your laptop and click on the track pad to advance your slides. You want the freedom to make gestures and keep your eyes on your audience while you advance the slides by simply pressing a button on your remote control device. There are a lot of good remotes available, but my two favorites are the Logitech Professional Presenter R800 ($79.99) and the Logitech Spotlight Presentation Remote ($129.99). The difference between the two is that the former has a green laser that allows you to point something out on the projection screen, whereas the latter creates a spotlight effect when you want to highlight something on the screen. I like the spotlight effect on the latter one, and it is the one I use. Always carry a spare set of batteries, because you never know . . .

5.3 THINK OUTSIDE THE BOX

In the courtroom, visual aids are rarely used, particularly when examining witnesses, but they should be used often, and they will affect outcomes. Consequently, don't follow the conventional wisdom; instead, think outside the box. For example, in Mark Lanier's trials, he is always looking for a visual aid that drives home a point. He always has a visual aid displayed on a document camera (he now uses an IPEVO) when he examines a witness. Often, he will display just a simple drawing to convey his message, which can be seen by the jury on a large projection screen.

In figure 2, Lanier made the drawing himself during the cross-examination of the defendant's expert witness to show how the metal hip implant would create nano particles of metal debris that would break off from the defective hip implant, enter the bloodstream, and travel throughout the body. Obviously, he could have paid a graphic designer to create an elaborate picture, but there is something about this very simplistic drawing that provides the perfect contrast to the defendant's complicated explanations, explanations that were supported by sophisticated graphics that revealed that the defendant would not address a simple problem. It makes Lanier and his clients seem relatable, and it makes his opponent seem overly legal and technical. It also humanizes Lanier and allows the jury to connect with him.

As seen in figure 3, Lanier used this drawing of a building during his cross-examination of an expert witness to show that DePuy did not conduct studies that were long enough to show the dangers of its hip implant. That failure was like

Figure 2. Lanier's drawing of a hip implant.

Figure 3. Lanier's drawing illustrating that DePuy's studies were too short.

asking a man who had jumped off the roof of a building how it was going after only travelling a few floors to the ground.

Lanier also made a drawing during cross-examination of the president of DePuy to show that DePuy had studies that had spin, and that DePuy spent more money on sales and marketing than research and development (depicted by see-saw illustration in fig. 4). He also used a see-saw to depict that DePuy had allocated more of its workforce to sales and marketing than to research and development. He made these drawings to prove that DePuy had put profits over safety.

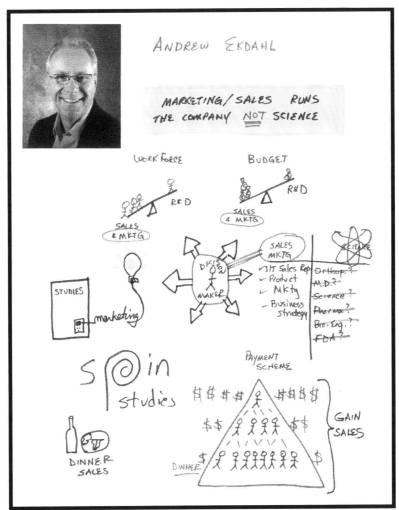

Figure 4. Lanier's drawing illustrating that DePuy puts profits over safety.

Lanier makes these drawings in court while the witness is on the stand. By doing so, he creates suspense in the courtroom because the jury—and the witness—is curious about what he is drawing. When he finishes, the jury experiences a feeling of clarity as the mystery is resolved, and it also senses that the trap has been set for the witness as Lanier begins to cross-examine on the topic of his drawing. In figure 4, Lanier made the drawing in parts. For example, he first drew the see-saw about the workforce, then questioned the witness about that topic, then drew the see-saw of the budget, then questioned the witness about that topic, and so on.

Lanier's trial team has also used drawings on direct examination to help jurors connect with the plaintiffs. In the talc powder litigation, which we will study more in chapter 10, there were 22 plaintiffs. Over a long trial, it is important to find ways for jurors to remember each plaintiff. Knowing this, Lanier's team wanted the jurors to associate a distinguishing quality with each plaintiff. Consequently, they created a drawing for each witness with an image the jurors could use to remember them by. The picture had the added benefit of serving as an outline for questioning, which helped the jurors pay better attention.

In figure 5, a drawing of a cake was used during the direct examination of Carole Williams. She loved to bake cakes, and the creative drawing was an image that the jurors would not forget. The three-tiered cake also provided a road map

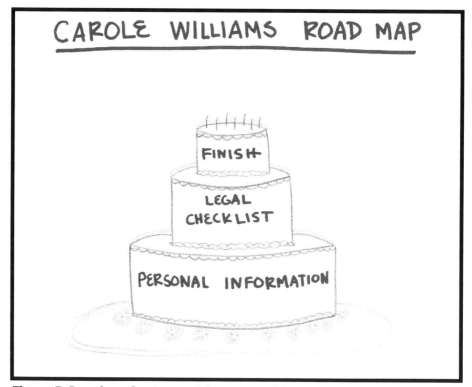

Figure 5. Drawing of cake used for cross of Carole Williams.

for the jurors to follow as the attorney asked her questions about her personal information, the facts to support her legal claim, and some concluding topics.

In figure 6, we see a drawing of a crossword puzzle that Lanier used on Janis Oxford's direct examination, knowing that Janice loved to solve crossword puzzles. The puzzle started off with blank squares, and as she was asked each question from the lists for down and across, her answers were filled in. It was an imaginative way to get the jury to not only remember that Janis loved crossword puzzles, but also to engage the jurors as they solved the puzzle along with Janis as she answered questions.

In figure 7, we see a drawing Lanier used to visually depict plaintiff Krystal Kim's fight with cancer. The hearts represent the ones who Kim was battling cancer for, her sons Bryce and Ross, because Kim always referred to her two sons as her two "hearts."

But Lanier, who may have no equal at using persuasive exhibits in the courtroom, does not limit himself to two-dimensional drawings. He has also shown jurors two different boxes filled with real donuts to make his point. He did this when he was cross-examining the head of DePuy's clinical research. The plaintiffs claimed that the version of metal hip implants they received had a different

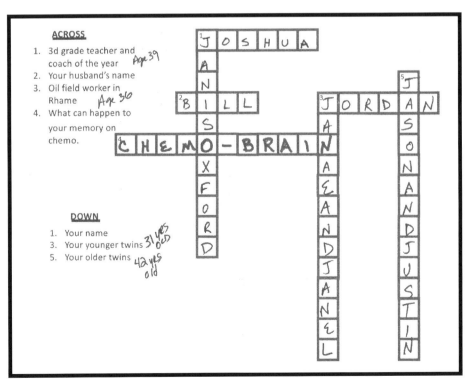

Figure 6. Drawing of crossword puzzle used for Janis Oxford.

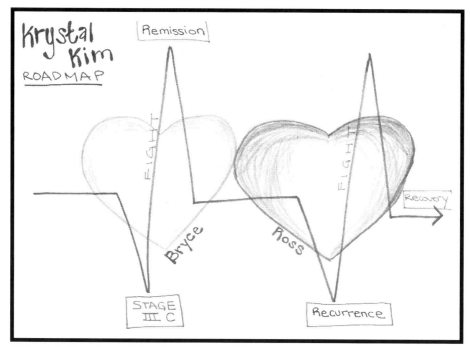

Figure 7. Drawing of two hearts used for Krystal Kim's questioning.

hardness, coating, and grain size than the previous version that DePuy had tested and claimed was safe. Lanier wanted to use a demonstrative exhibit to show the jury that DePuy should have tested the new hip implants before marketing them to the plaintiffs.

Accordingly, Lanier brought two boxes of donuts into the courtroom. One was from a national chain, Dunkin' Donuts, and the other was from a very popular Texas chain, Shipley's Do-Nuts. He gave a box of Dunkin' Donuts to the witness and kept a box of Shipley's Do-Nuts with him at the podium. Lanier told the witness that he thought Shipley's Do-Nuts tasted better than Dunkin' Donuts. Knowing that the witness lived in Indiana, where you could not buy Shipley's Do-Nuts like you could if you lived in Texas where the trial was, he asked her which donut tasted better. Obviously, she could not answer the question because Lanier had the box of Shipley Do-Nuts at his podium.

This demonstration served as a metaphor for DePuy's failure to test the new version of the metal hip implant. Lanier's point was that just as the witness couldn't say if Shipley Do-Nuts tasted better than Dunkin' Donuts because she had never taste-tested Shipley's Do-Nuts, she likewise couldn't say if the newer version of the DePuy hip implant was safer than the previous version because the newer version had never been tested. In other trials, Lanier has brought out a block of cheese and a bale of hay to prove his points.

5.4 DEATH BY POWERPOINT

PowerPoint burst onto the computer scene in 1987. If you don't know how to use it, you are decades behind. It is time to catch up. You also need to know how to use it effectively. In both cases, read on.

Most of us have heard the phrase "Death by PowerPoint." Even if you have not heard it, you almost certainly have been subject to such an experience. Since PowerPoint's launch, there are now an estimated 1.2 billion users, and millions of speakers use it every day. "Death by PowerPoint" is simply unavoidable. The phrase describes when a presenter shows a PowerPoint to supposedly help their presentation, but they use it so badly that you suffer a virtual death. You will experience boredom, impatience, frustration, and then outright anger over having had to sit through such a presentation. Below is a list of four deadly sins that lead to death by PowerPoint. After we examine these pitfalls, we will learn fail-safe skills that will bring any presentation to life.

The Four Deadly Sins of PowerPoint Presentations

The most common and worst mistake is putting almost all the words of your presentation on your slides. The naïve lawyer thinks that they have beaten the challenge of speaking in court without notes because they aren't using any. But the reality is that they are using PowerPoint as a teleprompter. The audience is not fooled. The slides are full of text, and when the lawyer is finished reading one slide, he waits for the next slide to appear, takes a moment to recognize what's on it, then begins reading it like all the other previous slides. Worse, he often has turned his back to the judge or jury as he reads what is on the projection screen.

To "spice" it up, the lawyer mistakenly believes that by putting bullet points before all of this text he is somehow highlighting important points instead of overloading the judge or jury with information that is hard to absorb and boring to follow.

In addition, while he reads his PowerPoint slides, the judge or jury is no longer listening to him but trying to read along with him. Why? Well, if he is looking at the slides on the projection screen, the audience is going to take its cue from him and do the same. Now everyone is trapped and forced to read together.

> *Most people use PowerPoint like a drunk uses a lamppost—for support rather than for illumination.*
> —David Ogilvy, known as the Father of Advertising

A close second to the sin of reading your presentation is using too small a font. In an effort to cram all the text of his presentation onto the slides, the lawyer has decided to use a font size that looks fine on his laptop (i.e., a 12-point font size) and allows him to put all of his argument on one slide, which a bigger font would not. The problem is that text in a 12-point font size is much too small for an audience to read. Instead, use a 32-point font size or larger.

A third sin is having too many slides. The lawyer makes no effort to rehearse and measure the duration of his presentation, so he runs the real risk that two-thirds of the way through his presentation he either has to stop to fast-forward through multiple slides to get to the last ones or just end his presentation without finishing it. While these slides are whizzing by, the jury or judge becomes more curious about what he has skipped over than what he has previously said. Either choice he makes is a mistake that cannot be overcome.

A fourth sin is to create a slide that takes the audience's attention away from what you are saying. Nancy Duerte, who wrote Persuasive Presentations posts for the *Harvard Business Review*, advises to "strip everything off your slides that's there to remind you what to say; keep only elements that will help the audience understand and retain what you're saying." As will be discussed further below, your slides should complement what you are saying, not overshadow it. Some examples of slides that would be too distracting are ones that create confusion, are inconsistent with what you are saying, are more interesting than what you are saying, or are too complicated for the jury or judge to absorb. Finally, some slides use graphics that are so clichéd, such as the handshake or thumbs up, that they are distracting.

The Most Commons Sins of Committing Death by PowerPoint

1. Too many words
2. Too small of a font size
3. Too many slides
4. Too many distractions

5.5 SEVEN POWERPOINT PRINCIPLES

Now that we have looked at the wrong things to do, how do we create a persuasive presentation that acts as a lamppost of illumination, rather than one that acts as a support for a drunk, as David Ogilvy so eloquently advised?

Principle 1: Each Slide Must Use Clear and Concise Images That Capture the Emotions of the Audience

The first and most important principle is that for any PowerPoint slide to succeed, it must be clear, concise, and capture the emotions of the audience. The remaining principles will show you how to accomplish this.

Principle 2: WIN

The second principle is WIN (remember this from chapter 2?). Win stands for What Is the Need of your audience. Who cares what your slide looks like on your computer if it doesn't look good on a projection screen in a courtroom? While a particular color might stand out on your computer, the result might be completely different in a courtroom with dim or bright lights. Likewise, the animations that you created might prove to be interesting to you when you see them on your computer, but other people might find them distracting when they see them displayed on a larger screen in a courtroom. Go to the venue where you will be presenting and test how your slides look. That is the only way to get the answer for WIN.

Principle 3: Properly Structure Your PowerPoint

The third principle is to properly structure your PowerPoint. Remember the Rule of Three, which declares it is best to only make three major points. With that in mind, think of a visual way to convey that you are going to cover three major points in your presentation. How are you going to let your audience know when you are transitioning from one point to another? One way would be to show a picture of a highway that has three signs, with one for each of your three points (see fig. 8). Another way would be to show a picture of a book and use a picture of a chapter for each of your three points (see figs. 9-10).

Principle 4: On Each Slide, Have One Picture On It That Conveys Your Idea

The fourth principle is to have one picture on each slide that conveys your idea. When you are making a comparison, a couple of pictures is fine, but in general, think of one picture on each slide. In short, think of your PowerPoint as being filled with images instead of text and you will immediately separate yourself from the pack. For example, in an opening statement when you might be talking about how the defendant company put profits over safety, instead of using a bunch of text or the words *profits over safety*, use a picture of a pile of money with the caption "profits" and a picture of a safety hard hat with the caption "safety." If you are going to quote someone famous, such as Lincoln, don't just put the quote of Lincoln on your PowerPoint, but also include a photo of Lincoln to give it even more importance. If the quote is a long one, leave the text off of the slide and just show his picture when you recite the quote.

There are many sources to get stock photos at very reasonable prices for your PowerPoint. Three of my favorites are www.stock.adobe.com, www.istockphoto.com, and www.123rf.com (best value).

Figure 8. Image of a highway with informational signs for each of your three main points.

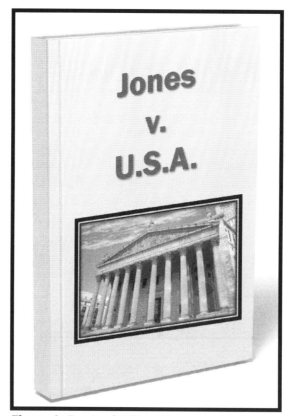

Figure 9. Book with its title named for your case.

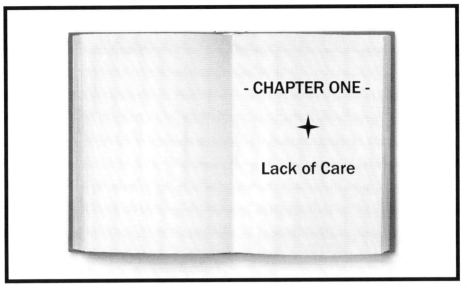

Figure 10. Book with Chapter One titled "Lack of Care" to highlight one of your main points.

Principle 5: Never Use Bullet Points

The fifth principle is to never use bullet points. This was mentioned earlier, but it bears repeating as a principle. Unfortunately, bullet points are appealing because they seem to help you avoid writing lots of sentences and force you to list your most important points in phrases. The problem is that once you start using bullet points to make lists, it is hard to have the discipline not to cram as many bullet points onto a slide as will fit. The caveat to this rule is that if you are going to make a list, limit it to three items. Preferably, don't use anything in front of each item, but if you must, at least use numerals. Bullet points are for losers. In any event, by limiting your text to three items, you will ensure that you have not crammed your slide with text and that your ideas are easy to understand.

> **Practice Tip**
>
> Almost everyone uses text in Power-Point the way closed captioning is used on TV. While closed captions work for a TV show, you should not use Power-Point to have the audience read along silently as you read aloud the text of your PowerPoint.

Principle 6: Remember That You, Not Your PowerPoint Presentation, Are the Main Attraction

A sixth principle is to remember that you, not your PowerPoint presentation, are the main attraction. With that principle in mind, think about using only the minimal number of slides necessary to effectively enhance, rather than overwhelm, your presentation. It is hard to delete a slide after you have spent a lot of time creating it, but you MUST. "Less is more" is true for public speaking and no less true for your PowerPoint presentations.

In addition, make sure that after you have used a slide you don't start speaking on another important point if you don't have a slide for it. The reason for this is that the judge or jury will still be reading what is on the projection screen and not giving their full attention to your new point. There is some popular advice that suggests that you insert a blank page into your PowerPoint that is colored black so that your audience focuses on what you are saying. You can also achieve this effect by pressing a button on some PowerPoint remote advancers (the Logitech remotes recommended above do not have this feature).

I disagree with this advice. Instead of having a black screen, always have something that supports what you are saying. If you don't have a picture or a piece of evidence, then just have a word or phrase displayed in large letters that captures the topic you are talking about. For example, if you end your hearing by talking about justice, you could display an image of a courthouse with the word JUSTICE in front of it (see fig. 11). Displaying that word with a picture of the courthouse you are in would add even greater emphasis to what you are saying, and it would certainly be better than a black screen.

Figure 11. Example of a one-word slide with a picture for emphasis.

Principle 7: Declutter Your Slides

The seventh principle is to declutter your slides. Make them easy on the eyes. Use color combinations that stand out as opposed to ones that don't, such as red or blue with green. Don't overload them with animations, arrows, and other symbols. As mentioned above, your text should be formatted in a 32-point font size or larger. Use the alignment tool to ensure that your text and graphics are centered (see fig. 12).

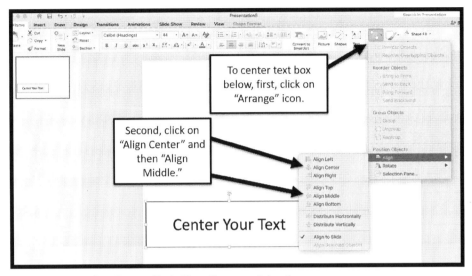

Figure 12. Using PowerPoint's alignment tools.

The Seven Principles of PowerPoint

1. Each slide must use clear and concise images that capture the emotions of the audience.

2. WIN: view your slides as your audience will see them.

3. Properly structure your PowerPoint.

4. On each slide, have one picture on it that conveys your idea.

5. Never use bullet points.

6. Remember that you, not your PowerPoint presentation, are the main attraction.

7. Declutter your slides.

As you were reading these principles, I bet you realized that reading a book about how to create PowerPoints is just a starting point. The best way to learn PowerPoint is to regularly use it. It needs to become a skill set that you have, just as you would for using Microsoft Word or Excel. Only by using PowerPoint routinely will you really learn how to use it effectively.

Consequently, think of creative ways to use it, so that you will have more opportunities to practice your skills. Instead of writing a memo to a colleague or superior, could you present those ideas more effectively in a PowerPoint or use a PowerPoint to illuminate what you are saying better? Or, for each new important case you get, create a PowerPoint slide for your bottom-line message (discussed in chapter 3) and insert a couple of photos or key exhibits. These opportunities that you create will force you to experiment with font styles and sizes, and with how to make pictures or exhibits look persuasive. Finally, when you get to mediation or a trial, you cannot delegate your PowerPoint creation to someone else. You are the one that needs to maintain creative control. It is very difficult for you to explain to someone else the vision you have for your case. That is perhaps the best reason why you need to have PowerPoint skills.

For a case study on how Mark Lanier used a PowerPoint in a record-setting trial, see chapter 10. For now, let's look at few of the PowerPoint slides Lanier used in his opening statement of the case and why they are so effective. Out of the 99 slides Lanier used in his opening statement, most of them contained one picture that represented one idea. Using that idea as a principle, he created slides that conveyed one idea in a variety of ways, as illustrated below.

The first and second slides (see figs. 13-14) illustrate Lanier's bread-and-butter technique: using one picture to convey one idea. In figure 13, he wants to show that just like it is difficult to catch fish in a lake, it is equally hard to find asbestos in human tissue. It is a simple picture that people can immediately relate to and will easily remember for the idea it represents. In figure 14, he uses a simple

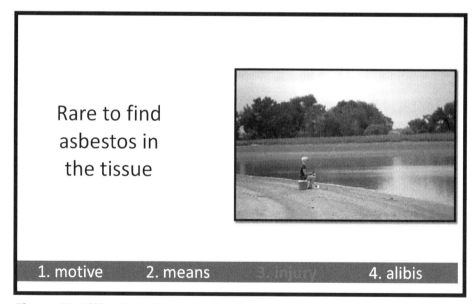

Figure 13. Difficulty in finding asbestos.

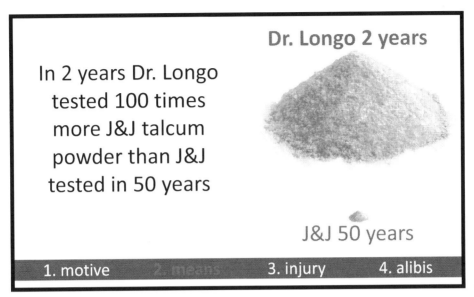

In 2 years Dr. Longo
tested 100 times
more J&J talcum
powder than J&J
tested in 50 years

Dr. Longo 2 years

J&J 50 years

1. motive   2. means   3. injury   4. alibis

Figure 14. Comparison of tests.

photo to compare the vast amount of powder his expert studied in only two
years with the amount that Johnson and Johnson's studied over a 50-year period.

In figure 15, Lanier uses a chart to convey one idea. He rarely uses charts, but
this is a powerful one. He wanted to show that Johnson and Johnson had many
people on its board of directors who were leaders of asbestos companies. Notice
how he has the danger sign above the asbestos companies. In the original color
version that the jury saw, the names under J&J are in red to signify danger. Also,

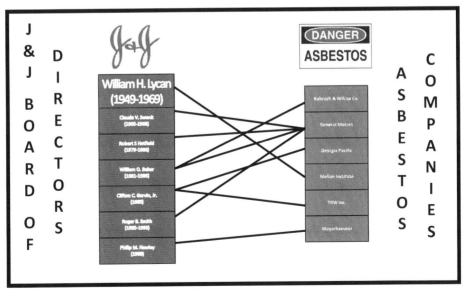

Figure 15. Chart of relationships.

the crisscross manner in which Lanier drew the lines highlights how intertwined the relationships are.

In the final slide (see fig. 16), Lanier concludes his opening statement with a countertheme to J&J's defense that it did not know there was asbestos in its Baby Powder. Using a large font, Lanier writes his countertheme that "'We didn't know!' is not a legitimate excuse!" and then uses simple pictures with just a few words to show the jury what Johnson and Johnson should have done. He also has a caption for the slide that tells the jury that he is on his fourth topic, "alibis," so that the jury has a reference point for his slide. Notice also that Lanier uses the Rule of Three to show that all J&J had to do was three things.

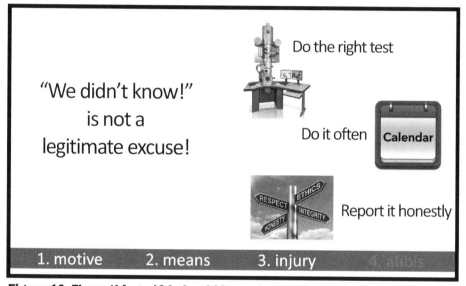

Figure 16. Three things J&J should have done.

SUGGESTIONS FOR FURTHER STUDY

1. Lynda.com has a wide variety of videos on how to learn specific tasks in PowerPoint.

2. *Presentation Zen: Simple Ideas on Presentation Design* (3rd Ed.), Garr Reynolds (New Rider, 2019). This is not a how-to book for PowerPoint but a book that explains the concepts behind using simple and powerful slides for storytelling.

3. *Beyond Bullet Points: Using PowerPoint to Tell a Persuasive Story that Gets Results* (Pearson Education, Inc., 2018). This book assumes a working knowledge of basic PowerPoint and guides you on how to tell a story through PowerPoint.

CHAPTER CHECKLIST

1. Don't be boring.

2. Whenever you can, use images to support what you are saying.

3. Three days after hearing a lecture, a person can only remember 10 percent of it. The retention rate increases to 65 percent simply by adding pictures.

4. The left side of your brain processes language, the right side processes visual images.

5. Use visual aids so that you don't ignore half of the brain of your audience.

6. Get the right equipment such as an IPEVO document camera and a Logitech Spotlight Presentation Remote for your PowerPoint presentation.

7. Think outside the box when creating visual aids. The more creative they are, generally, the more memorable they will be.

8. The four sins of PowerPoint are (1) too many words, (2) too small a font, (3) too many slides, and (4) slides with clichéd graphics that distract from what you are saying.

9. The seven principles of PowerPoint are (1) every slide should be clear, concise, and capture the emotions of your audience, (2) view your slides as your audience will see them, (3) provide structure for your PowerPoint, (4) substitute pictures for text whenever you can, (5) never use bullet points, (6) you are the main attraction, not the PowerPoint, and (7) declutter your slides.

CHAPTER SIX

How to Never Use Notes Again

"First he read his speech, second he read it badly, third it wasn't worth reading." —*Winston Churchill*

The topic of how much you should rely on notes for your presentation is usually given a couple of paragraphs or a small section at most in public speaking books. I want to emphasize what a difference it will make in your career if you don't use notes. Let's first look at the value of making eye contact, and then we will explore in depth the reasons for not using notes and learn surefire techniques to speak easily without them.

6.1 THE IMPORTANCE OF EYE CONTACT

Making eye contact is important for many reasons. Surprisingly, most lawyers don't do it very well. Next to a handshake, which physically connects you with another person, there is nothing more important than making eye contact with the person you are trying to persuade. And since we cannot shake hands with our audience in the courtroom, eye contact is of paramount importance. There is a saying, "Eyes are the windows to the soul." When we connect with another person by making eye contact, we have a chance to persuade them by touching their soul.

But making eye contact has another benefit. It forces the other person to look back at you and keeps them engaged with you. We all know that it is rude to look away when someone is talking to you, so use that custom to your advantage when you are presenting. When you are making eye contact with your audience, they will feel obliged to look back at you. Moreover, studies have shown that when one person makes initial eye contact with another, it triggers the firing of neurons in the recipient that leads them to mirror the emotions of the other person. If you are calm

> **CHAPTER ROAD MAP**
>
> - Understand why making eye contact is the key to speaking from the heart to persuade.
> - Easily master the skills to speak without notes.
> - Bonus: Learn an ancient secret to avoid speaking with notes that works as well today as ever.

and confident, you will trigger that emotion in the other person, but if you are nervous and uncomfortable, you can also trigger that mirroring effect.

When making eye contact with the jury, don't look too long at any one juror. First, you don't want to impose your visual will on someone else. It is not a staring contest, like two rhinoceroses sizing each other up before a charge. Second, you don't want to neglect the other jurors. Look at one juror for a few seconds and then move on to the next. Your social instincts will tell you when it is time to look at someone else. What do you do when you are telling a story to a group of people at dinner or at a party? The same rules apply in a courtroom. Also, instead of just looking at one individual juror, vary up what you do and look at several at the same time. That is, look in the general direction of several jurors. This is less intense for both you and your audience. It also allows you to include more people at the same time.

One way to think of this is that making eye contact with a group of people is like feeding bread to a bunch of ducks (see fig. 1). You want to focus on one duck here, one duck there, as many individual ducks as you can, then throw a bunch of bread to the group on the left, the group in the middle, and the group on the right. You are trying to reach every duck without focusing too much attention on one duck at the expense of the others.

Figure 1. Make eye contact with the group as if you were feeding ducks.

Making eye contact with judges is critical. Unlike jurors, who do not have anything before them to read, judges have your pleadings, your opponent's pleadings, and quite likely other case files at their bench. You'd better be interesting because you have some competition: judges can focus on your case or on the file of another case sitting right in front of them that they have yet to handle. Anytime you look away, you run the risk that judges will take that break as an opportunity to look away also. Once they have done that, you may not get their attention back. However, as in the discussion above concerning jurors, if you sense that a judge wants to take a break from your gaze, just look away briefly, like you would do at a party when talking to one individual person.

Likewise, making eye contact lets judges and jurors see your emotions and take in your character. They can see if you are confident, sincere, and trustworthy. Be vulnerable so you can gain their trust.

Finally, when you make eye contact, you get immediate feedback on how persuasive you are. Do the judge and jury understand what you are saying, or do they look confused? Do they look interested or bored? Take the feedback from their eyes and facial expressions and adjust your presentation accordingly. You may think you are making an important point, but if your audience is bored, you should either change up your delivery or move on to another topic.

> **Practice Tip**
>
> If the judge looks down at the case file or something else and you are about to make an important point, just say, "Judge Johnson, this is my most important point." Everyone answers to the sound of their own name.

Having said that, just because one or two jurors happen to yawn or look disinterested when you look at them does not necessarily mean that you are failing. You need to ask yourself if this is just a momentary expression, or is it a more sustained one that suggests they are disinterested. It may be that the juror or judge is actually enjoying your presentation but is tired for other reasons or is thinking of something else (multi-tasking). The key to knowing their interest level is acquired by noticing how long and how frequently they exhibit certain expressions. If the expression is not what you are expecting, focus on another juror for a moment and check back in a bit to see if that person has reconnected with you.

One piece of bad advice that is still taught quite often is that if you are hesitant to look directly into someone's eyes, you can use the crutch of looking at a juror's or judge's forehead. The advantage to this is that you will be less fearful because you are not looking into someone's eyes. But the disadvantages vastly outweigh that one positive. By not looking your audience in the eye, you will miss out on all the advantages discussed above. Second, the judge or jury is bound to notice that you are not looking at their eyes. That will be disconcerting to them. That is no way to build a bond with your audience. Would you ever talk to a friend, a client, or a supervisor by looking at their forehead? Then, why would you ever do that in court?

Andrew Lloyd Webber, arguably the most successful composer of musicals in history, instructs his singers to never close their eyes, because if they do, the audience cannot see what they are feeling, and vice versa.

As an aside, there is nothing worse than an insincere smile when you are speaking. But a sincere smile can go a long way on the road to success. First, it relaxes you. The more you smile the less nervous you will be. Second, a study from Penn State found that when you smile, you appear to be more courteous, likeable, and competent.

Let's look at a press conference from the world of sports to see the importance of eye contact. In January 2020, the Commissioner of Major League Baseball issued a report concluding that the Houston Astros illegally stole signs for pitches from opposing teams during its 2017 World Series title run. Before spring training in March of that year, the Astros's owner, Jim Crane, along with two of the team's top players, issued a statement to the press.

Crane has given countless speeches and had plenty of time to prepare for this moment. And what did he do? He read every word perfectly so that the press could repeat it verbatim correctly. Unfortunately, the style and credibility of his apology was criticized by the very media he was hoping would simply repeat his speech. You can see the clip at www.winningatpersuasion.com.

If he had spoken from the heart instead, he would have missed a few words, but he would have been much more credible. For example, it is not very good when you read aloud "I want to say again how sorry our team is for what happened" from a sheet of paper (see clip at 0:22), rather than talking from the heart, without notes, and looking the camera in the eye. It does not get any more sincere or credible when he reads aloud "I would like to personally thank all of our fans." (See clip at 2:15.) The problem with reading aloud is further exacerbated when he says, "I agree that our players should not be punished . . . who did not receive proper guidance from their leaders [manager and general manager]" (see clip at 3:00). That is the crux of his argument, that Major League Baseball has punished his team enough by suspending the manager and general manager for a year. To come across as more sincere, he should have let his audience look into his eyes to see his sincerity.

> No notes. You speak from deep in your heart. It's easy.
> —Manny Pacquiao

Compare Jim Crane's apology with that of J.D. Davis, the former Astro ballplayer (see clip at www.winningatpersuasion.com). He doesn't use notes, and unequivocally says—with conviction—that he knows that fans want to see a fair game and that the reporters want to cover a fair game. He admitted that the sign-stealing had given the Astros an unfair advantage and pointed out the obvious that a team should not cheat to win but that everyone who gets crowned world champion "has to earn it." He added, "It's terrible for baseball." Finally, he said that he felt "ashamed to be a part of it." When asked if he ever wore his World Series ring, he said once or twice, and you could tell by the look in his face that the reason he did not wear it is because the Astros had cheated.

Lastly, Cody Bellinger of the LA Dodgers responded to Jim Crane's apology. (See the clip at www.winningatpersuasion.com). Compare how Crane read from his notes with how Bellinger spoke from his heart. Crane rarely made any lasting eye contact with his audience; Bellinger looks directly into the reporters' eyes. More importantly, the audience can look into Bellinger's eyes and see the sincerity within.

6.2 DON'T FOLLOW THE CONVENTIONAL WISDOM THAT READING FROM NOTES IS GOOD

Now that we know the importance of eye contact, why would you ever use notes? One reason is that everyone does, even politicians who have given thousands of speeches. But it was not always like this. In the first half of the 1800s, the best politicians were the best orators because the best orators had the ability to persuade others and effect change. To name but a few, Abraham Lincoln, Henry Clay, and Daniel Webster all spoke without notes, knowing that such a crutch would completely undercut their credibility and persuasive powers.

Conventional wisdom suggests that by using notes you can carefully craft every word you want to say before your speech, write them all down, and ensure that the audience hears precisely what you intended to say when you read your speech (see earlier examples from the Astros). Furthermore, if you look up occasionally, you can make eye contact and seemingly have the best of both worlds: a written speech where you say exactly what you meant to say and a connection with the audience because of your occasional eye contact.

Another reason given for using notes is that by rehearsing the reading of the speech, you will be fairly certain of how long it will take because there won't be any variations or ad-libbing. However, you can be just as certain of the length of your presentation by rehearsing one that is not read.

The conventional wisdom also says you can also be very comfortable if all you have to do is read your words. In essence, you almost completely avoid having to overcome the fear of public speaking (see chapter 1). Finally, it takes a lot less time to prepare because you don't have to memorize your remarks. I mean a lot less time. In short, a speech read from your notes is more comfortable to deliver, takes less time prepare, and you are assured of saying exactly what you intended. That sounds like a winner, right?

Well, just because you say something is so doesn't make it so. For your words to have any power, they have to persuade (see discussion on eye contact above). In addition, the conventional wisdom is wrong because when you read from your notes and try to occasionally glance at the audience, it becomes likely that you will lose your place as you look up and down from your notes. Once you lose your place, the time it takes to find your place and recover can be a disaster for you if your audience is looking for an excuse to think about something else. While you can put feelings into words when you read them, you cannot put as much feeling into them as when saying them while looking someone in the eye.

Also, it can be quite nerve-wracking trying to keep track of where you are on the page you're reading from while also thinking about when it will be a good time to look up. It never really looks very engaging when you look up at the audience. The audience does not really have time to connect with you and is thinking about when you might look back down, which will be very soon.

A close but no better cousin of reading your presentation aloud is delivering one that you've memorized. There is a misconception that if you memorize your presentation, you really have the best of both worlds. You can say the exact words that you have written down and make flawless eye contact, because you are looking at the audience and not at your notes or script. But you are likely to fail. Dale Carnegie (1888-1955) was one of America's most respected experts on interpersonal skills, salesmanship, and public speaking. He was a firm believer in not using notes and of speaking from the heart to persuade.

He also explained why trying to memorize a speech word for word instead of delivering it in a conversational manner is problematic. When you try to recall a memorized speech, you are likely at some point to freeze under the pressure of public speaking and forget what you want to say. For that reason, it is a waste of time trying to memorize a speech. Instead, he points out that it is easier and more effective to build your presentation around ideas. He instructed, "All our lives we have been speaking spontaneously. We haven't been thinking of words. We have been thinking of ideas. If our ideas are clear, the words come as naturally and unconsciously as the air we breathe."

I want to share with you a viewpoint that I do not believe in, but in fairness you need to know it exists. Chris Anderson is the curator of TED Conferences LLC, the organization that created TED Talks. He explains that TED's cofounder, Richard Saul Wurman, was adamant that speakers could not use notes because he believed that's how speakers can best connect with the audience. However, over time, TED speakers were allowed to use notecards, and many of them now do. Interestingly, the video editors have hidden them on the internet feed you watch, so you don't see them.

Anderson believes that if you are more comfortable using notecards, that increased comfort level is worth the trade-off of losing some measure of vulnerability and connection with the audience by not using them. He recommends 5 x 8 inch notecards, with a ring punched through them to hold them together. TED speakers put key examples on their notecards, reminders of what to say to transition to another PowerPoint slide, or anything else of value. By having notecards in your pocket, you are free to move about the stage knowing that you have your notes with you. Anderson concludes that notecards are fine because most TED speakers only look at them occasionally.

I disagree with Anderson, and I hope I can convince you, too. I have been teaching trial advocacy at SMU's Dedman School of Law for over 20 years. I have yet to see a student in my class who was not capable of giving an opening statement or closing argument without notes. Would they have been more comfortable with notes? Yes. Having the benefit of notes, would they have read from them? Yes. Would their presentation have been worse? Yes.

The problem is that once you start using notes, the temptation to use them again will pull at you every single time you get ready for court. I have seen many lawyers using notes even though I know that they have the ability not to use them, but they have become too reliant on them to stop. My suggestion is to never go down that path.

> ### Practice Tip
> A five-minute speech with no notes is better than a 10-minute speech with notes. If you are afraid you can't remember everything, cut some stuff out. You'll perform better and your audience will appreciate it.

Here is the solution I came up with that raises my comfort level and allows me to benefit from not using notes. I create a one-page outline. But it is not a typical outline. If someone can take your outline and get the gist of your speech, you have way too much information on it. My outline is a topic outline and I limit myself to 5 topics and 15 words. On the outline I write the things I absolutely cannot forget. Perhaps it is the date of the dispute in issue or the exact number of something. I never look at it, but I put it at counsel table, close to the podium, so that if I need to look at it once during my speech, I can get a sip or water at counsel table and, while I get my water, I can glance at the outline without the judge or jury ever knowing.

Getting a sip of water achieves two goals. It buys you time as you walk to your outline to think of what you need to say. Second, everyone understands that a speaker can get thirsty. You will actually get some sympathy from the judge or jury while you are buying time to refresh your memory.

But here is the key: when you are nervous and looking at your notes, words get harder to read. As a result, think ahead. Instead of using an ink pen, write your words in large letters using a felt-tip pen. Make them easy to read from a distance. Use different colors for different topics. Use anything you can think of that will relax you by knowing that when you look for a cue word on your outline, it will be easy to find. If your outline is displayed for you from your computer, use an extra-large font size (32 points or larger). Practice using your outline so you will know what is on it and where to look so that when the time comes when you might need it, you will know where to look.

A second trick you can use is to place a visual aid that you want to use on counsel table, and as you walk toward it, glance at your outline that you have strategically placed beside it. A third trick is to plan at some point in your presentation to quote from a witness or case (if arguing at a hearing). At that moment, tell your audience that you want to get what you are about to say just right. Walk to counsel table, pick up a sheet of paper with the quote on it, and read it verbatim. While you are either picking up that sheet of paper or putting it down, glance at your outline.

Nonetheless, the reality is that if you are delivering an opening statement or closing argument, you should be using a PowerPoint presentation and exhibits as visual aids. Those slides will remind you of what to say. In addition, when you are in presentation mode in PowerPoint (see fig. 2), PowerPoint gives you a preview of the next slide in your presentation to remind you of your next topic. To the jury or judge, it appears as if you are talking without notes, when what you are really doing is using the visual aids and the pictures on the PowerPoint slides as visual cues for what to say next. (Remember, your PowerPoint slides should have primarily pictures on them instead of text.)

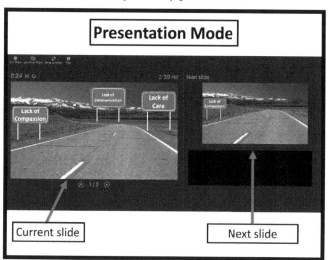

Figure 2. Use PowerPoint's Presentation Mode for Helpful Speech Reminders.

Here is some good news. Even if you have been relying on your notes at a hearing or a trial, you will find that not using them is a lot easier than you think—but I suggest you do it cold turkey. You won't find it that hard. And besides, you will quickly see that the extra time you put into practicing without notes will give you more confidence in what you are saying.

Another way to look at it is like this: When you asked for a raise or made a marriage proposal, did you have notecards with you? Of course not. You spoke from your heart to persuade. I believe that when you don't use notes you appear more confident—which you are—and more sincere. Those two qualities provide the motivation for me to not use them.

6.3 THE MEMORY PALACE

For the vast majority of my career, I was able to avoid using notes by practicing my presentation so many times that I could present it in a conversational manner without ever looking at them (see chapter 9). But in the past few years, I began to explore if there might be a better way. I investigated how memory experts learned their craft and found their techniques can be helpful in the courtroom. The memory palace, discussed below, is a proven technique that you will find fascinating and helpful. Use it to remember the topics and their order in your presentation, not every word of your speech, because then you will just wind up giving a memorized speech, which, as we have seen, is not persuasive.

At the most recent USA Memory Championship and as long ago as the fifth century B.C., people were using the same memory technique to succeed. It is a technique variously referred to as the memory palace, the method of loci, and the art of memory. According to legend, it was made famous by Simonides of Ceos in the fifth century B.C. He was in a large banquet hall for dinner. Simonides was a Greek poet who had just spoken in honor of Scopas, a Thessalian nobleman. After he sat down, a messenger told him to go outside to meet two men on horseback who needed to tell him something. Just as he stepped outside, the banquet hall collapsed, and hundreds of people lay dead beneath the rubble.

Instead of being distracted by the chaos, Simonides immediately remembered everyone inside in the exact location where they were before the collapse. In essence, he went back in time and pictured where everyone had been, instead of seeing the mangled bodies and rubble. For example, he saw a poet eating the last scrap of his meal with a piece of bread sitting across from him, and Scopus sharing a laugh at the head of the table. With these vivid pictures in his mind, he was able to direct those who came to the disaster scene to the exact location where their loved ones lay buried beneath the immense rubble.

Simonides then realized that he could use this technique to remember anything. For example, he could use it to remember the words of a poem if he pictured the words of the poem (rather than people) as being seated at the banquet table in a logical order. This memory technique used by Simonides became known as the memory palace. The technique is discussed in the bible of classical memory training, *Rhetoric ad Herennium*, which was written around 84 B.C. and was taught in Greek and Roman times in classical education on an equal footing with grammar and the arts.

Greek and Roman orators used this technique—whether it was called the memory palace or the method of loci or the art of memory—to give long speeches without notes. They did this by associating each part of their speech with a specific location they had created in their mind. For example, they might have associated the opening of their speech with an image of their home's front door, and the ending of their speech with their back door. These memory systems were used by monks and philosophers during the Middle Ages and by kings and even Shakespeare. However, with time, these techniques lost their popularity and necessity as the ability to mass produce books and writings became easier and made the reliance on memory less important.

Despite most people ignoring this technique today, it is still immensely valuable and practiced by competitors in national and world memory contests. If you decide to use the memory palace, you might consider using a different location for different presentations, just as the Greek and Roman orators did to keep their images fresh. For example, for one presentation you could use your home, another your childhood home, and another your college dorm. It does not matter what your "palace" is, as long as it is intimately familiar to you and has a sense of order that allows you to link one idea to another (i.e., a journey through your house from the front porch to the backyard).

Don't limit your palace to just your places of residences; it can be real or imagined, keeping in mind that you need to be intimately familiar with it and there must be a logical sequence on your tour of it. For example, you could use stops along a familiar road, things you see on a walk around your block, or your commute on a subway train. It could even be something you create in your imagination or that you adopt. For example, USA memory champion Scott Hagwood would look at pictures of luxury homes in *Architectural Digest* to create memory palaces.

However, it is important to note that there is no requirement that you have a different location for each presentation as was done by the Greeks and Romans. Whether you decide to use the same location for different presentations or different ones, it is entirely up to you. As one respected memory thinker pointed out, "The loci are like wax tablets which remain when what is written on them has been effaced and are ready to be written on again."

Should we really use the memory palace to speak without notes? Ben Pridmore, a winner of the World Memory Championship, uses it and similar techniques so that he can remember any poem that is given to him and so that he can memorize a deck of cards in 32 seconds. In five minutes, he can memorize permanently what happened on 96 different dates in history.

If he can use these techniques to remember very complicated facts, we can certainly use them to remember the major points and their order in our presentation for a court. Let me emphasize that you should not use the memory palace to memorize precise words or sentences, even though you could. That would defeat two of the main purposes of this book, which are to teach you to have a conversation with your audience and speak from your heart to persuade. Instead, here is how I have used it.

For a hearing where I could not use a PowerPoint to remind me of my topics, I would associate my bottom-line message with the front door. I would have a strong image of it in my mind and even see its words written on the door. The two exceptions to not memorizing the words of a presentation are its beginning and its ending, both of which you need to know cold. So, I recommend memorizing the exact words of your bottom-line message.

Then, I would associate my first point with the first room on my left when I enter my house, the dining room. Maybe there are two subpoints that I want to make, and I would associate one with the table and the second with the chairs. That would help me remember that when I get to the dining room, I want to make two points. I would then picture myself walking into the kitchen for my second major point and do the same thing. For example, I might want to remember to be candid with the court about a weakness in my case, and I might associate the dishwasher with my weakness about failing to unload it.

My third point would be associated with the garage, and my ending statement would be associated with the garage door that leads to the alley. By using this memory palace, I would know that I have three major points to make, and each of the three rooms would help me to remember them. Give it a try at least once.

Now that you know how to never use notes, let's learn in the next chapter how to use gestures when delivering your presentation.

SUGGESTED ADDITIONAL READING

1. *Moonwalking with Einstein: The Art and Science of Remembering Everything*, Joshua Foer (Penguin, 2012).

2. *The Memory Book: The Classic Guide to Improving Your Memory at Work, School, and at Play*, Harry Lorayne and Jerry Lucas (Ballantine, 1996).

CHAPTER CHECKLIST

1. "Eyes are the windows to the soul." When we connect with another person by making eye contact, we have a chance to touch their souls and persuade them.

2. By seeing a person's reaction to your presentation, you get immediate feedback, which allows you to make necessary adjustments.

3. Smile. It relaxes you and you appear to be more courteous, likeable, and competent.

4. One pitfall of memorizing a speech word for word is that as you try to recall each word, you will inevitably forget one and freeze under the pressure of trying to remember it.

5. Dale Carnegie said, "All our lives we have been speaking spontaneously. We haven't been thinking of words. We have been thinking of ideas. If our

ideas are clear, the words come as naturally and unconsciously as the air we breathe."

6. Although it is commonplace for politicians to read their speeches, the great orators in history, such as Lincoln, Henry Clay, and Daniel Webster, never did.

7. When you try and read from your notes and occasionally glance at the audience, it becomes likely that you will lose your place as you look up and down from your notes. Once you lose your place, the time it takes to find your place and recover can be a disaster.

8. Just because it takes less time to prepare a presentation if you don't commit it to memory is no excuse to read it aloud.

9. The problem is that once you start using notes, it is a temptation that will pull at you every single time you get ready for court.

10. It is perfectly fine to have a one-page outline with your topics in large lettering nearby, as long as you look at it only once or twice during your presentation.

11. When you are asking for a raise or proposing marriage, do you have notecards with the words you want to use? Of course not. You speak from your heart to persuade.

12. Greek and Roman orators used the memory palace—whether it was called the memory palace or the method of loci or the art of memory—to give long speeches without notes. They did this by associating each part of their speech with a specific location they had created in their mind.

CHAPTER SEVEN

Gestures and Delivery

"All the great speakers were bad speakers at first."
—*Ralph Waldo Emerson*

People who speak well are perceived as being intelligent and trustworthy. As a result, they appear more credible than those who don't speak well. That should be all the motivation you need to become the best speaker you can be. This chapter will give you the tools to deliver a persuasive presentation. However, don't get lost in the details below. Keep in mind that in chapter 2, we discussed the importance of being true to yourself and speaking from your heart to persuade your audience (the first and second principles of public speaking). With that as your starting point, what you read below will help you communicate better. But if you start to focus too much on the mechanics, you will not be true to yourself. As you read each section, ask yourself, "can I adapt the particular technique to my own unique style, and if so, how can I use it to help me speak better from the heart?"

> **CHAPTER ROAD MAP**
>
> • Learn the techniques and mindset for proper posture and breathing.
> • Master gestures that will make a real difference in persuasion.
> • Recognize how to use your voice to give words more meaning.

7.1 THE IMPORTANCE OF BODY LANGUAGE

Professor Albert Mehrabian of UCLA conducted some studies in the 1970s about verbal and non-verbal communication. He concluded that we judge a person overwhelmingly not by what they say, but by how they present their information. He found that personal communication could be broken down in the following way:

- 7 percent words,
- 38 percent tone of voice, and
- 55 percent facial and body language.

Unfortunately, trial consultants have promoted this study to emphasize how important body language is for communication. While that is true, this study overstates its importance. When Professor Mehrabian saw how trial consultants and others were misinterpreting his research, he cautioned that the percentages were derived from studies where participants were communicating their opinions about feelings, such as whether they liked something or not. He said that his analysis would not be applicable in a different context. Nonetheless, when we speak, whether it is at a hearing or trial, feelings are involved. The formula is at least consistent with our life experiences, in that the way someone carries themselves, expresses themselves through facial expressions, and the manner of their speaking can communicate a lot of information to us.

7.2 A RELAXED AND UPRIGHT POSTURE

Let's first look at the correct stance, and then at how to gesture. Do not to get caught up with the conventional wisdom that instructs that to stand up straight, you need to think about holding a position by pulling your shoulders back and pushing your chest out. This creates too much stiffness. Instead, think about your spine growing taller and lengthening and that you have a bungee cord connected to your head that is pulling you upwards towards the ceiling. Next, relax your shoulders and let them fall away from your neck. If you spend just a few minutes imagining this as you walk around, you will feel yourself getting into better body alignment by having a straight, but relaxed, posture.

7.3 A GROUNDED STANCE

Many speakers think that the task of speaking is an activity performed from the neck up. But it is a very physical activity that uses the whole body. Like successful stage actors and singers, you must use your entire body to be energetic, focused, and calm under pressure. The tips below on your stance and your breathing have proven successful for singers and actors. Take advantage of what they do for success and apply them the next time you speak.

Before you begin to speak, you need to be physically grounded. How should your feet be spaced? Your feet need to be right below your hips, which is their natural position anyway. But to make sure that you have got it, here is an easy trick. Point your left foot straight ahead. Then, take your right foot and put its heel into the arch of your left foot so that the right foot is now perpendicular to your left foot. Then, pivot on the ball of your right foot so that your right foot is now facing forward. This results in both feet pointing straight ahead, parallel to each other, and both feet being straight under your hips. However, stand naturally. Your toes don't have to be pointed perfectly straight forward. This is just a technique to give you a good feel for where your feet should be.

Now, feel your connection to the floor. You are not just standing on it: you are grounded to the earth. This helps give your body security. But be careful, you don't want to be a wooden soldier. Keep your knees slightly bent, or soft. How bent? Don't think about it too much. They should be in the default position, the way you have been standing your whole life. You should be able to immediately take a step if you had to without adjusting your knees. If your legs and knees are stiff, you may lose circulation and become light-headed or even faint. Not to mention you'll be uptight.

Keep your shoulders relaxed. The energy from the earth is going to go from your feet up your spine and out your mouth. One image that may help you is to see yourself as a tree. Your hands and voice are the limbs, your body is the trunk, and your feet have roots connected to the ground. The energy comes up from the ground, through your body, and then to your hands and voice.

From this position, depending on your talent level, you are ready to act in *Hamlet*, sing on Broadway, or, maybe more realistically, perform in court.

7.4 BREATHE DEEPLY WITH YOUR DIAPHRAGM

Your goal is to breathe so that you get the most out of your voice. The best way to breathe is to learn the techniques singers use. But first, here is a very brief explanation of how breathing works. The automatic part of your brain controls your everyday breathing. When you are at rest and talking normally, your breaths are fairly shallow, which is fine for conversation. But when your adrenaline is pumping—as is the case when anyone speaks in public—these normal breaths become more hurried and shallower. That result is not good for public speaking. The audience sees the muscles in your face and neck tensing up and the quality of your voice becomes strained.

However, by learning to consciously breathe by using the voluntary part of our brain, you can overcome the negative effects of adrenaline and relax your muscles and thoughts. Even if you aren't feeling the effects of adrenaline, conscious breathing provides a better tone to your voice, allows you to project your voice further into a courtroom, and prevents vocal fatigue.

Here is how singers do it. Most people have an image of their breath going in and out of their lungs very high in their chest. But your lungs extend from below your neck to just below your rib cage. Singers need to take advantage of every inch of this capacity to sing long notes and phrases. As a result, they picture something different. On your next breath, imagine that the air particles are colored and that they go into your mouth and travel deep down your torso, pushing your stomach out and filling your lower back. Consciously push out your stomach as you breathe in. What you are really doing is engaging your diaphragm. It is a dome-shaped muscle that is located below the lungs and rib cage and just above the stomach. Its tissue is attached to the spine in the back, the rib cage on the sides, and to an extension of the sternum in the front. The diaphragm contracts and flattens when you breathe in and expands to a dome shape to push the air up when you breathe out.

However, when you consciously breathe, you get the most out of your diaphragm muscle because you force it to allow more air into the bottom part of your lungs by creating more space for the lungs to expand. If you do it correctly, the diaphragm will collapse and cause the rib cage to expand, your stomach and abs will get pushed out, and your lungs will have more room for more air. You will feel like you have an inner-tube completely full of air around you that is resting above your waist. Spend a few minutes trying this and you will get the hang of it. To really feel the inner tube, breathe in quickly and push your stomach out. You will feel the outer walls of your stomach stretch, and even some muscles in your lower back, too, due to the expansion of air.

Now that your lungs are full, breathe out slowly. Your neck and shoulders should be relaxed. Push the air out not from your mouth, but use the front muscles of your stomach that were stretched when you took in your breath. Contract your stomach muscles until they feel like they are touching your back as you push the air out. When you are first practicing this, put your hand on your stomach to feel the muscles expand and then contract. Because you usually don't speak in long phrases, you will probably not need to exhale this completely when you speak, but this is how singers sing a long phrase, and will it give you an idea of how much air your lungs can really hold.

Most important, deep, full breaths relax your body when you breathe in, and when you use your diaphragm to push the air out, your body stays relaxed. This process is also easier on your vocal chords. It's the secret great singers know: breathe from your diaphragm and stay relaxed. Most people never take a full deep breath. They just start talking, their neck tenses up, and sooner or later they wear themselves out. In addition, when you don't use your diaphragm, your voice is not as full and as rich as it can be.

Nonetheless, don't get too caught up in breathing from your diaphragm. It takes some practice, and you may not want to spend too much time on it since there is not enough time to master everything, although I highly recommend it. Even if you don't spend the time practicing, at least remember to just breathe in and out slowly. That takes no practice at all and will go a long way towards helping you relax and have a better tone of voice.

Then, on the day of your next hearing, don't wait until you are about to stand up to think about your breathing. Practice it while you are getting dressed in the morning and on your commute to the courthouse. As you are walking to the courthouse, think about it again. And then, a few minutes before you start, take some deep slow breaths, or breathe from your diaphragm before you start. If there is a point in your presentation where you are feeling tired or uptight, briefly refocus on your breathing to get re-centered, then return to your presentation.

While you are speaking, there is no time to take slow inhales and exhales. But you can still get the benefits from conscious breathing. Do what all professional singers do: inhale quickly using the technique above. Then exhale and let the power of the air carry your words. You will find that you can project further and speak for a longer period of time without getting tired.

7.5 THE EVIL PODIUM

There is no greater disservice to a lawyer's presentation than using the object that most people, including me, call a podium, but what is actually a lectern. (As an aside, a podium is a raised platform for speakers to stand on so that they stand above the audience. A lectern—what most people call a podium—is the raised slanted desk that you stand behind when speaking. But since most lawyers—and people for that matter—refer to the lectern as a podium, I will use the term podium in this section.)

If I could reimagine the interior of the typical courtroom, I would replace the podium with an open space (i.e., no podium), and I would replace the podium's attached microphone with lapel microphones, one of which would be provided to and worn by every attorney at the hearing or trial. That way, when you first check in with the courtroom deputy to announce your presence for your case, the deputy would give you a lapel microphone. You would then sit at counsel table, and when it was your turn to speak, you would go to the center of the courtroom and find no podium at all but a wonderful open space in order to communicate (using your lapel microphone) with the judge or jury.

There are many reasons why a podium is so bad. First, it encourages you to speak from your notes, and from lots of them, because of all the room it has. There is even more than enough room on the podium for a big, fat, three-ring binder. There is even storage room underneath to put more stuff! I have never seen a courtroom podium made of transparent material, such as clear plastic. Instead, they are usually made out of wood. With this lack of transparency, you can bring as many notes as you want to the podium and the podium will help hide your notes from the judge or jury.

Second, the podium is a magnet for your hands. There is almost no way to stand at a podium and not put your hands on it. Think about it: you are nervous and the adrenaline that is causing your nervousness wants to escape through your hands. Instead of channeling that energy to make effective gestures with your hands, you grab the podium for dear life to prevent your hands from moving. Now, you are not gesturing at all. In fact, a lot of public speaking coaches mistakenly teach that you should hold on to the podium to prevent your hands from unnecessarily gesturing.

Then, once you put your hands on it, the rest of your body naturally leans forward and uses the podium to support its weight. Consequently, instead of standing up straight with good posture that conveys a sense of confidence and authority, you are slouched at the podium, conveying just the opposite.

Perhaps the worst part about a podium is that it creates a physical barrier between you and your audience. When you are trying to connect with a jury or judge, having a physical barrier just makes it that much more difficult to connect. Imagine if you were at a social gathering at a friend's house or a bar. Would people connect more if they each had a podium to speak from? Of course not. The same is true for the courtroom.

Another problem with the podium is that the microphone is attached to the podium and forces you to bend down—sometimes slightly, but sometimes more—in order to speak into it. That restricts your ability to make strong eye contact, because your head is tilted forward. It also prevents you from gesturing with your hands, because if you back away so that you have room to gesture, you will then be too far away from the microphone to speak into it.

Podiums have been around since at least the Roman times, so, they are not going away anytime soon. To say that they have stood the test of time is an understatement. To help me overcome this obstacle, I imagine that the podium is electrified and that I will get a terrible shock if I touch it. That helps me keep a safer distance from it. Since I am now also farther from the microphone, I just speak a lot louder so everyone can hear me. By standing away from the podium, I am forced to project my voice, which makes me more confident than if I am leaning over the podium, trying to speak softly into a microphone for fear of speaking too loudly because of the court's often sensitive sound system.

> **Practice Tip**
>
> If a judge requires you to stand at the podium during trial, just take a step back so that you are not leaning on it or grabbing it, and speak a little louder. When speaking to the jury, do the same thing, or if the judge will let you, stand to the side of it.

7.6 BAD GESTURES

Once you get into a good stance, you need to figure out what to do with your hands and feet. Let's look at the worst things you can do. Although it is not easy to rank them, I will try starting from worst to least worst—but still unacceptable.

1. The Wooden Toy Soldier

The worst thing you can do is put your arms straight down the side of your legs—like a toy soldier—and leave them there. Why? Because now you look stiff as a board, and you have prevented your arms and hands from gesturing at all. You have lost a key element of persuasion: the gesture.

2. The Fig Leaf Position

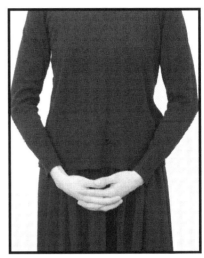

After the toy soldier impersonation, the fig leaf position comes in at a close second. This position is performed when a person clasps their hands in front of their body below their waist so as to act as a fig leaf to cover their private parts, as fig leaves did for nude sculptures for a period of time (see fig. 1). People keep their hands together as a security blanket throughout the entire presentation. Not gesturing is never an acceptable form of communication. Even if the speaker gestures from this position, the fig leaf position makes it difficult to get your hands up above your belly button to where gestures should occur (see discussion of the "Gesture Strike Zone" below).

Figure 1. The Fig Leaf Position.

3. Putting Your Hands Behind Your Back

Many lawyers decide to clasp their hands behind their back. This position brings endless comfort. The thought process is that if the hands are behind the back and out of sight, the audience won't be distracted by them. This position also allows you to squeeze them or fidget with them when you are nervous, and no one will be the wiser. In addition, speakers believe that they are also conveying a polite body position for the audience, almost one of submission. The audience has nothing to be afraid of because with the speaker's hands effectively tied behind their back, they are not a threat.

Like the toy soldier imitation, all you have done is destroyed any chance to communicate effectively with your arms and hands. Furthermore, being submissive in front of an audience is not the right image to project. You are a leader, a teacher, a persuader; not someone who is shyly going to give them some meek ideas to think about.

The opposite problem is having no control over your hands or arms and just letting them go all over the place. However, this fear is largely unfounded. By default, your hands and arms will naturally complement what you are saying with appropriate gestures.

4. Putting Both Hands In Your Pockets

Putting both hands in your pockets is distracting, prevents you from gesturing, and gives you the unfortunate opportunity to play with your phone, key fob, or whatever else you have in your pocket.

I have seen some very good public speakers put one hand in their pocket a majority of the time while they speak (see discussion under "Good Gestures"). Doing so allows you to gesture with the other hand and creates a relaxed mood by inviting the audience in for a casual conversation. I hesitate to mention this as being an effective gesture because I fear many people will be drawn to try it. If I were you, I would not try it, because a lot more fail than succeed at it. One reason is that speaking requires energy, and you can gesture better with two hands than one. With one hand in your pocket, you are going to be less energetic. Most presentations die for lack of enthusiasm and conviction. Your body language needs to set the tone for the energy you want to convey.

5. Crossing Your Arms

Crossing your arms is another bad trick people use to calm the nerves to prevent unwanted gestures. However, crossing your arms does just that, it prevents gesturing, which is essential to persuasion. In addition, crossed arms send a lot of wrong signals to the listener, such as that the speaker is judgmental, angry, or bored, even though the speaker isn't.

6. Holding a Pen or Notepad

Another bad habit includes holding a pen or notepad in one hand. Many professors teach this strategy as a way to give you something to hold onto while you are speaking. You can grip the notepad or pen as tight as you want if you get nervous. They act as a security blanket that you can literally hold onto if you need some comfort. The downside? Well, you already know one answer: it prevents you from fully gesturing. Second, you will likely start clicking the pen, playing with its detachable top, or waving your notepad around in a distracting manner.

7. Pointing Your Finger

A lot of politicians and some lawyers use their finger to point at their audience to emphasize their idea. Do you like having someone point their finger at you? Of course not. I don't know why this is ever done. It is patronizing and makes the recipient feel uncomfortable.

8. Pacing and Swaying

I think one of the hardest problems to solve is the tendency to pace back and forth while we talk. Why? It is the natural thing to do when you are nervous. Indeed, if you were asked to draw a picture of someone who is nervous, you would probably draw a person with sweat rolling down their face, or someone pacing back and forth. When you are nervous, that nervous energy needs to go somewhere, and walking off your nerves is a great way to relax, except when you are speaking, because it is distracting. You want the judge or jury to focus on what you are saying. But when you are pacing, the listener is devoting a certain amount of attention to following your pacing, which takes away from the attention they can devote to what you are saying.

The solution to all of this is to overcome your fears before you begin speaking, as discussed in chapter 1, and to focus on your stance, as discussed above. Your stance should be governed by Newton's first law of motion, often called the law of inertia: a body at rests stays at rest and a body in motion stays in motion until acted on by an external force.

A good stance will go a long way toward preventing pacing. But if you are one that tends to pace (I include myself in that group), think of yourself as having a duty to speak to the entire jury, and understand that if you are pacing, you are turning your back or side to jurors and ignoring the ones that you have walked away from.

In addition, realize that standing in one place produces a position of strength, and if you are grounded, that nervous energy can go right back into the earth,

---

List of Bad Gestures

1. Putting your hands and arms to your side like a toy solider.
2. Clasping your hands in front of your waist.
3. Clasping your hands behind your back.
4. Waving your hands in exaggerated gestures.
5. Putting your hands in your pocket.
6. Crossing your arms.
7. Holding a pen or notepad in one hand.
8. Pointing at a judge or juror.
9. Pacing too much.
10. Swaying from once side to the other.

instead of up into your brain, where it will encourage your feet to wander. The key is to think of yourself as not merely standing with your feet on the floor, but that your feet are firmly planted on the ground, and that this strong and secure connection to the earth extends from the earth up through your entire body. If you do this, you will begin to see that standing in one place is really a position of strength.

Swaying is pretty easy to fix. First, you need to be aware of whether you sway or not. Get some feedback. If you do sway, simply being conscious of it will be enough to correct the problem. Like with pacing, you don't want to distract your audience by your shifting weight from one leg to the other while you talk.

7.7 AVOID VERBAL PAUSES

Although it is not a physical gesture, the verbal pause is a close cousin. A verbal pause is when a speaker stalls for time before speaking their next thought. Speakers do this by saying words such as *um, uh, ah, like, so,* and, *OK.* We use these words constantly in our everyday speech. It does not bother our friends, because they are probably using them also, so no one pays attention to them. But when you are in a courtroom and the entire focus is on what you are saying, these verbal pauses can become not only distracting but very annoying to the listener. It is very typical for a speaker to use these verbal pauses at the rate of one per every other sentence. You probably are unaware of how often you use verbal pauses. To become more aware, record yourself speaking or look for the verbal pauses in one of your transcripts from a hearing.

One reason people use these words is to fill a one- to two-second gap between what they have just said and their next thought. In essence, these words indicate to the audience that you need a moment to decide what you are going to say next. Other times, the words are used for no good reason at all other than because it is a habit, and a bad one at that.

The solution is to embrace a brief silence instead of the annoying word. Rather than saying "uh" or "so," just remain silent and think of your next thought. Don't be afraid of the silence. While you are thinking of your next thought, your audience is actually thanking you for having given them time, through your silence, to think about what you have just said and actually catch up to you. Think of the silence as being an aid to both you and your audience, instead of as a sign of weakness that you aren't able to speak continuously. No one could, or should, speak continuously without pausing.

It takes practice, but this habit can easily be fixed. In order to first break it, you need to be aware of what you are doing. Record yourself speaking. Find out which word or words you use to fill the space. Then, deliver your presentation and listen to yourself as you speak and focus on the moments between sentences and phrases. Be determined not to say the verbal pauses. Instead, pause for a second and then just continue speaking your next thought.

Exercise

This exercise will also help you get rid of the verbal pauses. Read this passage below aloud and focus on the silence. Don't be afraid of it. You will see how silence actually helps you speak with more emphasis and, consequently, more persuasively. Without realizing it, your voice will highlight the word before the pause. That contrast will create an emphasis that is infinitely better than if you used verbal pauses.

Let me tell you the story of one of my favorite heroes, Benjamin Franklin. **[pause, consciously hold your mouth closed. When you are ready for the next line, breathe in and speak.]**

He was born on January 17, 1706, **[pause]**

and was one of the Founding Fathers of the United States. **[pause]**

He excelled at almost everything. **[pause]**

He was an accomplished political philosopher, **[pause]** *writer,* **[pause]** *inventor,* **[pause]** *scientist,* **[don't say "uh" or "ah" here]**,

and diplomat, among many other things. **[pause]**

For example, **[pause]** *as a scientist ,* **[pause]**

he discovered the theory of electricity, **[pause]**

and as an inventor, **[pause]** *the Franklin stove.*

7.8 GOOD GESTURES

Science Supports Communicating with Gestures

Perhaps the best argument for not gesturing is that since there is a risk it will be distracting, the safest strategy is to not gesture. However, given the findings of the previously mentioned study that indicated that when we speak about our feelings, 55 percent of our communication is through facial and body language, why would you give up this vital form of communication? It is obvious that good gestures enhance communication, but let me share a few more studies with you to get you motivated to learn the gestures discussed below. Judith Holler and Geoffrey Beattie conducted a study and found that the use of gestures could increase the value of what you are saying by 60 percent. Similarly, a study by

Adam Kendon that was published in the journal *Research on Language and Social Interaction* in 1994 found that people understood what someone was saying twice as well when it was accompanied by gestures.

Dr. Susan Goldin-Meadow studied people who were asked to memorize a list of words. One group was allowed to gesture when recalling the words, the other was not. The group that used gestures remembered 20 percent more than those who did not. Consequently, gestures can help you remember what you want to say.

The simple trick to deciding how you should gesture is to do what you do naturally. How do you figure that out? Next time you are telling your friends an interesting story at a meal, at their house, or at a bar, notice what your hands are doing. I'm certain they are not clasped behind your back or in the fig leaf position, or stuck at your side or in your pockets. Also, I'm sure your arms are not crossed. Instead, your hands will be naturally moving in front of your body to emphasize what you are saying. Better yet, notice how your friends are gesturing. Pay particular attention to the ones who tell really good stories. You will find that they are gesturing very effectively and you can imitate their gestures when you speak.

Often when I give feedback to a lawyer suggesting that they did not gesture enough—or at all— they will complain that they don't know how to gesture. For example, some will say, "I just didn't know what to do with my hands." To me, that was clearly true because they looked stiff and uncomfortable. But as they are explaining the problem to me, they are gesturing very effectively and naturally to me. This never fails to happen. Why? They are having a conversation with me, which is exactly what they should be doing with the judge and jury when they are in court. I cannot emphasize this enough. Concentrate on how you gesture naturally when you are telling a story to your friends and incorporate that into your presentation in court. That will get you 90 percent of where you want to be. Below is how to get the other 10 percent.

The Resting Position

Everyone wants the security of holding onto something while they speak. When I started out, I needed to hold onto a legal pad. It gave me something to channel my nervous energy onto, and I could quickly look at my notes when necessary. Then, I graduated from a legal pad to a pen. which I could hold onto for dear life. It was less noticeable and very comforting. But these tricks were not stepping stones to better public speaking. They were detours. Both the notepad and the pen—and what you are doing with them—are distracting to judges and jurors.

Instead of taking these detours, incorporate the tips below. One of the hardest things that I tried to solve was what to do with my hands in the moment right before I started speaking, when my hands are in what I will refer to as the resting position. The resting position is determined by where your hands are just before you begin to speak and also where they can return and "rest" between gestures while you are speaking. Nothing felt natural. If I looked at what people did when talking to friends at a party, they

> **Practice Tip**
>
> Don't worry about what your resting position is. Just find something comfortable. People will remember what you say. They won't remember—much less notice in real time—where your hands were between gestures.

sometimes had a drink in one hand. Well, that does not work in a courtroom. I have two good solutions for you to try, and one option to avoid.

The first solution is to slightly cup your hands, as if you were going to throw a baseball, and bring them in front of your belly button. Touch the tip of each finger on one hand with its matching fingertip on the other hand. That is, the tip of right pinky touches tip of left pinky, the tip of right ring finger touches tip of left ring finger, and so on. Once the fingers are touching each other, they remain slightly spread out and cupped. A lot of people like this position, but to me, it feels too rigid. My opinion is not important. Find something comfortable for you.

The second solution is to clasp your hands just below your belly button. To do this, put your left hand just below your belly button with the palm facing up. Take your right hand, with the palm facing down, and clasp your left hand so that both palms are touching and your fingers are wrapped a little bit around the back of the palms of your hands (see fig. 2). I have found this resting position very relaxing and reassuring. If you feel more comfortable, you can do it the opposite way, with your right palm up.

One option that I am not a fan of is to put both hands just below your belly button and interlock your fingers with the palms cupped towards the ceiling. It is like the fig leaf position, but moved above the waist. It does not look natural, and when the fingers are locked, it is hard to untangle your fingers to make a gesture.

Figure 2. The Resting Position.

The Ready Position

Once you begin to speak, go immediately from the resting position to what I call Ready Position #1, which is really a gesture in and of itself. It is a great way to get the hands and forearms moving, and it positions you for any number of gestures to follow.

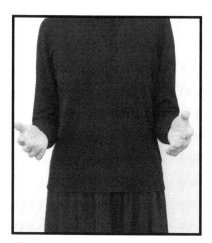

Figure 3. The Ready Position #1.

That is why it is called the ready position. To find Ready Position #1, put your arms to your side, and bend your elbows so that your forearms are at a 90-degree angle to your biceps. Picture yourself as relaxed but still ready enough to catch a basketball if it were thrown to you just above your waist, with your palms turned about 45 degrees upward from the ground (see fig. 3). In a lot of ways, this gesture is like "the give" discussed in the next section, but here you are using both hands.

It is a great way to start a presentation, because you are gesturing as if you want to reach out to your audience and give them something, which is exactly what you are trying to do with your words.

From this position, you are ready to transition to any other gesture. Don't worry about what your hands will do; they will naturally follow what you are saying.

Another ready position is one that I don't recommended, but since a few accomplished speakers use it successfully, I will briefly discuss it here. I call it Ready Position #2 (it can also serve as a resting position). It is very natural. Put one hand in your pocket and use your other hand as if you were going to shake someone's hand, but with the palm tilted upward at about a 60-degree angle to the ground (see fig. 4). The civil rights lawyer Bryan Stevenson did it when he gave his popular TED Talk (see it at: www.winningatpersuasion.com).The preacher Joel Osteen often does it too (see an example at: https://youtu.be/KSzTLJqi4Ck).

Figure 4. The Ready Position #2.

Nonetheless, I don't recommend it, because for most of us, the disadvantages are many and hard to overcome. Anytime you have your hand in your pocket, you will be tempted to fiddle with whatever is in it, which can become a distraction. Also, you need to gesture with both hands, and having one in a pocket will tempt you to keep it there and deprive you of the ability to gesture with both hands.

As I mentioned at the outset of the chapter, find out what position works for you and adapt it to your style so that you speak from your heart. For me, Ready Position #2 does not work because I feel like my left hand gets stuck in my left pocket, preventing me from gesturing with both hands. But you may find it works for you.

The Give

From the ready position, a great second gesture is "the give." This is accomplished by extending your arm in front of you with your palm almost completely open to the ceiling (see fig. 5). It is used when you are sharing an important point. It reinforces the idea that you are giving your audience something, and it also suggests that you are inviting them in to hear what you are saying. You can also use both hands in "the give" for additional emphasis, and to include the audience in your story by bringing your hands towards you after you extend them.

Figure 5. The Give.

It is also used when you are making contrasting points. For example, you might say, "On the one hand," while extending your left palm to the audience, followed by "On the other hand," while extending your right palm to the audience.

The Number

Your hands can be used to signal the number of points you want to make and what point you are on. For example, you could hold up three fingers when you tell the judge that you are going to give them three reasons for why your client should prevail. Then, as you go through the appropriate points, hold up the corresponding number on your hand.

Figure 6. The Chop (using just one forearm).

The Chop

Another gesture is the chop, which is performed when both hands and forearms move together from about a 45-degree angle to the elbows down to about a 90-degree angle. You can also do the chop with just one forearm (see fig. 6). Both are a way to emphasize the point you are making.

The Measurer

Another way to use your hands is to show the audience how big or small something is, or to describe what you are saying.

The key to performing all of these gestures persuasively is to make bigger gestures than you probably feel comfortable doing. Get some air beneath your armpits.

List of Good Gestures

1. *Resting position*, with hands clasped just below your belly button.
2. *Ready position #1*, as if you were about to catch a basketball, with palms facing upward about 45 degrees.
3. *The give*: an open palm facing upward to show the audience you are giving information.
4. *The number*: hold up fingers to emphasize the number of your points.
5. *The chop*: hand and forearm move together to emphasize a point.
6. *The measurer*: use your hands to illustrate or show how big or small something is.

Although most of your gestures will come naturally, it does not hurt to plan out what your gestures will be for your most important points. Make a note of when it will be a good time to describe something with your hands, point to your PowerPoint slide, or use your left hand to make one point with "the give" and your right hand to make a second point with "the give." Or, are you going to lean forward and speak softly so that the jury leans forward as well in response? Once you start thinking about your gestures, they will start to come naturally to you the more times you speak. Practice the gestures mentioned above and the others that you like. If some of them don't feel natural, practice them to get comfortable with them. The more you practice, the more naturally you hand gestures will start into motion. Remember Newton's law of inertia? Your hands and arms are going to stay at rest unless you force them to get moving.

The excerpt below provides an example of a spontaneous, natural gesture that was made in court by Daniel Petrocelli, the lawyer for the Goldman family in the wrongful death civil lawsuit against O.J. Simpson for the murder of Ron Goldman and Nicole Brown outside Nicole's home. The boldfaced and italicized words are Petrocelli's subsequent comments about his performance.

And by [Ron Goldman's and Nicole Simpson's] blood, they forced him [Simpson] to step, step, step, *[I just began stepping! I hadn't planned to, but I picked up my feet gingerly; you could almost hear the wet blood sticking to my soles]* as he walked to the back, leaving shoe prints that are just like fingerprints in this case, that tell us who did this, who did this unspeakable tragedy.

Clearly, not all of our gestures need to be done with our hands!

The Gesture Strike Zone

I don't like giving a vague answer like the one that I am about to give, because I never liked it when law school professors would try to avoid answering a direct question with, "It depends." However, in general, your gestures should be performed within an imaginary strike zone, like the one used in Major League Baseball, only the gesture strike zone is higher and slightly more rectangular. For speakers, the bottom of the zone starts at your belly button and the top of the zone ends at about your mouth. The zone extends on either side of your body to a point outside your shoulders, as if you were to stick your elbows into your sides and extend your forearms out from your sides (see fig. 7). If you extend your arms straight out to your sides from your shoulders, you have gone too far, unless you are in a large courtroom. However, this strike zone is not two dimensional. Feel free to extend your arms forward toward your audience as much as you want, as long as you don't invade their space.

Figure 7. The Gesture Strike Zone.

The reason I mention the strike zone is that most lawyers never use the full strike zone; instead, they only use very small gestures that stay within the boundaries of the torso and consequently have no impact. Use all of the strike zone when you are speaking. However, don't let the gesture strike zone limit you from making even bigger gestures when you need to—get your elbows away from the side of your body and put some space underneath your armpits. Whether to go outside your strike zone depends on the environment and what you are saying. Think about how close you are to the judge and jury and how big the courtroom is and make the necessary adjustments. To figure out what those should be, think of how you gesture outside the courtroom. For example, when you are speaking to friends at a restaurant, your gestures would be within the strike zone, and maybe even in only a small part of it, depending on how physically close you are to your friends. If you were gesturing outside the strike zone, above your head or extending your arms out to your side, you would get unwanted attention from the other tables and your friends would be embarrassed. On the other hand, if you were telling a story at a rehearsal dinner in a bigger room, where you were the sole focus of attention, you would certainly make some gestures outside the strike zone.

Practice Tip

Think of your gestures as being smooth and relaxed, not forced and choppy.

Consequently, when you are in court, think about using the entire strike zone as much as you can and don't be afraid to go outside of it when necessary.

7.9 MAKE YOUR VOICE INTERESTING (THE BASICS)

The Sound of Your Voice

If you focus on listening to the sound of your voice, you may cringe a little at what you hear, particularly if you have recorded it. It will probably sound different than you expected and more nasally. There are a variety of scientific reasons for this that don't need to be explained here, including the quality of the recording used. But the truth is that our ears hear our own voices differently than other people (our listening audience) hear them, and we hear our voices more critically than others. You will have to accept the fact that your voice is simply better than it sounds to you.

Nonetheless, your audience needs to be interested in what you are saying and how you are saying it. There are two common complaints about speakers: their delivery is boring, and they speak too fast. Let's explore the qualities of the sound of your voice and the pace of delivery and then do some exercises.

Volume

By virtue of your ears being closer to your mouth than anyone else's, you think you are speaking louder than you are. In a courtroom. where there are often microphones, be aware of how your voice is carrying. Are the jurors leaning towards you because they are not able to hear you? Or are you speaking too loudly, so that you are literally invading their personal space with the strength of your voice. All it takes is self-awareness to see the reactions of the judge or jury that you are talking to. If I am unsure, I never hesitate to ask, "Your honor, can you hear me okay?" It is always met with a kind reply.

Pitch

Pitch is the degree of highness or lowness of your tone of voice. We use variations in everyday conversation to convey meaning. For example, say the following without any variation in the pitch of your voice: "It is raining outside." By your tone, you are making a statement that it is raining. Now, say the same sentence but make a conscious effort to say the words "raining outside" with higher pitches than the preceding words. Imagine that your pitches are going up a staircase, with the syllables of "raining outside" getting higher on the staircase. By simply changing your pitch, you now have turned the statement with certainty that it is raining into a question. You will naturally change your pitch during conversation. The point is just to be aware that you do it. You may find moments in your presentation when you can do it with more emphasis to make a point.

Pace

Most people speak at a rate of 125-150 words per minute. But there is no perfect rate. Daniel Webster spoke at 90 words per minute, and JFK spoke at 180. Martin Luther King Jr. began his "I Have a Dream" speech at 92 words per minute but finished it at 145.

As discussed in more detail below, you need to have a deliberate pace. Like when running a race, before you start, visualize your pace. Your presentation will need to have plenty of pauses, but you want to vary your speed when it matters. What you are saying will dictate your pace. Obviously, if you are talking about something complicated, you need to slow your pace. But if it is a legal point or facts the judge already knows, speak faster so that you can spend more time on the important points.

Most important, think about the pace you want to set for your presentation. Start a little slower than you think you need to because you will naturally start speaking quicker once you get into your speech. If you are fast talker (see the following discussion), be particularly conscious of setting a slower pace than usual.

How to Stop Speaking Too Fast

People speak too fast for one of two reasons. First, they are nervous, and they feel that the faster they speak, the sooner the speech will be over. Second, some people speak too fast because they feel that they have so much information to share and not enough time to share it. Consequently, they overload their audience with so much information that the audience cannot process it as quickly as they are dispensing it. The overburdened audience quickly shuts down and tunes out.

Whatever the reason for speaking too fast, the solution is to first understand that you will fail if you speak too quickly. Instead, think about speaking in phrases with distinct stops between different ideas. Highlight with your voice what is most important and consciously insert pauses before important points that you want to make.

I have a persistent habit of speaking too fast in conversations and in court. I was told in elementary school that I spoke too fast, and it is a natural tendency that I still struggle with. In court, I used to take a notecard with me to the podium that had in big writing only two words: speak slowly. The notecard helped. But I now think these words are better: highlight and pause. These words are better because they give you something positive to think about.

> *The right word may be effective, but no word was ever effective as a rightly timed pause.*
> —Mark Twain

In addition, the exercises in the next section regarding "America the Beautiful" will also help. As you will learn in the next section, if you are thinking about emphasizing a key word in each sentence, you must necessarily slow down to emphasize it, and sometimes even pause. Those necessities will make your speech a measured and interesting journey for your listeners, rather than a runaway freight train ride. But for now, let's just do an exercise to specifically eliminate your urge to speak too quickly.

Exercise

As you read the lyrics below, pause at the end of each phrase (I have placed reminders for you). Make sure the thought sinks in before you go to the next line. This is the pace you should speak at. Reading aloud poetry and song lyrics is a great way to cure the problem of speaking too quickly because it forces you to focus on thoughts and phrases.

America! [**pause**] *America!* [**pause, let the emphasis sink in**]

God shed His grace [**pause**] *on thee.* [**this is an important idea, pause before you continue**]

And crown thy good [**pause**] *with brotherhood* [**let your audience enjoy this wonderful thought**]

From sea [**pause**] *to shining sea!*

Exercise

Another trick to help you speak slower is to sync your words with your gestures. You cannot speak fast when your gestures are slow. Consequently, consciously think about slowing down your arms and hands when you feel that you are starting to rush your words. Here are some sample gestures for the lyrics above.

[**Ready position**] *America! America!*

God shed His grace on thee [**use the give gesture with both hands**].

And crown thy good [**Bring your right hand towards you and then extend both arms out toward the audience in a circular motion that is parallel to the ground from the center of your body to show that everyone is included in the following words**]

with brotherhood [**bring your hands back to the center of your body and give a chop with both hands in front of you to emphasize "with brotherhood"**]

From sea to shining sea! [**chop with both hands on the left side of your body to indicate one coast and then take your right arm and move it across your body to demonstrate the width of the USA from one coast to the other**]

You will find that if you gesture, there is no way to speak quickly because your hands will slow you down.

7.10 MAKE YOUR VOICE INTERESTING (ADVANCED TIPS)

Alexis and your car's navigation system are famous for speaking in boring, monotone voices. Don't fail to take advantage of being human. Use the gift of vocal variety that you have been given.

Have you ever heard a professional singer sing a song at the same volume throughout? Of course not. Songs crescendo (increase volume) or decrescendo (decrease volume) at the most important parts. You should do the same.

Are there pauses before an important passage in your presentation? There should be. Have you noticed that singers slow down at the end of a song to emphasize a lyric and the finality of the song? You should employ these tricks with your voice. Think about your most important points. What is your voice going to do? Get louder? Softer? Slower? Faster? Be intentional about how you are going to say key phrases.

Another tip is to repeat important words or phrases throughout your presentation. Unlike a book that has a table of contents, an index, and written pages, there is no way for an audience to refer to a written page or table to remember what you said. By occasionally reminding them of what your presentation is all about, you will avoid the problem of not having written pages for your audience to refer to.

You also need to foreshadow what you will tell your audience and occasionally summarize what you have told them. Wouldn't it be refreshing if you told a judge at your next hearing, "Your honor, I want to talk to you about my three most important points," and then two thirds of the way into your presentation say, "Your honor, now that I have talked about [describe points one and two], let me end with the following point."

Let's do an exercise to see how we can change the meaning of a phrase by using several tools with our voice: speaking a word louder, slower, and pausing before or after it. By doing this, you will be forced to think about the meaning of what you say and what is important about it.

Below is the same portion of the chorus from "America the Beautiful" that we worked with earlier.

Exercise One

Say the words of the chorus. Now repeat the chorus by speaking the word in boldface with a louder voice.

America! America!

God *shed His grace on thee*

And crown thy good with brotherhood

From sea to shining sea!

Did you notice that by simply increasing the volume of that one word, you told your imaginary audience what the most important word in the chorus is?

Exercise Two

Speak the words of the chorus again, but this time emphasize with a louder voice *and* slower pace the word in boldface.

America! America!

God **shed** *His grace on thee*

And crown thy good with brotherhood

From sea to shining sea!

Did you notice that you have now shifted the meaning to the *giving* of God's grace? By saying the word "shed" more slowly and loudly than the others, you have given that word more emphasis than if you had just said it louder. Let's continue to see other ways to emphasize a word.

Exercise Three

Speak the words below, and just before you are about to say "grace" pause slightly, and then say "grace" just a little bit louder than the other words.

America! America!

God shed His **grace** *on thee*

And crown thy good with brotherhood

From sea to shining sea!

Did you notice how the slight pause added dramatic effect to the word that followed, in this case "grace"? Now repeat this exercise but pause after the word "grace." Repeat the exercise a third time but pause before and after the word "grace." You will notice that each way provides a different dramatic effect. Pausing in different places also provides variety.

Exercise Four

In this last exercise, pause slightly just before the word "thee" and then speak it softly.

America! America!

*God shed His grace on **thee***

And crown thy good with brotherhood

From sea to shining sea!

The point is that by varying the volume of your voice, the pace of your delivery, and adding pauses, you make the words that you are saying more interesting and you emphasize the important words for your audience. Would you like to see a master in action? Go to YouTube and search "Ray Charles America the Beautiful World Series 2001" [https://www.youtube.com/watch?v=1OTR RzSuWro]. There you will find Ray Charles displaying these techniques in their highest form.

CPRs

There is an acronym that will help you remember the tips in the previous section. In order to remember it, think of how you would inject your speech with some life. In order to resuscitate someone who has stopped breathing, you would apply CPR, or cardiopulmonary resuscitation. For speaking, it is not very different, except that you will make the CPR plural (i.e., CPRs). Here, **C** stands for "change pace, pitch, and volume," **P** stands for "pause for effect," **R** stands for "repeat important words," and **s** stands for "stress key words."

If you want to see the power of CPRs, watch Will Stephens' TEDx Talk on "Nothing" [https://youtu.be/8S0FDjFBj8o]. In his humorous short talk, he shows the power of using the gestures and techniques described in CPRs to make you think you are hearing something important, even when you are not. He is a great speaker and demonstrates the techniques very well. By watching him, you can see how helpful the techniques would be when you really have something important to say in court.

Speak with Conviction

I have already discussed the importance of speaking from the heart to persuade. Speaking with conviction is similar, but slightly different. When speaking to a jury, you need to keep in mind that the jury believes that you know *all* the facts in the case: the good, the bad, and the ugly. Jurors also realize that you know *more* facts than those that have been presented at trial. As a result, you need to speak the absolute truth and say it with confidence. If you are not convinced that what you are saying is true, you are not going to be able to persuade anyone.

7.11 HOW TO DRESS

I hesitate to even write a section on this topic because it should be obvious to everyone why it is important to dress properly. But let me share with you a few anecdotes. Jurors often discuss what the attorneys wear each day. What you wear matters. A famous plaintiff's attorney once told me that he learned his client had been awarded less damages because the jurors had noticed the gold watch the attorney wore at trial. Jurors will notice if you wear the same tie, a bad tie, a flashy tie, etc. Jurors have made comments during deliberations that an attorney's shoes were never shined. Is that what you want jurors talking about while they are deciding your case? These clothing faux pas are also true for women.

> *Clothes make the man. Naked people have little or no influence on society.*
> —Mark Twain

You never want your clothing to distract from your case. In short, dress conservatively. But just wearing something that you really like and that has a good feel will go a long way towards helping you feel confident.

7.12 VIDEO HEARINGS

The coronavirus pandemic of 2020 fundamentally altered the way courts conducted hearings, and that trend may continue well into the future. As we all know, courts were closed, and the necessity of video conferences for hearings forced many to have their first hearing via the camera on their laptop. Here are some tips to look your best on Zoom, or whatever video meeting application the court requests.

You can't do anything successfully unless you have a good internet connection. Check your internet speed at one of the many places such as www.speedtest.net. You need at least 10-20 Mbps for downloading and 5 Mbps for uploading files. If you need to get better Wi-Fi reception in your home, you should consider setting up a mesh network that spreads your signal throughout your living space. Eero makes my favorite one. You also need to be comfortable. LoveHome makes a wonderful lumbar support cushion for your chair ($26.99).

Next, you need a good webcam. Even if your computer has a camera, Logitech makes an HD webcam (Logitech C920s for $69.00) that will provide better video resolution. The difference it makes is well worth the cost. You should also consider a separate microphone that will make your voice sound better and also keep out background noise. One such microphone that I like is the Tonor TC-777 ($39.00). Another great microphone is Blue's Yeti ($130). I have found the Tonor does all I need it to and is as good as the Yeti, but the Yeti has a very strong following and has a few more functions. Both are better than the microphone on your computer or the one included with most webcams, including the Logitech recommended above.

As stated above, dress is important. Dress for the virtual hearing as if you were going to be live and in person. The next thing you need to consider is lighting. Access your camera on your computer so that you can see what you will look like before your hearing. You can also go to Zoom.com and select "Host a Meeting" and then select "with video on" and you will get a live video of yourself as your computer's camera sees you.

Here are some basics about lighting. You don't want the light coming from behind you as it will backlight you and cover your face in a shadow. You also don't want the light to come from the sides as it will cast shadows. Ideally, you want diffuse lighting in front of you. The easiest solution is to buy a ring light with a stand and place it in front of you. My favorite ring light is the UBeesize 10" Ring Light ($29.00). It comes with a stand and you can adjust the brightness to several settings in order to provide diffused light in front.

The second best way to get good lighting is to sit at a desk facing a window so that you get naturally diffused lighting from the outside, but not direct sunlight. If you can arrange that, just make sure that the lighting is in front of you and even on both sides. If you are in your office and all you have is overhead lighting, you should be fine as long as the lighting is bright and evenly dispersed. The key is to just experiment by taking your laptop to different rooms and positioning it in different directions to see what looks best.

Another important consideration is camera angle. Most people make the mistake of putting the laptop on their desk instead of putting the camera at eye level. It is shocking how many people don't make this simple adjustment. When the camera is at eye level, you avoid all the unflattering angles of your face when the camera is below your head, not to mention the fact that the ceiling or the upper part of the wall behind you becomes a distraction when the camera is angled up.

Instead, put your laptop on a couple of thick books so that the camera is just slightly above your eyes. Better yet, the non-swivel mStand by Rain Design

($44.00) is sturdier than a stack of books and more accurate for adjusting the height of your laptop. By putting the laptop camera just above eye level, you are looking slightly upwards when you are talking. Not only is this a better camera angle for your face, but you will also look more confident. You also don't want to be too close to the camera, since it has a wide-angle lens and will distort your face if you get too close. Stay about an arm's length from your laptop's keyboard.

In addition, look to see if your video meeting application has the ability to enhance how you look. Zoom has such a feature. Under video settings, select "touch up my appearance." This option will give you a softer and warmer look if you want it.

A common piece of advice is to look straight into the camera when you are talking and not toward the video stream of the person talking to you, who—depending on the software program—may be off to the side on your computer screen. The rationale is that you will be looking a little off to the side if you look directly at the person. But I think the trade-off is not worth it for the beginner. It is hard to connect with a judge or opposing counsel if you are talking to a camera on your computer. It is much easier to have a meaningful conversation if you look at their image on your computer.

Give some thought to your background. It should appear professional-looking, clean, and simple. Perhaps you want a bookcase behind you, or just a blank wall. Just be aware that people will notice your environment, and you want it to be a good reflection on you.

Finally, make sure there are no distractions. Turn your phone to silent and make sure people know not to enter your room. Take all the obvious precautions, such as putting your pets in a place where they cannot be heard. Also, be aware when your neighbor mows their lawn. It will often be at a regular time. If so, make adjustments.

SUGGESTED ADDITIONAL READING

1. *The Quick & Easy Way to Effective Speaking*, Dale Carnegie, (Pocket Books, 1977).
2. *TED Talks: The Official TED Guide to Public Speaking*, Chris Anderson (Mariner books, 2017). This is a very good book that pulls the curtain back on TED Talks and how speakers prepare to give these talks.
3. *The Articulate Advocate: New Techniques of Persuasion for Trial Lawyers*, Brian K. Johnson & Marsha Hunter (Crown King Books, 2009). A very good book if you want to explore in-depth how to gesture.

CHAPTER CHECKLIST

1. As Emerson said, "All the great speakers were bad speakers at first."

2. People who speak well are perceived as being intelligent and trustworthy.

3. A study found that personal communication could be broken down as follows: 7 percent words, 38 percent tone of voice, and 55 percent facial and body language. Although the study applied to people who were talking about their feelings, the percentages provide general guidance for lawyers in court.

4. To stand up straight, think about a posture that feels as if you are being pulled upward, starting from the top of your head. Imagine a flexible bungee cord is attached there. The bungee cord pulls gently upward. As your head pulls up, your spine straightens and lengthens.

5. Before you begin to speak, you need to be physically grounded. Your feet need to be underneath your hips and you should feel that you are not standing on the ground but that your feet are connected to the earth. One image that may help you is to see yourself as a tree. Your hands and voice are the limbs, your body is the trunk, and your feet have roots connected to the ground. The energy comes up from the ground, through your body, and then to your hands and voice.

6. Breathe deeply with your diaphragm.

7. Never touch the podium.

8. There are several bad gestures, including the wooden toy soldier, the fig leaf position, putting your hands behind your back, putting both hands in your pockets, crossing your arms, holding a notepad or pen, and pointing your finger.

9. To avoid pacing, remember Newton's first law of motion: a body at rests stays at rest and a body in motion stays in motion until acted on by an external force.

10. Avoid verbal pauses such as *um* or *OK* by embracing a brief silence instead.

11. Studies show that gestures can increase the value of what you say by 60 percent.

12. Concentrate on how you gesture naturally when you are telling a story to your friends and incorporate that into your presentation in court.

13. The Resting Position is determined by where your hands are just before you begin to speak and also where they can return and "rest" between gestures while you are speaking. My favorite resting position is performed by clasping my hands just below my belly button.

14. The Ready Position is the position where your hands go immediately once you start to speak. To find the Ready Position, put your arms to your sides, bend your elbows so that your forearms are at a 90 degree angle to your biceps. Picture yourself as relaxed, yet ready to catch a basketball if it were thrown to you just above your waist, but with your palms turned about 45 degrees upward from the ground.

15. To accomplish "the give," extend one of your arms in front of you with your palm almost completely open to the ceiling. This gesture is used when you are sharing an important point. It reinforces the idea that you are giving your audience something.

16. "The number": Your hands can be used to signal the number of points you want to make and what point you are on.

17. "The chop" is performed when a hand and forearm (or both) move together from about a 45-degree angle to the elbows down to about a 90-degree angle.

18. "The measurer" shows the audience how big or small something is, or to illustrate what you are saying.

19. The gesture strike zone is the area in which you should gesture. The bottom of the zone starts at your belly button and the top of the zone is about at your mouth. The zone extends on either side of your body to a point outside your shoulders, like if you were to stick your elbow into your side and extend your forearm out to your side.

20. Make sure you use the full strike zone when you speak, and don't be afraid to go outside of it when the venue or what you are saying demands it. Get some air beneath your armpits.

21. To make sure you are speaking loud enough, be aware of your audience's reactions. It also never hurts to ask, "Can you hear me OK?"

22. By using a higher or lower pitch, you can change the meaning of a phrase.

23. You need to have a deliberate pace. Like running a race, before you start, visualize your pace. Your presentation will need to have plenty of pauses, but you want to vary your speed when it matters.

24. To avoid speaking too fast, take a notecard to the podium that says, "highlight and pause."

25. To avoid a boring voice, remember CPRs. C stands for "change pace, pitch, and volume," P stands for "pause for effect," R stands for "repeat important words," and S stands for "stress key words."

26. Speak with conviction. The jury believes that you know all the facts in the case: the good, the bad, and the ugly. Jurors also realize that you know more facts than those that have been presented at trial. As a result, you need to speak the absolute truth and say it with confidence. If you are not convinced

that what you are saying is true, you are not going to be able to persuade anyone.

27. Dress conservatively and wear something that you really like and that has a good feel.

28. For video hearings, you need at least 10-20 Mbps for downloading and 5 Mbps for uploading files. Make sure your camera is at eye level. Get a good webcam such as the Logitech C920s. You also need a good microphone such as the Tonor TC-777 or the Blue's Yeti. The UBeesize 10" Ring Light will help get rid of unwanted shadows.

29. For video hearings, make sure your laptop camera is just above eye level and that you have a clean and professional-looking background.

CHAPTER EIGHT

Pulling It All Together Through Practice

> "My father taught me that the only way you can make good at anything is to practice, and then practice some more."
> —*Pete Rose*

Now is a good time to learn how to pull it all together. You have learned how to overcome your fears, execute the principles of public speaking, write a compelling story, support your story with visual aids and PowerPoints, and speak persuasively without notes. However, none of the lessons you have learned will bring you success unless you learn how to practice and have a structure for doing so.

Consequently, let's pull everything together from the previous chapters and develop a surefire routine to get you from the starting line to the finish line of your next presentation. After you learn this process, we can examine some famous masters of persuasion in Part III.

8.1 THE PROCESS FOR TURNING YOUR COMPELLING STORY INTO A PRESENTATION

1. Set Aside Enough Time to Practice

First, you must make time for practice. Surprisingly, based on a large number of discussions with lawyers after their performances, I have found that they never practiced enough to ever have a chance for success. The lawyers fall into two groups. The first group admits that they did not practice at all and just winged it because they were confident that they could speak extemporaneously. The second group admitted that they ran out of time to practice. This latter group would tell of similar situations where they wrote their brief or opening statement, read it over a couple of times, and then hoped it would go well once they got to court. Of

---

CHAPTER ROAD MAP

- Learn how to develop your story from the first draft to a final presentation.
- Recognize how to practice effectively and avoid the mistakes others make.
- Learn essential tips for what to do on the day of your presentation.

course, they were disappointed in their performance, and for good reason. As Francis Bacon said, "Hope is a good breakfast, but it is a bad supper." I believe that if you haven't practiced enough, there is no reason for you to feel confident, and certainly no reason for you to succeed.

The best way to ensure that you have enough time to practice is to get your presentation in its final form several days before you need to deliver it. That way, if you need more time, you'll have it. Once you set your deadline, here is a process that works.

2. Write Your Compelling Story Once and Then Practice It Orally

Let's assume you have an upcoming opening statement. Once you have written a first draft of your compelling story, put it away and start practicing it orally. (If you have a hearing based on written briefs, obviously you will have to write a final brief for the court. Then, follow the same steps.) Your first draft will probably not be very good. That doesn't matter. The point of oral practice is that the real creative process begins when you get away from the written page. When you practice speaking your presentation after the first draft, the trick is not to try and recall the exact words that you have written, but to practice saying out loud the ideas in your draft. Each time you go through it, you will come up with different phrases and metaphors to articulate your ideas. Sometimes they will be better than they were in the last practice, sometimes they will be worse. It doesn't matter, just keep practicing. If you come up with a particularly great phrase that you are afraid you will forget, make a note of it. After going through your presentation many times, you will start using similar phrases for your ideas each time, and you will grow very comfortable with them. During the last rounds, you will notice that you give a similar presentation each time, but not the exact same one. That is exactly what you want, because instead of a memorized speech, you have now internalized it so that when the moment comes, you can "talk" to your audience instead of delivering a stilted delivery of memorized words.

> *He who loves practice without theory is like the sailor who boards a ship without a rudder and compass and never knows where he may cast.*
> —Leonardo da Vinci

One of my favorite ways to practice aloud is while I am walking my dog early in the morning or in the evening. I am relaxed, it feels good outside, and there is no more supportive audience than one's dog.

3. Create Images to Support Your Story

For me, once I feel like the compelling story is headed in the right direction, it is time to think about how I want to visually support it with PowerPoint slides, exhibits, or both (see chapter 5). At what point in your practice you decide to think about visual images depends on your particular creative process. Some people like to think of them when they first begin to create a compelling story, others like to wait until the structure is more complete.

4. Get Feedback from Family, Friends, and/or Colleagues

Test the persuasiveness of your compelling story with your family, friends, and colleagues. For instance, do they like your bottom-line message? Do they like the structure? Have you made complicated ideas simple? Do your PowerPoint slides touch their emotions?

Then, ask them to assume the role of opposing counsel and come up with responses to your story. Remember that for every hour you spend preparing your case, you should spend 20 minutes looking at it from the other side's perspective. Getting feedback from others is a great time to brainstorm how the other side will attack your story.

A lot of lawyers never practice in front of others, and the few that do often do it before their lawyer friends at the office. The problem is that it is very unlikely that you will have lawyers on the jury. So, their opinions aren't likely to mirror your potential jurors. Moreover, it is probable that the lawyers in your office (i.e., defense lawyers at a primarily defense-oriented firm) will think similarly about the type of case you have and not give you the diverse opinions that you need. For example, they will probably compare your facts to similar cases that they have handled and therefore not be good candidates for giving you critical feedback. They will also be inaccurate judges about how well you explained the case, since they will easily understand what you are talking about.

Ideally, you would practice before a focus group that would mimic your potential jury. This is highly recommended. But for many, the cost can be prohibitive. For those preparing for oral arguments, you need to have a moot court with lawyers who will be motivated to study the written briefs and ask the pointed questions you will get at the hearing. Sometimes that is easier said than done. Nonetheless, whatever type of practice you conduct at the office, include non-lawyers so that you can get diverse feedback on your presentation.

Also, practice before your family and friends. Your group will certainly not be familiar with the law, so you will be forced to explain your story clearly to them.

However, it can be very daunting to practice in front of friends and family, particularly if it is early in your process. I have found that it is one thing to deliver your presentation in court after it has been polished with relentless practice, but it is another thing altogether to perform an unfinished product in front of friends or family. I have a heightened sense of self-awareness and fear of failure when practicing in front of people I know well.

Here are four things I think about to ease my mind that I think will help you, too. First, your friends want to help. Second, they know that it is not a final rehearsal because you have told them that. Third, if you wait to get feedback until you have finished your presentation, there will be no time to take the feedback from the rehearsal and make your presentation better. Fourth, you need to practice. As John Wooden, the legendary basketball coach at UCLA who won 10 NCAA championships in a twelve-year period, said, "What I always loved about coaching was the practices. Not the games, not the tournaments, not the alumni stuff. But teaching the players during practice was what coaching was all about to me." He also said, "If you're not making mistakes, then you're not doing anything. I'm positive that a doer makes mistakes."

Cut yourself some slack. Learn to enjoy the practice and what you learn from it. In many ways, that is where you will become a great lawyer, not in the presentation that you finally give.

Finally, don't neglect the opportunity to get feedback on your gestures, in addition to your content. You can also get helpful tips on your verbal pauses. To that end, give a friend or family member a clicker (like the ones used to train dogs). If clickers aren't available, they can have their knuckles at the ready near a table. Tell your friend to use the clicker anytime you use the words uh, um, ah, OK, and so. You will be surprised how often you use one of those words. The clicker is a staple of a critique in any Toastmasters talk. Take advantage of it wherever you practice.

> *Even now, at 82 years old, if I don't learn something every day, you know what I think? It's a day lost. . . . I'm doing something musically all the time. And my ears are wide open for anything I can hear.*
>
> —B.B. King

5. Final Run Through

In an ideal world, my final formal rehearsal is in the courtroom a couple of days before I am scheduled to appear so that I don't become overly stressed the day and night before the presentation with a feeling that I haven't practiced enough. This will usually need to be arranged during regular business hours when the court is open but not in session. You will be hard pressed to get anyone to open the court for you outside of regular hours. If you cannot make that arrangement, find an alternative place at your office or home.

The day before the presentation, focus on the parts that might need a little more practice and then do a final run through. Since you have already done a formal final rehearsal a couple of days before, this is just a time to reinforce how good you feel about it. My final practice is usually on a late night dog walk. Obviously, I cannot take my PowerPoint on the walk, but I speak aloud the presentation and visualize the PowerPoint slides that accompany each point. Although

I have been doing this for years, I recently found out that Abraham Lincoln did the same thing, except without a dog. He was known to recite passages of his speeches aloud as he walked down the city streets of Springfield. If it worked for Abe, you ought to give it a try. What you should do on the day of the presentation will be discussed in section 8.3.

8.2 DO'S AND DON'T'S OF PRACTICING

Here are some general ideas for practicing public speaking that you can incorporate into the process above.

Practice During Normal, Everyday Conversations

A great way to get better at public speaking is to practice during your normal conversations. For example, practice speaking in phrases and emphasizing words when you tell a story, say grace at dinner, or are out with friends. Focus on making good eye contact when you talk. All these things can be practiced and will not only make you a better courtroom speaker, but also a better communicator in your everyday life.

Also, ask your friends and family if you speak too quickly, too softly, or too loudly. Those around you all the time will probably be grateful that you asked! Ask what your verbal pause is. Almost everyone has one. Mine is "so." Also, notice what gestures you use in casual conversations and get some feedback. Then use those gestures in the courtroom.

Don't Use a Mirror to Practice

I used to think that the conventional wisdom was correct about needing to practice in front of a mirror so that you can see how you are doing in real time. However, there are a couple of reasons why this conventional wisdom is wrong. As we all know, a mirror reflects our image in a way that when we move our right hand, we see our left hand moving in the mirror. That is confusing in and of itself.

But there is a more important reason not to use a mirror. When you are practicing in front of a mirror, you will become very self-conscious about what you are doing. For example, you may focus on your eyes and mistakenly think you blink too much, or think you have too many wrinkles, or not like the way your face looks when you speak. These are all stupid reactions, because no one else will even notice what you are hypercritical of.

Being self-conscious is completely at odds with being a persuasive public speaker. You want to lose your inhibitions and be in the moment, not self-reflective, so that you can connect with your audience and convey your client's story. You don't want to be focused on trying to connect with your reflection. It is so much better to rehearse to an imaginary audience that you can picture in your mind than to be distracted by the reflection in the mirror that is literally mirroring what you are doing.

Video Yourself

One of the best steps you can take to improve your skills is to use your cellphone to video record yourself. I have to admit, I hate doing this. I cringe at the thought of having to critique myself. I have a tendency to focus on all the negatives and not on any of the positives. But there is no better way to see and hear how you are doing. Unlike a mirror, which gives an inaccurate impression of what you are doing, the video recording does not lie. However, your perception—as I just mentioned—can affect how you see your recording. As a result, watch the video and learn what you can, but more important, watch it with someone else. Pause it at certain places and get their specific feedback. Look for the skills that you should be doing. For example, are you pausing enough, gesturing appropriately, and making your voice interesting? But above all, are you speaking from your heart to persuade?

8.3 THE DAY OF YOUR PRESENTATION

Warm-Up Exercises

On the day of your performance, get relaxed and get your voice warmed up. You never want to go into a speech cold. One of the best things you can do is perform your favorite exercise in the morning before your presentation. Go for a jog, walk the dog, work out in the gym, or do some yoga. Expending some physical energy will help get rid of the nerves and get you in a good mood before your presentation. It will also give you some time to review in your head what you are going to say while you are exercising.

Here are some other exercises that should not take more than five minutes to perform. One is to stretch your neck. Move your right hand over the top of your head and place it on the left side of your head, above your left ear. Then, slowly pull your head toward your right shoulder and feel the muscles on the left side of your neck stretch. Repeat this stretch by using the left hand to stretch the right side of your neck.

Second, raise your left arm straight up to the ceiling. Raise your right arm up, bend your right elbow and grab your left arm so that your right forearm is on top of your head. Then, use your right arm to pull your left arm—keeping your left arm straight—to the right so that you are stretching the muscles in your left arm and the left side of your torso. Repeat this exercise by stretching your right side.

Third, roll your shoulders forward five times and then roll them backward five times. You have now gotten your upper torso, neck, and head relaxed.

Fourth, to warm up your voice, begin by humming one verse of your favorite song. If you don't want to try to carry a tune, just hum several different sounds for 30 seconds. Next, wet your lips, take a deep inhale using your diaphragm, and close your lips, but leave a slight opening between them. Exhale and make the sound of a motorboat by touching the inside of your lips with your tongue. This takes a little practice to get the right tension in your lips, but the exercise helps warm up the vocal cords.

Fifth, say any tongue twister a few times. "Peter Piper picked a peck of pickled peppers" will do.

Practice Routine

On the morning of your hearing or trial, relax and focus on the big picture. You have practiced your presentation enough that you should feel very confident. You just need to get rid of the last butterflies (see chapter 1 for more details). First, practice your transitions between topics one last time. That way, you will have the confidence that you can move from one idea to another. Another reason to do this is that if you forget something while you are speaking and don't know how to finish the topic you are on, you will remember how to transition to the next topic because you have practiced it relentlessly beforehand and refreshed your memory on the morning of.

Second, review your beginning and ending. Not only do you want to start and end strong, but you will gain confidence in your public speaking if you have certainty that you know exactly how you will begin and how you will end.

Third, go over your cheat sheet which should contain your goals for your presentation (see chapter 1). Those goals might be to have a conversation with the court, make good eye contact, and emphasize key words in each sentence (see chapter 1).

If you have a PowerPoint presentation, look over the printed sheets that have multiple slides on them to get an overview of the presentation (see fig. 1). If you are not using a PowerPoint, review your outline one last time. Finally, get to the courtroom early so you can get comfortable with the formality of the particular court that you will be in.

Final Thoughts

Always take a quick look (front and back) in the mirror before you enter the courtroom to make sure you look fine. Make sure that you are not thirsty and have water available in the courtroom. Nothing can send you into a panic

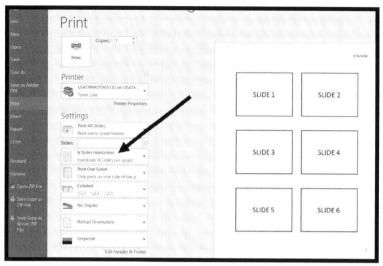

Figure 1. Printout of multiple PowerPoint slides onto one page.

quicker than getting a dry mouth before you speak and not having water nearby. Be positive, remember to breathe slowly and deeply, and focus on your cheat sheet (see chapter 1).

8.4 AFTER YOUR PRESENTATION, GET FEEDBACK

This was mentioned in chapter 2, under the section titled "Always Strive to Get Better," but it bears discussing a little more. You will never reach your fullest potential as a public speaker unless you get feedback. No one likes to be criticized, but you must see feedback not as something to fear, but as an opportunity for learning that you cannot afford to miss out on. After you have a hearing or trial, approach the court personnel at a break and ask them for their opinions. They will be thrilled to give it to you. They obviously see lawyers perform all the time and will be accurate sounding boards for advice and ideas. Moreover, you will make their day. Most lawyers don't even bother to seriously engage with the court reporter, courtroom deputy, or bailiff. Most lawyers just quickly check in for their case, conduct their hearing, and quickly leave. Instead, if you sincerely ask for their help, they will be glad to give you feedback.

CHAPTER CHECKLIST

1. Don't forget what Pete Rose learned, "My father taught me that the only way you can make good at anything is to practice, and then practice some more."

2. Most lawyers simply fail to practice enough to succeed.

3. Develop a process to get your presentation in final form. First, write one draft of your compelling story and then put it aside. Second, speak aloud your story until you get comfortable. Don't memorize it word for word. Lincoln was known to recite passages of his speeches aloud as he walked down the city streets of Springfield. If it worked for Abe, you ought to give it a try.

4. At some point in the process, think of the images you want to use to support your compelling story.

5. Test the persuasiveness of your compelling story with your friends.

6. Brainstorm with your friends about how to attack your case, so that you get the other side's perspective.

7. In addition to getting feedback on your content, get feedback on your gestures and verbal pauses.

8. In an ideal world, rehearse in the courtroom a couple of days before your scheduled appearance. Otherwise, do it in an alternative setting.

9. A great way to get better at public speaking is to practice during your normal, everyday conversations.

10. The conventional wisdom to practice in front of a mirror is wrong because it makes you too self-conscious and is literally not an accurate reflection of your speaking skills.

11. Video record your presentation in order to improve.

12. Have your friends use a clicker when you practice to alert you as to how many times you use words such as *um* or *OK*.

13. On the day of your performance, exercise to expend some physical energy to get rid of the nerves and get you in a good mood before your presentation.

14. Warm up your voice. Stretch your neck, roll your shoulders forward five times and roll them backward five times, hum one verse of your favorite song, and say any tongue twister a few times, such as "Peter Piper picked a peck of pickled peppers."

15. Always take a quick look (front and back) in the mirror before you enter the courtroom to make sure you look fine.

16. Make sure that if you get thirsty, you won't get dry mouth by having water available in the courtroom.

17. After your presentation, get feedback.

PART III

How the Masters Persuade

Now that we have learned the skills of persuasion and public speaking, let's look at how the masters, both old and new, have used these skills to achieve greatness.

CHAPTER NINE

History's Greatest Orators

"Every man I meet is my superior in some way. In that, I learn of him."—*Ralph Waldo Emerson*

This chapter could well be an entire book—which I might write one day—if I tried to do justice to all the great orators in history. Instead, I wanted to keep it short and focus on just a few of the greats. First, Aristotle has influenced in some way every great speaker. Lincoln is discussed because he was not only a great public speaker but also a great lawyer. Churchill not only spoke very well, but also shared his thoughts about what makes a great speaker. Finally, I included Paul McCartney because he knows a thing or two about communicating his feelings.

9.1 ARISTOTLE: THE TRUTHS THAT HAVE STOOD THE TEST OF TIME

Aristotle was not only one of the greatest philosophers of all time, but he also invented formal logic, organized the arts and sciences into a curriculum for learning that became the foundation of the modern university, and formulated the keys to public speaking. For trial and appellate lawyers, Aristotle's importance is that he was fascinated with public speaking and the art of persuasion. As democratic governments were being born in Greece and other places, individuals called *rhetores* sought to persuade the public with their ideas about politics and governance. Much like New England town meetings in the colonial era, people were expected to be conversant about political issues and convey those ideas orally. More than anyone else, Aristotle best understood the importance and the mechanics of this developing art of persuasion. His book *On Rhetoric* is widely regarded as the primary

> **CHAPTER ROAD MAP**
>
> - Learn Aristotle's three principles of persuasion for public speakers.
> - Examine what made Lincoln a great public speaker and lawyer.
> - Incorporate Churchill's teachings to become your best.

source of our modern understanding of effective communication skills. The principles he set forth are as true today as when he first declared them around 350 B.C.

Aristotle declared that *pisteis*, or the means of persuasion, was made up of three elements: ethos, logos, and pathos. Ethos refers to the character of the speaker. There is persuasion "through character whenever the speech is spoken in such a way as to make the speaker worthy of credence; for we believe fair-minded people to a greater extent and more quickly than we do others on all subjects. . . ." In fact, Aristotle remarks that character is "the controlling factor in persuasion."

Let's take a moment and look at ethos, or the moral character of the speaker. You must be a trustworthy person; otherwise, the jury won't believe you. Trust-worthiness can't be developed on the day of trial, but instead it is the result of a lifetime of making the right decisions to be a sincere and honest person. Earlier in this book, you were introduced to Bryan Stevenson. Desmond Tutu proclaimed, "Bryan Stevenson is America's Nelson Mandela, a brilliant lawyer fighting with courage and conviction to guarantee justice for all." Stevenson gave a TED Talk that has been viewed more than 7.5 million times. In that talk, he explained that he created the Equal Justice Initiative to help people who have been wrongly convicted, confront bias and discrimination in the administration of criminal justice, end life without parole sentences for children, and end mass incarceration, among other things. He believes that "Ultimately, you judge the character of a society, not by how they treat their rich and the powerful and the privileged, but by how they treat the poor, the condemned, the incarcerated."

He ended his talk with a story about when he was representing a 14-year-old child who was being tried as an adult (you can watch his TED Talk at www.winningatpersuasion.com. The story begins at 17:05). He admitted that he sometimes gets tired and frustrated from the battles he fights and was up late one night when he was wondering how a judge could certify his client as an adult for trial when he was just a child. Stevenson reasoned:

> If the judge can turn you into something that you're not, the judge must have magic power. Yeah, Bryan, the judge has some magic power. You should ask for some of that. And because I was up too late, wasn't thinking real straight, I started working on a motion. And I had a client who was 14 years old, a young, poor Black kid. And I started working on this motion, and the head of the motion was: "Motion to try my poor, 14-year-old Black male client like a privileged, White 75-year-old corporate executive."
>
> And I put in my motion that there was prosecutorial misconduct and police misconduct and judicial misconduct. There was a crazy line in there about how there's no conduct in this county, it's all misconduct. And the

next morning, I woke up and I thought, now did I dream that crazy motion, or did I actually write it? And to my horror, not only had I written it, but I had sent it to court.

Months later, when he was walking up to the courthouse, Stevenson relates:

And as I was walking up the steps of this courthouse, there was an older Black man who was the janitor in this courthouse. When this man saw me, he came over to me and he said, "Who are you?" I said, "I'm a lawyer." He said, "You're a lawyer?" I said, "Yes, sir." And this man came over to me and he hugged me. And he whispered in my ear. He said, "I'm so proud of you." And I have to tell you, it was energizing. It connected deeply with something in me about identity, about the capacity of every person to contribute to a community, to a perspective that is hopeful.

Well, I went into the courtroom. And as soon as I walked inside, the judge saw me coming in. He said, "Mr. Stevenson, did you write this crazy motion?" I said, "Yes, sir. I did." And we started arguing. And people started coming in because they were just outraged. I had written these crazy things. And police officers were coming in and assistant prosecutors and clerk workers. And before I knew it, the courtroom was filled with people angry that we were talking about race, that we were talking about poverty, that we were talking about inequality.

And out of the corner of my eye, I could see this janitor pacing back and forth. And he kept looking through the window, and he could hear all of this holler. He kept pacing back and forth. And finally, this older Black man with this very worried look on his face came into the courtroom and sat down behind me, almost at counsel table. About 10 minutes later the judge said we would take a break. And during the break there was a deputy sheriff who was offended that the janitor had come into court. And this deputy jumped up and he ran over to this older Black man. He said, "Jimmy, what are you doing in this courtroom?" And this older Black man stood up and he looked at that deputy and he looked at me and he said, "I came into this courtroom to tell this young man, keep your eyes on the prize, hold on."

Both the story and the video of his speech reveal Stevenson's character. Stevenson speaks from his heart, his character shines through, and because of that he is able to persuade.

Logos refers to the logic of the argument. Logos is the persuasive technique in which an audience is persuaded through arguments that "show the truth or the apparent truth from whatever is persuasive in each case." Pathos refers to the emotions of the audience. For example, audiences will arrive at different conclusions depending on what emotions the speaker awakens in them, friendly or hostile. Consequently, from no less an authority than Aristotle, we know that our presentations in court should convey our truthful character, provide a logical argument that is persuasive, and awaken the friendly emotions of the judge or jury.

9.2 ABRAHAM LINCOLN: USE INTEGRITY TO PERSUADE

As mentioned throughout this book, you should find and follow great lawyers to study and learn what made them great, and see what you can take from them and incorporate into your own skill set. One of the greatest lawyers was Abraham Lincoln, and one of the best one-volume biographies, *A. Lincoln*, was written by Ronald C. White, Jr., and it is the source of much of what follows. In this section, we will learn what made Lincoln so great.

Most importantly, Lincoln was a powerful persuader because he had ethos, or integrity, one of the three qualities required by Aristotle. He had the nickname Honest Abe for a reason. Lincoln's integrity was like a tree trunk from which all the branches of his life grew. His integrity had "many roots—in the soil [in the rural area where Lincoln grew up], in Shakespeare, and in the Bible." His speeches are the embodiment of his integrity, and "Even when Lincoln disappears in his speeches—as he does in the Gettysburg Address, never using the word 'I'—[the speeches] reveal the moral center of the man."

One trait that made Lincoln such a great lawyer was that he "delighted in approaching a question or problem from as many sides as possible, helping him appreciate the views of others, even when those opinions opposed his own." This approach would help him later when he would persuade the country about the evils of slavery.

For example, Lincoln, a Republican, needed to decide how to counter the Democrat's argument that the Republicans were a sectional party with anti-slavery beliefs that represented the North and parts of the West and would never be able to govern a nation that included the South and an expanding Western frontier that was divided about slavery. Lincoln realized that the issue of sectionalism, more than any other raised by the Democrats, was causing voters who opposed slavery's extension in the West to hesitate to vote Republican.

Lincoln systematically went through the Democrat's argument and wrote answers in a note to himself regarding every point that was raised. White discerns that this note "demonstrates a major reason Lincoln was becoming such a persuasive public speaker. He was willing to engage in the hard task of examining an opponent's arguments fully and fairly."

It was no less true in the courtroom. Leonard Swett, who had seen Lincoln practice law as they travelled around the Eighth Circuit, observed that Lincoln could "state the case of his adversary better and more forcibly than his opponent could state it himself." Lincoln did this by obviously understanding his opponent's argument, but he would add his own words to them to make them even stronger so that he could respond more forcibly. He was also keenly aware of the local attitudes where he presented his case.

His delivery was as persuasive as his content. Consider how one reporter described one of Lincoln's stump speeches: "Mr. Lincoln has a very tall and thin figure, with an intellectual face, showing a searching mind, and a cool judgment." Lincoln's oration was a "truly masterly and convincing speech." In another speech, a reporter commented, "Argument and anecdote, wit and wisdom, hymns and prophecies, platforms and syllogisms, came flying before the audience like wild game before the fierce hunter of the prairie." Yet another reporter observed, "His language is pure and respectful, he attacks no man's character or motives, but fights with arguments."

While his speeches appeared extemporaneous, the truth was that they were the result of painstaking preparation. This was also true of the metaphors he used. One of his more famous metaphors was used to explain the problem with slavery in the South and its opposition in the North. He borrowed from the Bible and proclaimed, "A house divided against itself cannot stand." It was a metaphor that he had used on different occasions and developed over many years.

You can do the same. If one of your metaphors works well in one case, improve its use in another case. Or, maybe you'll see someone in court or on TV using a captivating metaphor. Make a note of it and see how you can use it.

One might think that such a master orator as Lincoln would be calm and relaxed. But he was always nervous when he gave a speech. Also, his mannerisms are not something to be emulated, but they were genuine, as they should be. A reporter remarked, "He used singularly awkward, almost absurd, up-and-down and sidewise movements of his body to give emphasis to his argument . . . . [But he was] a thoroughly earnest and truthful man, inspired by convictions." Another observation came from the famous Lincoln-Douglas debates: "His voice was not melodious; rather shrill and piercing, especially when it rose to its high treble in moments of great animation. His figure was unhandsome, and action of his unwieldy limbs awkward. He commanded none of the outwardly graces or oratory as they are commonly understood. His charm was of a different kind. It flowed from the rare depth and genuineness of his convictions and his sympathetic feelings." But there is more: He "swung his long arms sometimes in a very ungraceful manner. Now and then, to give particular emphasis to a point, he would bend his knees and body with a sudden downward jerk and then shoot up again with a vehemence that raised him to his tiptoes and made him look taller than he was."

Let's look a little closer at the content of Lincoln's speeches. As his first inauguration grew closer, Lincoln deleted superfluous words from his speech. He tied words together by using alliteration—five times in the last two sentences of the speech—and assonance, which is the device used to associate words together that have the same or related sounds. He used symbolic imagery and opposition, which was one of his favorite rhetorical devices. For example, he once declared, "In your hands, my dissatisfied fellow countrymen, and not in mine, is the momentous issue of civil war. The government will not assail you. You can have no conflict, without being yourselves the aggressor."

Lincoln also knew the power of descriptive language. In September 1863, he wrote a letter to be read by a surrogate (as was often done at the time) at a large meeting in Springfield, Illinois. The main purposes of the letter were to praise Black soldiers, who fought for the Union but had been met with resistance by some White Union soldiers, and to defend his Emancipation Proclamation. Look at the following passage and notice the descriptive words (bolded) Lincoln uses to persuade:

> And then, there will be some black men who can remember that, with **silent tongue**, and **clenched teeth**, and **steady eye**, and **well-poised bayonet**, they have helped mankind on to this great consummation; while, I fear, there will be some white ones, unable to forget that, with **malignant heart**, and **deceitful speech**, they have strove to hinder it.

Through descriptive words, Lincoln heightens the contrast between some Black and some White soldiers.

One interesting trick you might want to try that Lincoln used was that in order to better remember what he was reading, Lincoln would read everything he read aloud, whether it was the newspaper or a book. He did this so that his eyes and ears could catch the ideas.

9.3 WINSTON CHURCHILL: HOW TO PERSUADE

Throughout this book, I have put Churchill's sayings about public speaking in text callout boxes. Now, let's take a moment and look at those quotes and some of his others to make sure we learn from one of the greatest orators of all time.

1. "First he read his speech, second he read it badly, third it wasn't worth reading."

   Churchill made this comment after listening to a speech delivered at Parliament. I felt it was such an important comment that I used it at the beginning of chapter 6, advising not to use notes in your presentations. I think it bears repeating with this additional thought: If you have notes, you are really just on the wrong path. Under Churchill's formula for failure, even if you had a speech worth reading and read it well (his second and third criticisms), you would still fail because you read it (his first criticism) when you should have had a conversation with the audience instead.

2. "Harold, when you rose you didn't know what you were going to say, when you were speaking you didn't know what you were saying, and when you finished, you didn't know what you had said."

Harold Macmillan, a member of Parliament, gave his first speech to the House of Commons in 1925. Although he would later become Britain's prime minister in 1957, the delivery of his speech did not give any indication of his future success. After the speech, he asked Churchill what he thought of it, and Churchill delivered the above quote. Churchill had no patience for speakers who did not make their points clearly.

3. "If you have an important point to make, don't try to be subtle or clever. Use a pile driver. Hit the point once. Then come back and hit it again. Then hit it a third time—a tremendous whack."

This quote goes hand in hand with the previous one. How many times have you listened to a presentation and walked away not really knowing what the main point was. That was not your fault, and Churchill has given every speaker the solution. As an aside, a pile driver is a machine used to drive supports into the ground as a foundation for structures such as buildings.

4. "The report, by its very length, defends itself against being read."

Churchill believed that brevity speaks loudly. Another one of his more famous quotes is actually an entire speech that he gave which was only one sentence long. Upon returning to his secondary school in 1941, he had been given a very long introduction from the school's headmaster. The headmaster droned on and on about Churchill's accomplishments. Sensing the difficulty in keeping the students' attention after such a long introduction, Churchill approached the dais, began in a soft voice, and then pointed at the students and said, as his voice rose in volume and authority, "Never, never, never, never, never give in—except to dictates of honor and good sense." I have never seen a lawyer give a one-sentence presentation at a hearing. But if what you had to say could be summed up in one sentence and you said it with authority and sincerity, it would certainly be worth trying. More realistically, the point is to be brief, because as we have seen earlier in this book, human beings' attention spans are short.

5. "Broadly speaking, the short words are the best, and the old words best of all."

No matter who your audience is, speak to them in a language that they will understand. Don't speak to a jury or a judge and try to impress them with legalese or use legalese because you have not taken the time to find more understandable and persuasive words. Churchill knew that old words—a.k.a. familiar words—are the best. Also, simple words are better than complicated ones. In fact, studies have shown that if you use a word that the listener doesn't know, the average person will miss the next seven words you use. So, if you use that unfamiliar word, you need to pause and also explain it.

6. "Opening amenities are often opening inanities."

We saw earlier how Mark Lanier sincerely thanks the jury before he begins his opening statements. Being sincere is the key to avoiding the failure that Churchill describes. Almost every lawyer or speaker perfunctorily thanks his audience at the start of his presentation. Such a beginning, in contrast to Lanier's, falls flat. Another way to make the "thank you" more sincere is to insert it not at the very beginning but a little later. It may sound less contrived, more sincere, and you will already have captured the audience's attention by starting with your best point. Nonetheless, if you're comfortable connecting with your audience at the very beginning, I would do it then.

Quoting Edward R. Murrow, John F. Kennedy said that "Churchill mobilized the English language and sent it into battle." Notably, Churchill even created an acronym for making a speech memorable and persuasive: C-R-E-A-M. It stands for contrast, rhyme, echo, alliteration, and metaphor. These ideas have been discussed in chapter 3, but Churchill's acronym is easy to remember, and a brief review here of how Churchill used it in some of his famous quotations and speeches will help us to learn it. Keep in mind, it is no coincidence that the reason his speeches are so famous is that he used the techniques from his acronym.

First, a contrast of opposites is a not only a way to highlight a comparison but it frames your argument in a stark way. One tool to help you find contrasts is to use a thesaurus. Once you find a word you want to use in your presentation, look for its antonym in the thesaurus. Churchill used opposites when he spoke the words "There is only one answer to defeat and that is victory." Or, simply just make a contrast between opposing ideas as Lincoln did above when he said, "In your hands, my dissatisfied fellow countrymen, and not in mine, is the momentous issue of civil war," or when he contrasted some Black soldiers with some White soldiers.

The second tool is rhyming. Common sense tells us this is a powerful technique because the use of rhymes is the reason why we remember so many of the stories from our childhood. Moreover, imagine trying to remember a song if it did not rhyme. There is no reason you should not use rhyme in your presentations.

Echo is an underutilized rhetorical tool and is like anaphora, which we discussed in chapter 3. When you are speaking, one way to hammer home your point is to repeat it. It is very helpful for the listener, since unlike a book where there is a table of contents and index to refer to, a listener must rely on the speaker to present ideas more than once so that they are easier to remember. When the Germans overtook France in WWII, Churchill gave his famous Dunkirk address where he said, "We shall fight on the beaches, we shall fight on the landing grounds, we shall fight in the streets, we shall fight in the hills, we shall never surrender."

Alliteration is the fourth technique that makes up the C-R-E-A-M acronym. This technique has been discussed at length, so I won't summarize it again here, but it is interesting that Churchill used alliteration in the advice he gave on how to deliver a speech. He said, "Vary the pose and vary the pitch and don't forget the pause."

Also, don't forget to use metaphors, the last tool represented in the acronym. We have talked about the need to create images for the points you want to make. If the metaphor makes sense and is memorable, it is a wonderful tool to use because it engages listeners' minds and helps you connect with them. Churchill would go on long walks or even to the zoo to jumpstart his imagination before writing a speech. Here is one of his more memorable metaphors, which he used to describe the danger in appeasing the Nazis: "An appeaser is one who feeds the crocodile, hoping it will eat him last."

9.4 PAUL MCCARTNEY: IT TAKES EFFORT TO CREATE SOMETHING MEANINGFUL

I am not going to suggest you wait until you have created a perfect story before you complete it, but let me share with you something that will inspire you to put more time into its creation than you might otherwise do. In February 1965, the Beatles had just completed a whirlwind transformation from being an unknown band to the most famous band in America. They had written huge hits such as "Can't Buy Me Move, "She Loves You," and "A Hard Day's Night."

Around this time, McCartney completed a song that had been two years in the making. In 1963, he woke up in the middle of the night and rushed to the piano to work on a melody that was in his head. Sometime later, he was playing the tune at a friend's house when his friend's mother walked in and asked if they wanted scrambled eggs for breakfast. With that prompt, McCartney put these words to his tune: "Scrambled eggs, oh, my baby, how I love your legs, not as much as I love scrambled eggs."

For over a year, McCartney could not complete his song, despite dedicated effort. During the filming of *Help!*, he worked on it so much during breaks that the film's director and the other Beatles became annoyed with him. George Harrison commented, "He's always talking about that song. You'd think he was Beethoven or something."

His breakthrough came while on vacation with his girlfriend, Jane Asher, in late May 1965 when the word "yesterday" came into his thoughts. With that one word, the song began to write itself. The scrambled eggs lyrics were replaced with "Yesterday, all my troubles seemed so far away, Now it looks as though they're here to stay, Oh I believe in Yesterday." The Beatles' producer, George Martin, saw the song as a turning point for the Beatles as they began to experiment with using more than the four instruments the Beatles played. "Yesterday" became the most covered song ever.

Here is my point: with patience and work, you can turn a forgettable song or story into something that has staying power. Obviously, we don't have two years to work on a presentation for court, but with effort we can make something special that stands out and is persuasive.

McCartney has also spoken about the importance of creating memorable tunes and lyrics. He tells the story of how his band, Wings, was working on the album *Band on the Run*. He and the band were walking down a street late at night when a car stopped and several men got out and stole all their belongings, including their demo tapes for the album *Band on the Run*. So, McCartney had to recreate the whole album. How could he do it? He explained that John Lennon and he had created music for the Beatles when there was not a lot of recording equipment. Their philosophy was, "If we can't remember it, how can we expect the people to remember it." The same is true for your presentations. Speak it, don't memorize it. The more you orally rehearse a conversational presentation, the more creative you will become and the easier it will be to remember it.

SUGGESTED ADDITIONAL READING

1. *Speak Like Churchill, Stand Like Lincoln*, by James C. Humes (Three Rivers Press, 2002).

CHAPTER CHECKLIST

Tips from Aristotle

1. Aristotle declared that the means of persuasion was made up of three elements: ethos, logos, and pathos. Ethos refers to the character of the speaker. Logos refers to the logic of the argument. Pathos refers to the emotions of the audience.

Tips from Lincoln

1. Lincoln's integrity was like a tree trunk that had many roots in the soil (in the rural area where Lincoln grew up), in Shakespeare, and in the Bible.

2. One trait that made Lincoln such a great lawyer was that he "delighted in approaching a question or problem from as many sides as possible, helping him appreciate the views of others, even when those opinions opposed his own."

3. Lincoln felt it was so important to understand his opponent's argument that he would add his own words to them to make them even stronger so that he could respond more forcibly.

4. Lincoln was always aware of the attitudes of the audience he was presenting his speech to.

5. Lincoln's oratory was filled with anecdotes, wit, wisdom, and syllogisms.

6. While Lincoln's speeches appeared extemporaneous, the truth was that they were the result of painstaking preparation.

7. Lincoln was always nervous before a speech.

8. While his gestures could be jarring, he was a thoroughly earnest and truthful man, inspired by his convictions.

9. Lincoln relied heavily on descriptive language to make his points.

10. In order to help him remember what he was reading, Lincoln would read everything aloud.

Tips from Churchill

1. Churchill believed that reading a speech could never make it a good speech.

2. Churchill had no patience for speakers who did not make their points clearly, and he advised using a pile driver to make your point.

3. Churchill remarked that "short words are the best, and the old words best of all."

4. Churchill created an acronym for making a speech memorable and persuasive: C-R-E-A-M. It stands for contrast, rhyme, echo, alliteration, and metaphor.

Tips from McCartney

1. Putting effort into your presentation pays off. It took McCartney two years to write "Yesterday."

2. When creating new songs, McCartney understood the importance of remembering their words and thus did not write them down. He believed in the power of oral repetition. His theory was that if he could not remember the song as he was creating it, how could he expect his fans to?

CHAPTER TEN

The Master Trial Lawyer, Mark Lanier

"I really do believe I represent truth, and I've got this burning belief that truth is important."—*Mark Lanier*

Let's take a deep dive to explore how the principles in the preceding chapters work in a high-stakes case by learning from Mark Lanier.

Although Lanier has been mentioned in various parts of this book, here is some more background information about him. He is one of the best lawyers in the United States. In 2018, the *National Law Journal* recognized Lanier as the "Outstanding Trial Lawyer of the Year." In 2015, *National Trial Lawyers* named him "Trial Lawyer of the Year." In 2010, the *National Law Journal* declared Lanier as "one of the decade's most influential lawyers." After a record-setting verdict against the pharmaceutical giant Merck, *The New York Times* reported that Lanier's victory "cemented his place as one of the top civil trial lawyers in America." In 2017, he was inducted into The National Trial Lawyers' Hall of Fame. He has achieved many record-setting verdicts, including the one we will study below.

> **CHAPTER ROAD MAP**
>
> - Learn candid insights from Mark Lanier on how to reach your full potential to persuade others.
> - Examine the transcript and video of Mark Lanier's opening statement to understand the story structure he used to win a landmark verdict against Johnson & Johnson.
> - Study the one-of-a-kind visual aids Mark Lanier uses to win at trial where others have failed.

10.1 INTERVIEW WITH MARK LANIER

Before we study one of Lanier's opening statements, let's get his take on some of the major topics in this book.

No Fear of Public Speaking

Although many of the greatest actors and professional athletes will tell you that they get nervous before a big performance, Lanier is an outlier. To my surprise, he doesn't get nervous at all. In fact, he never had to overcome the fear of public speaking. I asked if he got nervous before giving an opening statement, he replied, "Heavens no. I get to do what I do well on a major stage in a way that makes differences in this world, not just in the lives of my plaintiffs, but in the corporate culture that produces this problem, and in the lives of other people that will be touched. Why should I be scared? I am so thankful and excited to get to do this. So, it doesn't scare me. It thrills me. It invigorates and energizes me. So, I'm a weird one on that."

This gift of not being nervous was something he had even at a young age. When he started high school, he already loved speaking. He was on the debate team, and even before the first tournament, he was never nervous. He had a lot of success in debate tournaments and the affirmations that he received gave him even more confidence. For Lanier, the chance to speak in public was "an appetite to be sated, not anything to be feared." I pressed him on the idea that he must be afraid of something before trial, and he responded, "The idea of arguing, the idea of cross-examining, the idea of speaking publicly doesn't scare me. The only thing that scares me is do I know the rules well enough."

How to Create an Opening Statement

I asked Lanier how he knew when his opening statement was ready to be delivered, and, as you will see below from the way he explains ideas to a jury, he responded by using an analogy. He said, "I have elements that I have to put together. It's like a recipe. How do you know when the cake is ready to go in the oven? You follow the recipe." His recipe has five ingredients, and he warned that if you don't put all the ingredients in, your cake will flop.

> *I don't ever want to say something in opening statement that I can't prove.*
> —Mark Lanier

The first ingredient is a *three-columned* list that he writes, in which he lists all the good facts, the neutral facts, and the bad facts. He then tries to see if there are any arguments that can be made that will move as many bad facts as possible into the neutral column or the good column (see discussion in chapter 3).

The second ingredient is *the story* that he will use to tell the facts. As we saw in chapter 3, Lanier summarized one trial this way: "The plaintiffs trusted their doctors, trusted a product, and got terrible results."

The third ingredient is *the themes* that he will use. "I've got to have my themes, I've got to have the defense themes, and I've got to have my counterthemes to those themes figured out to integrate them into the opening as time allows also." Lanier knows the importance of being trustworthy with the jury. His opening statement is going to include the good, the bad, and the ugly, but he is going to develop counterthemes to the opposing lawyer's best arguments so he can attack their credibility if the opportunity arises.

The fourth ingredient is *structure*. "Element number four, I need to structure the opening in a way that makes sense, but also features three basic points because I believe in the rule and the power of three. So, I've got to put a structure together that incorporates all of the facts, all of the themes, and does it in a way that allows you to tell a compelling story." In the trials that I have studied or seen, Lanier has structured his story around asking jurors to be detectives in a show like *CSI*, where they need to find the motive, means, injury, and alibi of the defendant corporation; asking jurors to join him on a journey on a road with four stops; asking them to put together a jigsaw puzzle and looking for the misfit pieces; pretending to be home inspectors who must fill out a report about the shoddy "house" that the defendant corporation built; and comparing the trial to a book that will have three chapters.

The fifth ingredient is *the opening presentation*. To create it, Lanier changes the "opening from an opening statement into an opening presentation. That's my mentality of how I put together the slides that will accompany the voice over to make it a presentation, visually appealing, as well as linguistically appealing. So, hitting both hemispheres of the brain. That fifth step is an important step because it's also a step of creativity that forces you to think through how to say something in the right way. So, I do those, boom, boom, boom, boom, boom. The cake is ready to go in the oven."

Handling Pressure

I asked Lanier how he handled the pressure of conveying his clients' claims in the case discussed below, one that had very high stakes. He responded that he doesn't feel pressure from outside circumstances. "I perceive pressure because there's this internal drive to win. That pressure is there whether I represent 22 women or one woman, whether they're dying of cancer or whether they had a fender bender, whether it's property damage or personal injury damage. That's just this drive that's in me."

Finding Your Voice

As discussed in chapter 2, two of the principles of public speaking are to be yourself and to speak from the heart to persuade. As Lanier continued his answer from above, he revealed how he stays true to himself and speaks from his heart. Lanier explained that the pressure from his internal drive to win is "tightly interwoven with the drive for truth. I really do believe I represent truth, and I've got this burning belief that truth is important. So, if there's pressure, that's the pressure. Now, does that mean that when I've got 22 women with terminal conditions, many of them, that it doesn't affect me? Oh, it does, but I wouldn't say it affects me by putting more pressure on."

What he said next reveals where he finds his tone of voice. He said that his search for truth "affects me by recognizing the serious nature of what we're about. It sets the serious tone that will drive my presentations and what I do. I'm not talking about what did we have for breakfast, whether Chick-fil-A has a better chicken biscuit than Whataburger. I'm not talking about something that's an incidental in life. I'm talking about something that merits that greatest serious concerns and attention, but it doesn't drive pressure for me because that pressure is already there at 100 percent. It drives tone that we're in the middle of a very serious case. The gravity of what we're about is palpable. So, it will drive tone, not pressure."

> *If someone tries to be Mark Lanier, they will seem disingenuous, and that violates rule one of being authentic. My goal is to share with lawyers so that they can do a better job at what they do. I've been told, "Don't share your secrets." There's plenty of food to go around. I'm not starving.*
> —Mark Lanier

Winning Is Everything?

If you remember from chapter 1, we compared the Lombardi Rule and its sole focus on the result (winning) with the Rice Rule and its focus on the process of winning. Although Lanier talks about how the result of winning drives him, I believe that it is really his focus on the *process* of winning that is the key to his success. As you read his comments below, a good exercise would be to decide for yourself whether Lanier follows the Lombardi Rule or the Rice Rule, and in this process, you can revisit chapter 1 and determine which approach works best for you.

As I explored the idea of winning with Lanier, he shared that his father, who was a very successful athlete, instilled in him the importance of winning but also being a good loser. His father believed it was important to keep score but also be gracious in defeat. The lesson his father instilled in him about being a good loser is evident when I have seen Lanier in court. No matter how heated the battle, whether it is with opposing counsel or a witness on the stand, Lanier is always gracious. There is a kindness that envelopes everything he does. For example, when Lanier heard the verdict in the first DePuy hip implant trial, he immediately went over to defense counsel and said, "You all tried a tremendous case. Congratulations. Well done for you."

> *I have in my psyche not just the desire to win, but a desire not to lose. But I also have within me a recognition that you need to be a good loser.*
> —Mark Lanier

If an athlete or lawyer believes winning is everything, by definition there is no room for graciousness when one loses. The score or verdict is all that matters. There are three things that help Lanier deal with a loss. First, he learned from his father that it was important to be a good sport. Second, Lanier "believes in the jury system." Third, Lanier is determined to learn from a loss so that it won't happen again.

I wanted to probe this idea of winning one last time before moving on to another topic. I asked him if his faith in God influences how he views winning and losing (Lanier teaches a Bible class every Sunday that has more than 700 students). He responded:

> I do believe I'm responsible for doing the very best that I can. God has given me talents and opportunities, and I'm to use my gifts and talents and opportunities for justice, for truth, for things that count to do the tasks before me as if I were doing them for God himself.
>
> So, I believe all of that, but the nice part about all of that is it's the lesson of Noah and the ark. God told Noah, "Build an ark. Here's how I want you to build it. Get all these animals. Get them in the ark. Shut the door, and I got it from there." Noah was not responsible for bringing the rain or the weather.
>
> I do my stuff. I get in the ark. I shut the door, and God decides how much it's going to rain, when, where, and when that ark is going to be done because I can only do what he's charged me to do and I try to do it to the best of my abilities, but the results, they're in his hands. When I win, praise the Lord. When I lose, praise the Lord. So, that's how I live with it. I know that there's some divine machinations and plans of which I am only a little bitty cog. So, my part is to be the best cog I can be, but not to devise the whole machine of how it all works.

> *We do the best we can do, but God's the weatherman. We just build the ark.*
>
> —Mark Lanier

Could Lanier Have Won the Trial for Johnson & Johnson?

In an interview with Lanier for my book *Turning Points at Trial*, he told me that while a lawyer's persuasion skills are important, you cannot give them too much importance, because the facts matter. Consequently, I asked him if he could have won the case if he had been hired by Johnson & Johnson. He told me, "I hope not because I think we were right. I think justice prevailed. I don't think I would have agreed to try it for the others."

I then asked him what if Johnson & Johnson's trial team—instead of getting lost in the details or being in denial about the bad facts in his case—had simply highlighted the two facts that (1) none of the treating doctors who diagnosed the plaintiffs with ovarian cancer suggested that their use of Baby Powder was a cause, and that (2) after over a hundred years of using Baby Powder, very few women have ever even claimed that Baby Powder caused their cancer.

Lanier said he was ready for such a defense, even though it was never made (being prepared for anything is the key to success). He said that he prepared two charts. One showed the countries that used baby powder, indicating where the usage was high and where the usage was low. A second chart would have then been overlaid on the first chart to show the number or percentage of women who got ovarian cancer in each country. Those maps overlaid each other perfectly. He explained:

> The countries that have the most intense use of baby powder are the countries that have the most intense number of ovarian cancer cases. There are some countries where baby powder has never been sold. In those countries, there's almost no incidence of ovarian cancer among women. The reason there aren't a lot of women or doctors marrying that up to the baby powder is because J&J has kept it silent for so long. They've lied for decades about the presence of asbestos in the baby powder. If the doctors even remotely had a clue there's asbestos in the baby powder, they'd have no trouble saying, "All asbestos causes cancer."
>
> The whole reason they don't, to me, is a good fact, not a bad fact. I'm moving it over to the good column. It shows they've been secreting this information and they'll continue to secret it to the jury and hope the jury issues an opinion that secrets it even more because they don't want the word out. I think it would have fed right back into what I was arguing.

Rules for PowerPoint Slides

We will study Lanier's PowerPoint slides below, but we will get a great head start by learning his three rules for slides. Rule number one is to educate. "Think presentation. Don't think speech. Don't think statement. Don't think argument. Think presentation. So, your slide is presenting something. One point per picture, no more. Avoid distractions." Rule number two is to persuade. Your slide needs to be crisp and emotive. Rule three, the slide needs to be memorable.

Don't Overpromise in Opening Statement

Lanier believes the worst mistake you can make in opening statement is to overpromise what you will be able to prove at trial. He recalled a trial where the defense lawyer in their opening just said a bunch of things that were wrong. As a result, Lanier changed who he was going to call as his first witness and called the defendant's corporate representative as an adverse witness, which allowed Lanier to cross-examine him. The following exchange took place.

Q. You're the corporate representative?
A. Yes.

Q. You were sitting next to the company's lawyer during his opening statement?
A. Yes.

Q. *You are the company.*
A. Yes.

Q. *You're the person who stands for who I'm suing.*
A. Yes.

Q. *So, he's your lawyer?*
A. Yes.

Q. *You listened to his opening like the rest of us?*
A. Yes.

Q. *Then here's the question. I counted 17 times he misrepresented stuff to the jury in his opening. How many did you count?*
A. What?

Q. *I counted 17 times. I don't want to use the word lie because that seems unfriendly. So, I'll just say 17 times he misrepresented stuff to the jury in his opening. How many did you count?*
A. I didn't count any.

Q. *Well, let's write them down on the flip chart and see if you caught these. Number one.*
. . .

Lanier then made a list of the 17 misrepresentations and asked the witness if he heard his lawyer say them. Lanier then showed the witness a document to prove each statement was not true.

Prior to trial, Lanier had offered to settle it for $10,000. The jury returned a verdict for $118 million.

Unlike most lawyers, Lanier is very careful about the words he uses in his opening statement. "I don't want the defendant to ever be able to get up in their opening and say, 'Lanier said this. Let me show you why he's lying.'"

> *If there are iffy things where I take it one way but you could take it another way, I'm very careful on how I say those things because I want to acknowledge the truth.*
> —Mark Lanier

10.2 CASE STUDY: LANIER'S OPENING STATEMENT IN TALC POWDER TRIAL

Twenty-two women sued Johnson & Johnson (*Ingham v. Johnson & Johnson*) claiming that talc powder in the Baby Powder and Shower to Shower products they used contained asbestos, which caused their ovarian cancer after extended use. After a six-week trial in 2018, the jury returned a verdict of $4.69 billion, including more than $4.1 billion in punitive damages. The verdict is by far the largest jury verdict of the many that have gone to trial against Johnson & Johnson on these claims. The jury deliberated eight hours before returning their verdict on compensatory damages and then 30 minutes after punitive damages arguments were made before returning with their $4.14 billion punitive damages award. In June 2020, an appellate court found that plaintiffs had proven that Johnson & Johnson had acted with "reckless disregard of the health and safety of others." For jurisdictional reasons, some of the plaintiffs' claims were dismissed, which resulted in the compensatory and punitive damages being reduced to a total of $2.12 billion. The judgment is now final.

There are several complicated ways to analyze Lanier's opening, but I want to show you how we can use the Rule of Three and alliteration to not only make presentations as discussed in previous chapters, but also to provide a simple framework for an analysis. Consequently, I will structure the discussion around the story Lanier told, the slides he used, and his style.

A couple of technical comments before we begin. Each side was allowed one hour and fifteen minutes for opening statements. You can view Lanier's entire opening statement and a lengthy excerpt of the defendant's opening statement at this book's website (www.winningatpersuasion.com). The transcript below has been minimally edited for length and readability. The time-stamps for the video refer to YouTube's counter found at the bottom of the video, not the very small grey one imbedded in the video from Courtroom View Network. I have bolded important parts of the transcript that will be discussed at a later point, and I have put in brackets my analysis of a particular statement.

Thanks the Jury

[0:17] MR. LANIER: *May it please the Court.*
THE COURT: *Yes, sir.*

MR. LANIER: *Counsel. Good morning, y'all. Thank you for being here. Thank you for being willing to serve on a jury. Thank you for making a difference. And you do make a big difference. It's my honor to get to try this case, and I am delighted to do so. . . .*

Story: Most lawyers begin their opening statement with a perfunctory thanking of the jury. For that reason, I have instructed attorneys to skip it and get right to the point. But Lanier does it sincerely, and he has convinced me that if you give thanks from your heart, it is well worth doing. In addition to common sense, there is research that supports its effectiveness.

Lanier referred me to a study that was done using waiters at restaurants to determine if the manner in which they presented the bill would affect the amount of their tip. It revealed that the waiter's interaction could raise the tip by 23 percent. When each waiter brought the bill to a table (and did nothing else), the tip received—whatever it was—became the study's baseline tip. Then the study's same waiters, when bringing the bill, included a mint for each of the table's patrons, so, for a four-top table, one mint per patron was provided with the bill. The tips went up 4 percent. (That is, if a waiter had earned $100 that night without delivering mints, he now earned a 4 percent increase that totaled $104.)

Then, the same wait staff provided two mints per patron when they dropped off the bill. The tips rose 13 percent. Then they took the same wait staff, had them give the mints, two per patron, but in the following manner: Lay down the bill with one mint per patron, turn and take one or two steps away, turn back and say, "You guys have been such a great table. I am going to give you all some extra mints," and then leave the second mint per patron.

The tips increased 24 percent from the baseline. You've almost doubled the tip given for the same two mints simply because it became unexpected and the customers were shown true appreciation by the waiter.

The key is to be sincere and not just say things perfunctorily.

Bottom-Line Message and Countertheme

*The case is very different than what Mr. Bicks tried to indicate yesterday. In Mr. Bicks' voir dire, he told you some things that **I hope you remember** [Lanier says with emphasis], because I think the facts of this case are going to wind up being very different than some of the things he said, and I've got typed out what he said from the court reporter, and during the trial I'll be able to show it to you.*

*[1:20] This case boils down to something as simple as A, B, C. [**Lanier displays slide (see fig. 1)**] This case is as simple as asbestos, when you breathe it, or you put it inside of yourself in another way or around yourself where it will be taken up in body parts and cavities. Asbestos breathed or internalized becomes cancer. And it's no more apparent than in this case.*

That's the entire case. If I prove that asbestos is in that Baby Powder, you're going to know why these women had ovarian cancer, at least what a cause of the cancer was.

*[1:56] The big fight really [**Lanier pauses to emphasize "really"**] is whether or not asbestos is in the powder. And I think you're going to see quite readily that it's in the Baby Powder, the Shower to Shower powder, and the other things as well.*

I've got out here my plaintiffs, and I want to tell you about them. They come from all over the United States.

Story: Lanier uses the Rule of Three for his bottom-line message. He has boiled down a six-week trial with 22 plaintiffs and very complicated scientific issues to just three words and a simple mathematical equation.

Remember how in chapter 4 we discussed that in many ways, a countertheme is more powerful than a theme? We learned that your bottom-line message

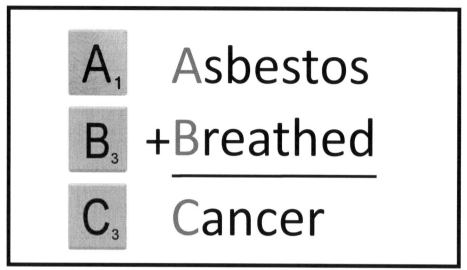

Figure 1. PowerPoint slide with Lanier's simple but persuasive bottom-line message.

should not only incorporate the theme of your case but also act as a counter-theme to your opponent's theme. As Cialdini advises in his book *Pre-Suasion*:

> "[I]n contests of persuasion, counterarguments are typically more powerful than arguments. This superiority emerges especially when a counterclaim does more than refute a rival's claim by showing it to be mistaken or misdirected in the particular instance, but does so instead by showing the rival communicator to be an untrustworthy source of information."

By citing Bicks's statements in jury selection, Lanier directly counters Bicks's theme. Lanier's simple ABC theme strikes at the heart of Bicks's complicated defense. But using a countertheme does much more, as Lanier related to me. "Any lawyer that overreaches in voir dire or overreaches in opening, I'll go after it immediately. If they overreach in voir dire, it's easy because I've got opening statement. Once I start hurting their credibility in opening statement, then when they get up and get their defense opening, their credibility has already been dinged, and so people will listen with their arms crossed because they're not quite so convinced that that person is telling the truth."

Slide: What separates Lanier from the pack is that not only is his bottom-line message clear and memorable, but his visual aids—as you will see throughout his opening—are always inspired and enhance what he is saying. Instead of just using the letters A, B, C on a PowerPoint slide, he uses Scrabble tiles to make his theme more interesting and easier to remember (fig. 3). I asked Lanier how he came up with Scrabble tiles. He said he wanted a picture of something familiar.

He associated A, B, C with the alphabet and then thought he could find some Scrabble tiles in a good clean picture.

Style: Lanier begins by gesturing with both palms up, or, as we learned in chapter 7, the give gesture. He is literally opening himself up through the gesture of his hands. Also, you can see by the way he turns his head from side to side that he is making eye contact with all the jurors.

Lanier's words are not rushed. He has well-timed pauses. For example, when he talks about what Bicks said in voir dire, Lanier pauses before each word when he says, "I hope you remember," because he wants the jury to clearly understand that he will prove that what Bicks said is wrong and therefore Bicks is untrustworthy. He also pauses before he shows the slide with the Scrabble tiles so that the jury will pay attention to his bottom-line message, which is displayed on that slide.

WIN (What Is the Need of the Audience?)

[2:16] *I'm going to take this out if it [the hands-free microphone] continues to be intermittent. Because that's just driving me crazy. Y'all can hear me without it? Thank you. Excuse me, your Honor. I don't mean to disrobe in Court. I promise it stops there. Thank you, Judge. Ladies and gentlemen, I hope you all can hear me out there as well. I'll speak up, I'm not trying to shout at you. I'm just trying to make sure my clients can hear what I've got to say to you this morning.*

Style: Remember that it is important to know WIN, What Is the Need of your audience (see chapter 2). Here, Lanier listens to his speech through the jurors' ears and notices that his headset microphone is breaking in and out so he takes it off.

Lanier Creates an Emotional Connection Between His Clients and the Jury

As each plaintiff below is introduced, their picture appears on a map of the United States with a line connecting the picture to the state that they are from (see fig. 2). After all the plaintiffs are introduced, the montage conveys that the ovarian cancer has struck a wide-ranging demographic of women from all over the country (see fig. 3).

[2:55] *I'm here on behalf of my team, but before I introduce my team, I want to introduce the plaintiffs. So, Andrea Schwartz-Thomas is not here anymore. She was diagnosed in 2014 with stage IV ovarian cancer. She's currently on very intense chemotherapy and has travel restrictions. She's from Virginia. Her son Izzy is here.* **Izzy is a pizza guru in Nashville, Tennessee.** *If you ever get there, go check out his pizza.*

Figure 2. PowerPoint slide with Plaintiffs' photos appearing on U.S. map.

Figure 3. Slide that links plaintiffs to the J&J product and the specific cancer.

> She's been on chemo for the past five years, which is really kind of nice and a blessing. She had been told she had two months to live, so her being on that is a good thing....
>
> Annette Koman is the next one. Annette, can you stand up? And your daughter Kimmy's here too. Kimmy, would you stand up next to Annette? Thank you. Annette was diagnosed in 2009 with stage III cancer. She had a recurrence in 2016 of that ovarian cancer. Interestingly enough, **she was diagnosed the day her son graduated out of boot camp**. And thank you for being here. So, Annette is here from Pennsylvania. We're delighted to have her and her daughter Kimmy here....

I next want to introduce to you Donna Packard, through her husband, Commander Robert Packard. **Commander Packard, 40 years in the Navy,** *and he is here on behalf of his wife, Donna. Donna passed away last November. She didn't get to live to see the court date, but we're glad that Robert is here. They were married for 37 years, and have been around for a long time. You'll get to hear from Donna, his wife, the deceased plaintiff, because she* **gave a deposition four days before she passed away.** *And the deposition gets played on the video screen. And you'll get to hear it, and you'll get to hear her testimony. She did that in this case, and so we've got that as well.*

Here, Lanier connects his client with the jury by mentioning not only that her husband was in the Navy, but also that she gave a deposition four days before she died. Imagine the strength it took for her to do that. Such courage would not be lost on the jury.

Next I want to introduce to you Eleita Walker. . . . Eleita passed away in December of last year, and she was diagnosed in 2012. Was in remission for 18 months, but then she had a recurrence that happened in July of 2017, and it took her life in December.

Marvin [**her husband**] *is an administrator in the correction office* [**of a prison**]*, but I've got him herding all the plaintiffs together because he's got that training. He's doing a good job. They don't get out of line, Judge.*

Slide: As he does with each plaintiff that he introduces, Lanier shows a Power-Point slide like the one in figure 2.

. . . . Next I want to introduce Laine Goldman. Laine, you're here on behalf of your now deceased wife, Johanna. Johanna passed away 11 months ago, and she had ovarian cancer. They've got an eight-year-old son named Lex, who is at art camp. **Johanna was an artist, and she's passed that on to her son.** *And she was diagnosed in 2014. Thank you for being here, Laine.*

Next I want to introduce to you Krystal Kim. Krystal? There you are there in the back. Thank you, Krystal, for being here today. You've got Bryce with you; is that right? Hello, Bryce. Glad that you are here. That's her son Bryce, and we're thankful that y'all are here. Krystal was diagnosed in 2014. She went into remission, and then had a recurrence in 2016. And gratefully she's in remission right now as well, but **she's a favorite of many because she has a Boxer, that is an adorable dog.** *So if you're a dog person, that's serious stuff. Thank you very much, Krystal, and thank you for being here.*

I also want to introduce to you Tracey Baxter and Chelsea Hillman. Would y'all stand up? These are the two daughters of Marcia Hillman. Marcia passed away in December of 2016. And so these are her daughters. They're here on her behalf. Chelsea, by the way — **Chelsea, wave. Chelsea actually did a promotional photo shoot for Johnson & Johnson as a baby for their Baby Powder. And we've got her here.**

Story: Lanier not only starts strong with a bottom-line message, but he continues to build momentum with a lightning bolt (as mentioned in chapter

3). One of the most powerful ways to structure the first part of your opening statement is to introduce your clients to the jury so that the jurors can relate to your clients and their experiences. Lanier is also meeting the sixth element of a compelling story discussed in chapter 3 by connecting his clients to the emotions of the jury.

Marcia Hillman's connection with Johnson & Johnson makes her a particularly sympathetic plaintiff. Her daughter Chelsea unknowingly helped promote the very product that killed her mother.

> *Next I want to introduce to you Karen Hawk. Karen is here with her husband Mark. She's diagnosed in 2003. She is still in remission. **They are having their 48th anniversary this month**. Five kids as well, 16 grandkids.*
>
> *And when the trial is over, she'll tell us how she has managed to stay married to—him for 48 years. Gail Ingham. Gail Ingham is—where are you, Gail? I can't see. There you are. I'm sorry. Gail is not the tallest one of our plaintiffs. So you might have to look, but she's right over there. Gail was diagnosed in 1985. She's been in remission for 33 years. So we've got a good span here for you to get a good feel for this. Married also 48 years, if I'm correct. And Gail is going to be especially important for you to hear. **She wrote a book on how to survive ovarian cancer.** And so that will be something that I think you'll find interesting.*
>
> *In addition to her, we've got Stephanie Martin from South Carolina. Stephanie, is Ken with you? And Ken is her husband. She was diagnosed in 2014 with stage 1 cancer. They met, by the way, in sixth grade. They've been married for 24 years. They've got two kids. **They've got a three-legged cat that was brought in by their daughter. Their daughter only has four fingers, and so she felt an affinity for the cat**.*
>
> *We've got to get 22 plaintiffs on and off the stand in a period of just a few days to make this trial fit inside our schedule, **but I'll make it a point with each of the plaintiffs to give you something special that you can remember them by** so that each one will stand out in your mind because each one is, very special, you'll really enjoy that.*

Story: Notice that Lanier links a memorable trait to each plaintiff that helps create a connection between the jurors and the plaintiffs. It is the essence of storytelling that the narrator gets his audience to care about the characters. Lanier wants each of his 22 plaintiffs to stand out. For example, the first plaintiff has a son who is a pizza guru in Nashville. As the other plaintiffs are introduced, their key description is in bold in the transcript above.

For brevity, the transcript has been edited so that it does not include Lanier's introductions of all 22 plaintiffs. But in the text box on page 189, you will see the attribute he told the jury about each plaintiff in order to distinguish them.

Style: This is the only time in the opening statement that Lanier looks at notes. He has notecards with the names of the plaintiffs and pertinent information about them and their battle with cancer. The notecards help him keep the

Plaintiffs and Their Unique Attributes

1. Andrea Schwartz-Thomas: her son is a pizza guru.
2. Annette Koman: she was diagnosed the day her son graduated from boot camp.
3. Cecelia Martinez: her son, interestingly enough, is taking the law school admissions test this Friday.
4. Donna Packard: Husband is a Commander in the Navy, and she gave deposition four days before she died.
5. Elaita Walker: husband is administrator in a correction office and is in charge of herding plaintiffs.
6. Janice Oxford: has two sets of twins.
7. Johanna Goldman: is an artist and passed on her passion to her son.
8. Krystal Kim: she's a favorite of many because of her adorable Boxer.
9. Marcia Hillman: daughter did a promotional photo shoot for Johnson & Johnson.
10. Marcia Owens: has had 18 rounds of chemo and still works at Coca-Cola.
11. Olga Salazar: like one of jurors, she has five children.
12. Sheila Brooks: Also five kids, 10 grandkids. Works with special needs.
13. Annie Groover: passed away in 2016. [no additional details]
14. Karen Hawk: is having their 48th anniversary this month.
15. Gail Ingham: wrote a book on how to survive ovarian cancer.
16. Stephanie Martin: has a three-legged cat that was brought in by their daughter. Their daughter only has four fingers, and so she felt an affinity for the cat.
17. Toni Roberts: her son Zach is a professional hockey referee.
18. Pam Scarpino: has two daughters. [no additional info given]
19. Sherise Sweet: has adopted five-year-old twin girls and has five dogs.
20. Clora Webb: Clora passed away in 2014. Her son-in-law is the representative of her estate.
21. Mitzi Zschiesche: Her daughter did a photo shoot for Johnson & Johnson's Baby Powder.
22. Carole Williams: husband is in the Army.

information about the 22 plaintiffs straight, but he rarely looks at the cards. It is obvious as he introduces the plaintiffs to the jury that he knows about their struggles and their interests. He really is having a conversation with the jury and you can almost imagine that you were at a small gathering at Lanier's house as he introduces the plaintiffs to make sure they feel comfortable, and that everyone knows them.

> [16:33] [**Lanier's tone changes from conversational to serious. As he speaks, the montage seen in figure 3 (shown earlier in this chapter) is displayed for the jury: it shows all the plaintiffs and a map of the USA.**] *All of these women, they have **different** names. They come from **different** parts of the country. They come from **different** educational backgrounds. They have got **different** social lives. **Different** skin colors. **Different** ethnic heritage.*
>
> *But all of these women have **something in common**. All of them **used regularly and extensively Johnson & Johnson Baby Powder and had to listen when a doctor said to them: You've got cancer.***
>
> *And not just any cancer. You've got ovarian cancer.* [17:19] [**A picture of Baby Powder and a diagram of ovarian cancer is inserted into the middle of the map**] *A cancer that has a mortality rate of almost 50 percent. And even if you go into remission, you always have an increased risk of a reoccurrence.*

Story: Lanier uses, anaphora, the technique of using the same word—here the word was "different"—in successive phrases in order to emphasize how diverse the women are and to highlight what they all have in common and how they got it.

Slide: The map of the United States that Lanier showed the jury earlier is now dominated by the photos of the plaintiffs. He then adds two pictures, one of Johnson & Johnson Baby Powder and one of ovarian cancer. Visually, the plaintiffs are linked to the product, the product is associated with the cancer, and the entire PowerPoint slide is the perfect complement to what Lanier has been talking about to the jury.

Style: Lanier varies his pace, pauses for emphasis, gestures with both hands, and changes the volume of his voice to emphasize the climax that he has been building to as the 22 plaintiffs have been introduced.

CSI St. Louis

> [17:31] *Now, all of these women have had that, it's what has taken the lives of a number of them, and what you've got to do in your position in this case is figure out why. You're the detectives in this trial.* [**Lanier displays slide (see fig. 4)**] *You've got to do some detective work.*

Figure 4. Slide that describes the jurors' role as detectives in the trial.

I thought it was interesting when Mr. Bicks asked one of the potential jurors, Ms. Smith, about science interests, she said I watch those shows, CSI, and a number of you all murmured yeah, yeah, yeah.

[18:03] This is like CSI St. Louis. This is your chance to do the show. And I think while this isn't a criminal case itself and we don't have a criminal burden of proof and we're not alleging criminal wrongdoing, I still think you can use this and understand, and the evidence will show that Johnson & Johnson is responsible for this. And the responsible party needs to be brought to justice.

[18:28] And the way you do it as jurors is the same way you do it if you were on the TV show. You're just going to follow the evidence, and I think the evidence I'm going to show you will fall into a couple of categories. We're going to have evidence of what the **motive** *was. We're going to have evidence of what the* **means** *was, we'll have evidence about* **the injury** *itself that we'll examine, and then we'll have evidence about the defenses, or the* **alibis** *that Johnson & Johnson's going to give you. [18:57]* **[Lanier displays fig. 5.]**

Story: Lanier uses the mystery structure for his story (see chapter 3). He not only tells a mystery, but he further connects with the jurors by asking them to take on the roles of detectives. The structure of the mystery story is one that Lanier has used before. In July 2005, Lanier tried a case against Merck alleging that the drug Vioxx killed Bob Ernst. The trial took place in Angleton, Texas. He told the jurors that they were detectives in CSI: Angleton. Lanier won a record-setting verdict at the time of $253 million for one plaintiff.

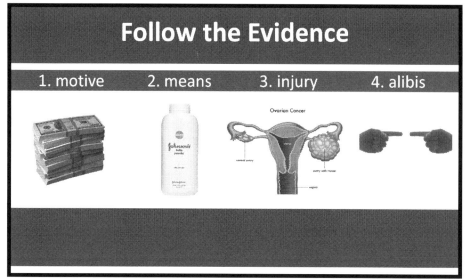

Figure 5. Slide illustrating the four categories that the evidence will fall into.

Slide: For each of the four points that the detective jurors will need to examine (motive, means, injury, and alibis), Lanier has a simple picture that enhances what he is saying. For example, he shows a picture of a stack of money with the title "motive," a picture of Baby Powder with the title "means." But what picture would you use to convey the meaning of alibi? You would have to get creative. Lanier succeeds by using two fingers pointing at each other to show the inconsistency of the alibi.

For the remainder of his opening, as Lanier goes through the four points, he uses slides that are remarkable for their clarity and simplicity. On the left of each slide is the number of the point and a description of the point. On the right side is a picture of the point (see fig. 6). These slides provide the perfect transition as Lanier moves through the four points during his opening statement. With the large number on the left and the simple picture on the right, there is no mistaking what point Lanier is talking about.

Motive

And that's where we are, and that's what the trial will be about, and that's the case that I plan on putting in front of you. So I want to start with the motive. Johnson & Johnson had the motive. The motive was clear. The motive was money. [**Lanier displays figure 6.**]

*[19:13] Now, money itself is not a bad motive. We work for money, we do things for money, but you've got to be careful because the **love of it can be the root of all evil. It can be something that causes you to do things you wouldn't do otherwise**.*

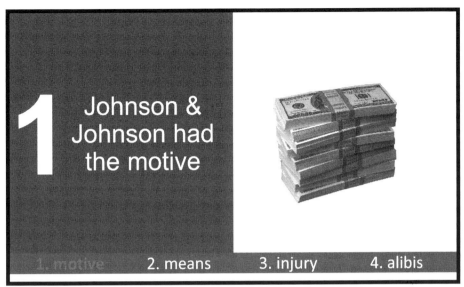

Figure 6. Slide with text and an associated image to illustrate Lanier's first point.

Discusses Weakness

Story: Perhaps the biggest weakness in Lanier's case is that everyone trusts Johnson & Johnson. The company has produced a lot of good products, and its Baby Powder is one of the first purchases anyone makes after having a child. Is Lanier going to make the mistake of being in denial about this? Notice how he tackles the problem head on and changes a bad fact for him into a good fact.

> [19:31] *And this is not—the Johnson & Johnson I'm talking about in this trial is not the Johnson & Johnson of yesteryear. It's not the Johnson & Johnson that started in the 1800s with two fellows named Johnson & Johnson, who figured out how to do civil war casts.*
>
> *No. Johnson & Johnson's a multibillion dollar, multinational corporation, that's got pharmaceuticals under Janssen's name. They've got transvaginal mesh and other things under Ethicon's name. . . . They do hip replacements and other orthopedic things through DePuy. They've got Animas Corporation. They've got LifeScan. They've got McNeil. They've got **57 different countries** where they have headquarters of over **250 different subsidiary companies.*** [Lanier increases his volume to emphasize the bolded words to contrast the current company with the two founders of Johnson & Johnson in the 1800s.]

Baby Powder Is the Sacred Cow

Story: Lanier also discusses a second weakness. After pointing out that Johnson & Johnson is not a small family business anymore, he needs to explain why it would care so much about its Baby Powder when it is making billions of dollars from other products. Watch what he does.

[20:31] *Now, one thing that these companies all have in common, Johnson & Johnson understands from them that the **sacred cow was their Baby Powder**. Because this is what people know them for. People know them for the Baby Powder. I've got a large one here.*

And it's [Baby Powder] one that engenders an emotional connection is what the company says because people think of it and the smell alone makes you think when you were with your mom or when you were a baby, or when you were taking care of your baby.

And so the smell they recognize is a powerful emotional connection. And when people think of Johnson & Johnson, they want you thinking of the products Mr. Bicks talked about in his voir dire where he talked about baby shampoo and Band-Aids and things like that. And they do those things.

*But that's not the big—that's the sacred cow. That makes everything else seem good. You see that Johnson & Johnson on the label and you feel good about it. You feel like this is a good thing, and the company plays on that. What I'm telling you, by the way, is not lawyer conjecture. **I've got documents that back this stuff up**. I've got documents where the company calls it their sacred cow. Where they talk about the trust relationship and how important it is because it runs over to the rest of their products.*

Story: It is one thing to tell a good story, but to be persuasive as a lawyer, you have to back it up. Lanier uses foreshadowing, a powerful storytelling device, to indicate that he will prove it through documents.

Johnson & Johnson Had the Means

[22:45] *They not only had the motive to cause the problems that these ladies and their families have endured, but they had the means. And that's because this Baby Powder had asbestos in it.*

Asbestos Explained

[22:56] *Now, I want to talk to you for a minute about asbestos. And I want you to understand what this is. Asbestos is a mineral. It's—it's like—it's typically found underground or in a mountainside. But it is a mineral, and there are different types of asbestos. . . .* [**Lanier spends five minutes explaining the different types of asbestos so that the jury will understand the testimony that will come later in the trial.**]

Story: Lanier uses his opening statement not only to tell a story but also as a presentation to explain which types of asbestos cause cancer and how it happens. Lanier recognizes the unique opportunity an opening statement provides for a lawyer to simply explain difficult concepts so that the jurors can not only understand what the case is all about but also be given key knowledge of scientific terms so that they can easily understand the testimony at trial that will follow.

Asbestos and an Onion

[26:34] *Asbestos, when it hurts you, doesn't have what I call onion properties.* [**Lanier displays fig. 7.**] *You do not smell it. There's no smell to asbestos. You can't see it when it's going to be the kind that hurts you. It's invisible to the naked eye. You don't sneeze when it's around because it's so small it bypasses all of the body's defense systems and goes not just in through the nose, not just in through the throat, not just into the lungs. **It goes down into the deepest part of the lungs.** Into the little alveolar sacs that look like grapes if you put them under a microscope. Down in the very bottom, those are the little sacs and the walls are so thin where that asbestos goes in, that those sacs are the place where carbon dioxide comes out of the blood and oxygen goes into the blood.*

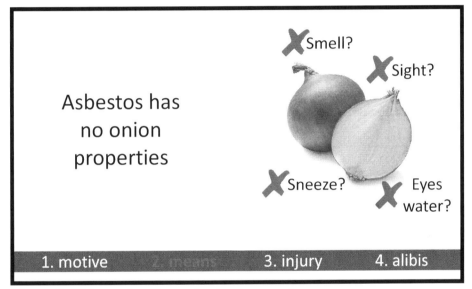

Figure 7. Slide contrasting asbestos to an onion.

It just passes through the wall of those little sacs, and that's where the asbestos goes. And the body can't get rid of it. It's indestructible. So it doesn't make you sneeze, it doesn't make your eyes water, it doesn't do anything. All it does is live forever.

Story: After explaining the different types of asbestos, Lanier creates one of the many highlights of his opening. He simplifies a complicated idea through his words and the visual aid he shows. He does this through a visual image to contrast its qualities to the characteristics of asbestos. Not only is the visual image powerful, he clearly explains the differences.

Slide: From now on, the jury has the idea-image of a well-known vegetable and its properties in their heads to contrast with asbestos and its invisible properties. Lanier has used this comparison of asbestos to an onion for years. For this slide, he wanted to find a clear and clean picture of an onion that might make the jurors' eyes water.

Style: Lanier uses both hands to dramatically show how asbestos enters the lungs and can then penetrate their tissues.

Asbestos and Cockroaches

Story: Lanier creates images and associations throughout his opening. He wants jurors to use both the left and right side of their brains so that they will remember what he says. He wants them to remember that asbestos is invisible, it is bad, it survives for years, and where you find one asbestos fiber you will find more. To help them remember it is invisible, he has contrasted it with an onion. Now, he needs to pick an image that will help them remember the remaining characteristics. Watch.

> [27:49] *I call it the cockroach of the mineral world.* [**Lanier displays fig. 8.**] *I mean, I don't know if it's true, but you read on the internet that after a nuclear war everything will die except cockroaches. I do know where you see one cockroach you probably got a whole bunch more.*

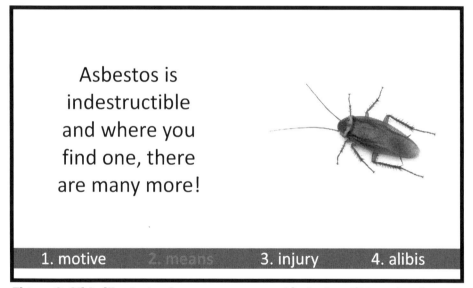

Figure 8. Slide illustrates how numerous and indestructible asbestos fibers are.

> *Both of those facts are true about asbestos. And you'll hear from the experts if they find asbestos in the Baby Powder, there are going to be millions of fibers in that powder, if they find one.* **If they find one, there are going to be millions.** *And so asbestos is just something that can't —your body can't destroy it. You don't get rid of it. It is really, really bad.*

Slide: Lanier told me that in addition to the comparison he made, he liked the "visceral reaction the picture of the cockroach causes."

Asbestos and Steaks

[28:29] *And this asbestos is marbled into the talc mines.* [**Lanier displays fig. 9.**] *I heard Mr. Bicks say there's not asbestos in the talc mines. He's going to tell you that. I am dying to show you the documents on this. There are—there's asbestos in the talc mines.*

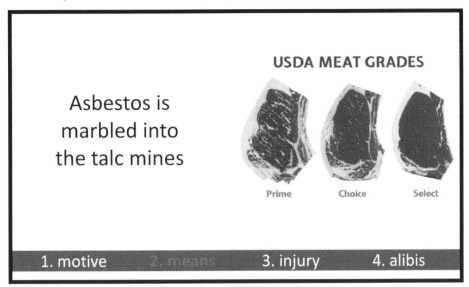

Figure 9. Slide that illustrates asbestos in talc mines.

The asbestos, it depends on what the talc mine is as to how much asbestos it's got in it. Some of it—it's like meat and fat marbled into meat, some of it's got more than others, but nobody's going to stand up and say that steak, it's fat-free, because it's in there.

Story and Slide: Lanier is really on a roll with creating powerful images. We have gone from an onion, to a cockroach, and now to steaks. It is one thing to try and describe that talc mines can have asbestos in them. But to use descriptive words and analogize the mines to marbled steaks creates a visual image that will long be remembered.

Rigged Tests

[30:15] *Now, Johnson & Johnson can get up here, and I firmly expect Mr. Bicks to get up here and to tell you over and over, and show you document after document, give you a pretty PowerPoint that says, look, we've tested this every which way to Sunday, we've got hundreds and hundreds of tests, and it's never shown asbestos.*

[30:46] *They rigged the tests.* [**Lanier shows fig. 10**] *They rigged the tests. Here's what they did. They took a **bathroom scale and they tried to weigh a needle on it**. They're using a test that will not detect the asbestos unless the asbestos is at a certain level. Which it's not. . . .*

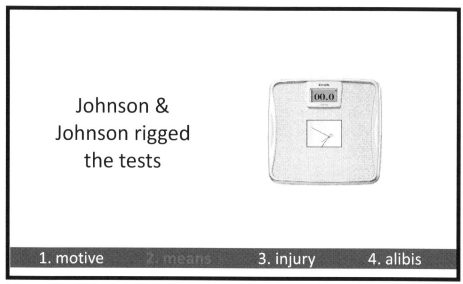

Figure 10. Slide that illustrates how J&J rigged tests.

Story: Here again, Lanier is using a countertheme (rigged tests) to undermine Johnson & Johnson's theme (tests did not reveal asbestos).

Slide: Lanier's ability to find an object to represent the idea he needs to explain is unmatched by any lawyer that I have seen or studied. Instead of trying to explain the components of a complicated piece of equipment used to look for asbestos, he compares it to something very familiar. Everyone knows that a bathroom scale is not very sensitive and would never register the weight of a needle. Lanier shows this image to create a lasting impression on the jury.

Style: Lanier mimics what defense counsel will soon say. He has to walk a fine line between being aggressive and not mocking Bicks. He accomplishes it by using a very slight sarcastic tone and with gestures as he suggests the many points Bicks will make. Then Lanier pauses, folds his arms as if he—and the jurors—will have heard enough, and emphasizes, "They rigged the tests." Then he shrugs his shoulders, and repeats the answer for emphasis.

The Right Test

Another test that Johnson & Johnson conducted sampled only an extremely small part of the contents of a bottle of Baby Powder.

[32:16] *There's a way to test more of the bottle. You can take it and concentrate it down and dilute it and put it in a centrifuge, one of those things that spins those test tubes around. And it's going to shoot the asbestos down to one end, and then you can take that out and test it.* [**Lanier puts his right hand up to his mouth to mimic a whispering gesture as he relates the next allegation.**] *The company knew about* *that for 40 years, 50 years, since the early '70s, but they refuse to use that test because, quote, that's too sensitive* [**Lanier uses both hands to make a quotation mark gestures**]. *It will show asbestos.*

We've used that test. And it's the—you know, I told you they used such a little bit. I asked one of the witnesses who was working with these tests, I said, based upon all the tests you've done in 40, 50 years, how long would it take you for this—this really small electron microscope test, how long would it take you to test this entire bottle based upon the pace you've been going so far? [**Lanier holds up a very small bottle of Baby Powder that fits entirely in one hand.**]

Just one of these 1.5 ounce chiquita, small. **600,000 years** *before they'll even test one full bottle at the rate they're going. . . .* [**Lanier raises his voice considerably to emphasize the outrageousness of Johnson & Johnson's testing procedures.**]

Lanier Summarizes Witnesses' Testimony

Lanier next tells the jury what he expects his first witness, Dr. Alice Blount, to say. She used to work for J&J and found asbestos in the Baby Powder. He then summarizes the testimony of other witnesses, which is where the transcript picks up below.

[36:40] *And as soon as she's done* [**Dr. Blount**], *I'm going to put on Dr. Longo. Dr. Longo is a world-renowned expert in asbestos testing for over 30 years. You might be saying, well, you know, he's what Mr. Bicks called the plaintiffs' expert.*

Well, he's our expert in this case, but he's been against me before too. I've brought him stuff before and said what do you think. And he said, no, there's no asbestos in this. He has no trouble doing that because he doesn't just do it for me.

He's worked with or been affiliated with and done work for or consulted with and been a part of the Environmental Protection Agency for the U.S. The FAA, Massachusetts Institute of Technology, MIT. The Department of the Treasury, NASA. . . . This gentleman has tested over 300 to 400,000 pieces of analysis over the last 30 years for asbestos. He's got a million-dollar electron microscope.

And he has, in two years that we've been trying to get him as many samples as we can, we've got them off eBay, we've got older ones. We've got them out of the Johnson & Johnson museum where they've kept them. We've gotten them out of some of our ladies' homes. He's gotten some from all these different places. **And in two years he's tested over a hundred times more Johnson & Johnson talcum powder than Johnson & Johnson has in 50 years** *if you're looking at volume. . . .* **Dr. Longo found asbestos in over half the bottles he examined.** *Didn't find it in all. Found it in over half.*

And then as I told you, if you use the right method, you'll hear this deposition of a consultant for Johnson & Johnson. At least they're lawyers. **Because Alice Blount wrote a letter to the Johnson & Johnson lawyers back in the 1990s, saying quit telling everybody your Baby Powder doesn't have asbestos in it. I've tested it and it does.** *She published on it. . . .*

*[39:58] You will even hear from the expert for the company, that's been the company man for almost 50 years, Dr. Pooley, from Wales, over in England, Great Britain. He's testified by deposition, and he wants to tell you—he gives a good company line that there's never been anything. **But if you look at his documents, his documents even show that he's found it in the mines. It's just a question of doing the right test. He told the company the right test to do, and the company said, no, we're not going to do that.** We're not going to concentrate it before we test it. We want to just test little bits.*

[40:36] See, Johnson & Johnson knew if you wanted to test it right, you needed to take a good chunk and concentrate it down so that you're testing the concentrated form, otherwise you'll never get through the bottle. You never test enough to know. **[Lanier shows fig. 11.]** *But we know that you can—you can reduce a gallon of orange juice down to a can. You can really reduce this down and you can look for the asbestos.*

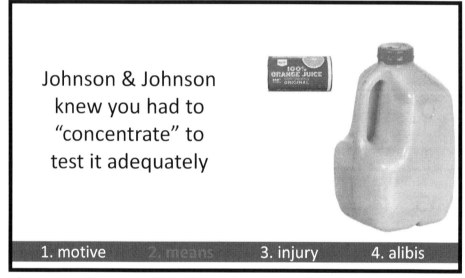

Figure 11. Slide illustrating J&J's failure to use the correct test.

Story: Lanier's first witness will be a former J&J employee. By talking about her first, he inoculates his second witness—a paid expert—from accusations from the defense attorney that Lanier's expert witness's testimony is untrustworthy because Lanier paid the expert. The defense attorney will seem disingenuous when he argues that Lanier's expert is only giving an opinion he has been paid to give by Lanier when Lanier's first witness is a J&J employee who also found asbestos in the Baby Powder. In addition, Lanier mentions all the reputable organizations that have relied on Lanier's expert witness and how much better the tests were that he conducted compared to those conducted by the Johnson & Johnson's experts who will be called to testify.

Slide: The image of the orange juice containers perfectly complements what he is saying. Lanier had to think of an image that would convey how easy it would be to concentrate the Baby Powder so that the right test could be conducted. He could have done it with mathematical formulas that would have confused the jury. Instead, he used a powerful image that will have a lasting impact on the jury.

Johnson & Johnson's Baby Powder Has Asbestos

[41:06] *And so when I tell you Johnson's Baby Powder has asbestos in it, it's not just me. It's in the powder and it's in the mines. . . .* **You get it from Dr. Pooley at Cardiff University.** *He'll say, no, it's not; no, it's not; no, it's not; 30,000 times, but once I finally put the record in front of him, the record speaks as to what he found. . . .*

The FDA has found asbestos in it, regardless of what Mr. Bicks will tell you in his opening. Not only has the FDA done it, but their own research lab, McCrone Research Institute, has found asbestos in the Baby Powder and in the products from the mines, the talc. **[With each person or company he lists, he adds their picture to a slide that is titled, "Johnson's Baby Powder has Asbestos." (See fig. 12.)]** *The mining company, Imerys, found it. There was a TV station in Sacramento, California, that sent some off to one of the national testing labs, Forensic Analytical Labs. They found the asbestos in the Baby Powder. Not only that, but the Colorado School of Mines, another school that's hired by this company to test their product, they found it.*

Figure 12. Slide showing those who have found asbestos in Baby Powder.

[42:28] **[Lanier discusses "word games."]** *Now, Mr. Bicks will put up here all these things that say no asbestos, no asbestos. That's because they* **start playing word games.** *They change what they call asbestos. Or they change the rules. We're not going to count it as asbestos if there's less than five fibers that we saw. So they just change the rules so they can tell everybody it doesn't have asbestos in it. . . .*

[**Lanier returns to the slide**]

[42:55] *Even Pfizer did a study that found it. RJ Lee, Sanchez, one of their experts that's going to come in here,* **he'll have to confess under oath, even with all of their games, with all of the definitions and everything else, yes, he's seen asbestos fibers in their product.** *. . . . You're going to get it from the MSHA. You're going to get it from Alice Blount at Rutgers University. You're going to get it from Bain Environmental.* **You're even going to see it in some Johnson & Johnson documents.** [**Lanier quickly rattles off the organizations, then slows down to emphasis that J&J's documents will admit it.**]

Story: As Lanier is filling the slide discussed above with organizations, he addresses a weakness—J&J's tests did not find asbestos—and overcomes it by providing a memorable label for the defense's anticipated argument. The label "word games" is effective because if you can show a party is changing the rules of the game, no one on the jury is going to like that.

Slide: Lanier creates a powerful slide as he mentions all the scientists and organizations that have found asbestos in Baby Powder. By the end of his discussion, he has filled the slide with 16 logos so that the slide is bursting with images from reputable groups. This crowded slide visually supports Lanier's story of overwhelming evidence. By design, the largest logo is Johnson & Johnson because Lanier will prove the company knew of its dangerous product in what he discusses in the next section.

When you look at the defense's opening statement on video, you will see that Bicks has a similar slide to prove the opposite point. I asked Lanier about this slide because I wanted to get his reaction when he saw that Bicks had copied his slide. It turns out that Lanier had done the copying, not Bicks. Lanier told me that in a previous case between his firm and Bicks's firm, Bicks displayed a similar slide. Lanier anticipated that Bicks might use a similar slide in the talc trial, and he stole Bicks's thunder. Remember from chapter 3 the importance of spending time figuring out how your opponent will attack your case? Lanier shows here how that can pay off.

Style: After he says Johnson & Johnson is "not going to count it as asbestos if there's less than five fibers," he pauses to let that reality sink in with the jury [42:42]. Lanier pounds his left hand with a fist to emphasize that J&J's own expert will have to "confess under oath" [43:01], raises both arms and waves them to demonstrate the amount of word games J&J has played, and even so [43:06], the expert will have to admit "yes, he has seen asbestos fibers in their product."[43:11] Lanier slows down and emphasizes each word of this last phrase. His gestures support what he is saying, and the variety of them makes his story more interesting.

Johnson & Johnson's Documents Reveal That There Is Asbestos

[43:40] *This is just a smattering*. *I don't have a lot of time, so I've got to do this fairly quickly. But if we can go to the ELMO, please, Juan. This is a summary of what we're looking at. . . . [45:06] Because the other reports, like Exhibit Number 93, your Honor, which I'm displaying now, that comes to the Johnson & Johnson research center that has the examination of the Baby Powder,* **they say "don't use this report. Replaced by another version."** [These words are written in ink at the top of a J&J report. Lanier slows down as he says each word and pauses afterwards to make sure the jury sees and hears what her says.] *And they'll milk down the words and all the rest.*

This is one [**Lanier shows another document**] *which shows the presence of trem-olite content, this is a Johnson & Johnson document. The total tremolite content of the two samples, .5 percent for one sample, .2 to .3 percent for another. That's asbes-tos. That's tremolite asbestos.* [**Lanier highlights the finding with a yellow high-lighter.**] *They found it. They looked and they found it. These are fibers, asbestos fibers . . . . It's not just in that report Exhibit Number 93. We've got it in others. The Dutch Consumer Group. Your Honor, this is Plaintiffs' Exhibit 6163.* [**Lanier summarizes this Johnson & Johnson memo.**] *Johnson & Johnson goes crazy because during the month of August, the Dutch Consumer Organization informed [Johnson & John-son]. They determined asbestos in Johnson's Baby Powder. According to their first test it was 1.59 percent. They tested another sample and it was .3 percent. [Johnson & Johnson] asked them, "don't tell anybody about this unless we agree. They didn't accept our arguments against their method of testing."*

[46:52] *Because Johnson & Johnson's got this elaborate scheme, if this doesn't work or they find it here then we look there. And if it's not there then we're done. We say there's none. But if it's there too then we'll look here.* [**Lanier uses both hands to gesture the different areas where J&J will hide test results.**] *And they call this being "overly careful."* [**Lanier makes quotation marks with both hands.**] *They'll say, oh, we do more than the minimum required. No. That's a trick. What they do is if the test shows it, they'll do more to try to find a test that won't show it, and once they get a negative result, they shut it all down and say, okay, now we've proven there's no asbestos here.*

[47:27] *I've got three boxes of positive findings* *that I'll be trying to show as we got time to do so. It goes on and on and on. FDA, et cetera.* [**Lanier drops a large folder full of tests that he has been showing the jury on a table and the weight of it makes a thud.**] *So, let's go back to the PowerPoint, please, Juan.*

Story: To be persuasive, you must be credible. There is no better way to back up what you are saying than with facts. Here, Lanier shows the jury documents that will be introduced at trial showing that J&J knew its products contained asbestos and tried to hide it from the public.

Style: Lanier's word choices and his gestures are really brilliant in this section. He tells the jury that what he is going to show them is just a "smattering" of what he has. He whets their appetite by showing them a document that says "Do Not Use This Report. Replaced by Another Version." He also leaves the J&J document on the document projector. As a result, while he is talking, the jury sees highlighted in yellow what J&J wrote: "We also asked them clearly not to make any publications about asbestos in Baby Powder, before we agreed with their findings. Because they did not accept our arguments against their method of testing. . . ."

Slide: Lanier switches from his PowerPoint to show the jury documents from J&J. He highlights in yellow the important admissions. The variety of switching back and forth from the PowerPoint to the document camera makes his visual presentation more interesting.

[47:44] *Where does that leave us? It leaves us with asbestos in the Baby Powder. It leaves us with asbestos in the mines. Asbestos in the mills.* [**Lanier uses anaphora—using the same word or phrase in successive phrases—to make his point stand out.**] *And it leaves us with a company that doesn't tell the truth. They suppress the scientific truth.* [**Lanier displays fig. 13.**]

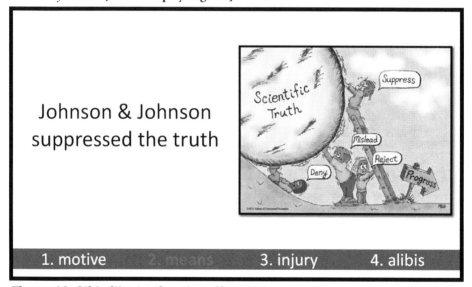

Figure 13. Slide illustrating the effort J&J made to suppress the truth.

I'm glad that we've got a full range of people on this jury. Because common sense is going to dictate the day. But there is some good science in here that you'll enjoy look-ing at. . . . You see, what the company did is the company manipulated the science in more ways than I can count right now. Oh, from changing what they call it, what they measure it by and playing the word games and all this kind of stuff to one gentleman, Dr. Langer, was going to present a paper in England, showing that he tested Johnson & Johnson Baby Powder and it had asbestos in it.

Johnson & Johnson stopped him from producing the paper. . . . There's a mine in Italy that publishes an Italian publication. This is a mine that supplies their Baby

Powder. And the publication says, "We've got asbestos in talc mines." And the company sends two of their big dogs over to Italy to get in front of that company and say, "please stop this English translation from going out until we can work on it and take out the asbestos section. We don't want that in English. We're telling everybody it doesn't have asbestos in it. . . ."

[49:38] I thought it was interesting when Mr. Bicks said, "Have you ever taken a document and seen a sentence out of context in a document?" **I'm not going to take sentences out of context. You hold it against me if I do. I want to show you the documents because the documents reveal the truth.** *. . .*

Style: In the last sentences of this section, Lanier executes the second principle of public speaking (speak from your heart to persuade) at its highest level. He builds an emotional bond with the jury when he says, "I'm not going to take sentences out of context. You hold it against me if I do." He is saying in effect, "Trust me and I will deliver the truth to you and if at any time I don't, you no longer should believe me." It is a bold statement, but it really shouldn't have to be. We should be able to trust professionals such as doctors and lawyers we rely on to tell us the truth, but our life experiences have taught us that they don't always do so. Lanier gains the jurors' respect by making this promise in such a straightforward manner.

Slide: For figure 13, Lanier told me he thought about Sisyphus, the figure from Greek mythology. "I thought about rolling a boulder uphill. So, then I just started looking for cartoons that had something similar, then I can add any writing I want. This just seemed to work. So, I was just shopping on Google images, looking on the internet for something that I could co-opt and modify and make it work."

Injury

Slide: As he transitions to a new topic, Lanier makes it very clear to the jury that he is on his third point (injury) with a slide that spells everything out clearly (fig. 14).

[51:58] You'll see the motive, you'll see the means, and then we'll get to that third area, the injury. You see these women were **targeted***. Johnson & Johnson targeted women for this product. Not simply to use on babies. But to use themselves.* **They targeted non-baby use** [**Lanier displays fig. 15**]. *They targeted use by any number of different groups. Overweight. African Americans. Hispanics. Teenagers.*

Let's go to the ELMO, please, Juan. Here's Plaintiffs' Exhibit 8214, your Honor. This is the Media Recommendation for 2010. Baby Powder. Here's their program overview. "Target overweight women living in hot climates during the key summer season." [**Lanier reads verbatim from the exhibit and then continues to summarize from it.**] *So they're going to print their ads in Weight Watcher magazine. They're going to "focus*

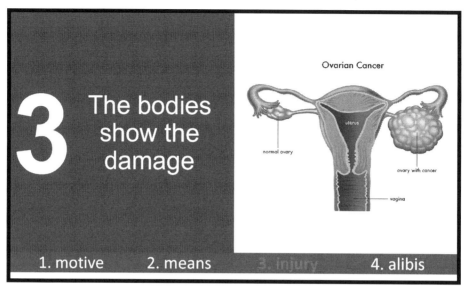

Figure 14. Slide illustrating the damage caused by asbestos.

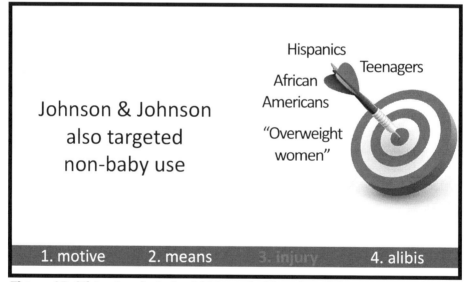

Figure 15. Slide showing who J&J targeted in advertising.

on overweight women living in hot climates, a/k/a, plus-sized Southerners." Because they hold a high school diploma. They live in cities, and they have friends with similar body types. They didn't only target overweight women. **They targeted teenagers.** *These are ads put out in the 1970s, or this is information put out about their ads in the 1970s, about your baby market. And they talk about their history of success with adult advertising. And how the sales of a major competitor has gone since 1965, but how Johnson's sales have skyrocketed. How have they done it?*

Well, now they're working on teenagers. Look at how important they are. There are 13 million teenager girls, and the number's going to increase dramatically. They spend 7 billion a year. 23 percent cosmetic stuff. They're receptive to Baby Powder. 75 percent of them use a body powder. 50 percent exposed to our advertising will buy Johnson's Baby Powder.

So they're going to advertise in Teen, Co-Ed, Seventeen, Ingenue. They're going to give out over two million and a half free samples. They're going to have these ads that tell girls, "You start being sexy when you stop trying. If a boy is interested in you, it should be because you're you, not because you wear musky perfume or makeup or anything that makes you something you're not. Johnson's Baby Powder won't make you something you're not. It won't make you smell like a siren. Stop trying, just try it." [**Lanier displays advertisement to jury and quotes from it.**] *Wasn't just that. Evidently teenage girls, when they're coming naked out of the river from bathing, are supposed to know, "If you'd rather be fresh and natural, you're our baby. You're one of the natural people." [1:07:03] "What you put on your body has to be fresh and **pure**."* [**Lanier reads from the advertisement.**] ***When they know it's got asbestos in it?***

Style: Lanier emphasizes the word "pure" and says it with a tone of disbelief.

They target Hispanics. They target black people. *I'll show you Plaintiffs' Exhibit 43. "Johnson's Baby Powder has a high usage rate among African Americans, 52 percent, and Hispanics. This brand can increase volume in 1993 by targeting these groups." They find the groups that they think they can best sell this to and they go to work on those groups and they figure out how to do it. And that's what they've done.*

No Warning Labels

[55:52] *Now, some companies actually put warnings on their bottle. You go to Angel of Mine. Angel of Mine's got a warning on the back. "This product contains talcum powder, it's intended for external use only. Frequent application of talcum powder in the female genital area may increase the risk of ovarian cancer."* [**Lanier displays picture of Angel of Mine's talcum powder and its warning label.**] *Johnson & Johnson didn't want to put that down there.*

[56:15] *Now, the doctors themselves, the treating doctors, most treating doctors don't know the role of asbestos in ovarian cancer. Most treating doctors don't. But there's no question that asbestos causes ovarian cancer. It's been determined by the International Agency Research on Cancer, that's the World Health Organization. They are the global authority because, as Johnson & Johnson put it, it's really hard to influence them. It's really hard to, they don't really take lobbying money and stuff. The National Cancer Institute in the U.S.A. says asbestos causes ovarian cancer. The American Cancer Society says it. . . .* [**Lanier displays a slide with a picture of ovarian cancer surrounded by the logos of all the organizations that have concluded that asbestos causes ovarian cancer.**]

Story: Lanier addresses a potential weakness in his case. That is, none of the doctors who diagnosed the plaintiffs told them that their cancer could have been caused by long-term use of Baby Powder. By admitting that fact, Lanier ensures that jury sees him as the truthteller in the courtroom. He then brings them facts to prove that although the treating doctors did not know, other very credible medical authorities did.

Latency

[59:02] *I've got a fellow named Dr. Felsher from Stanford University, who you're going to want to shake his hand, the judge won't let you until the trial is over maybe, but this man will cure some form of cancer in his lifetime. He is an amazing, amazing man, and he is all over this stuff. And both he and Dr. Moline [another plaintiffs' expert] will explain that asbestos cancer takes time to develop. They call it latency.*

You don't breathe it in and then get the cancer tomorrow. It takes decades to affect those mesothelial cells like mesothelioma; 20, 30, 40 years after you're exposed is when the cancer comes in.

*Now, the company says, well, it's background. Background's the cause. [***Lanier displays fig. 16.***] No, here's—Krystal Kim, there you are, back there. Stand up so they can see you. Krystal Kim [***Lanier points to one of the plaintiffs***]. We did— had our experts look at this. Thank you, Krystal. That line right there is how much background asbestos she's been exposed to. Just in the air. Mr. Bicks said everybody's exposed to it. Everybody's exposed to it. Her lifetime exposure is the 66,000 fibers. Her exposure based upon her uses of Johnson's Baby Powder, 67,300,000,525 fibers. [***Lanier slows down and raises his voice to emphasize the large number.***] Background asbestos. That's not going to be reasonable. Now, Mr. Bicks [in voir dire] said, "Wouldn't you expect the plaintiffs to show you asbestos in every tissue?" No. That's not the way it works, it's rare to find asbestos in the tissue. [***Lanier displays fig. 17.***]*

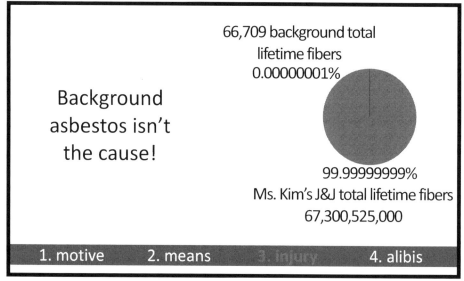

Figure 16. Slide depicting asbestos exposure.

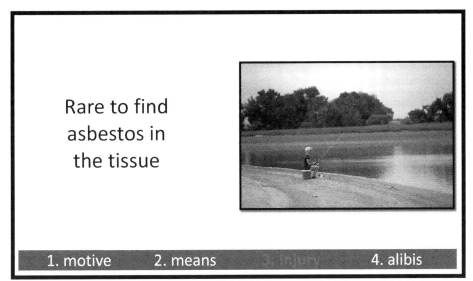

Figure 17. Slide showing how hard it is to find asbestos in tissue.

[1:00:51] *We've had Dr. Rigler look at it, he'll testify. And he's been able to look at, I don't know, 10 or 12 slides, and he's found it in a remarkable number. But the way asbestos works is our expert will teach you, it causes—it's the cause of cancer in three ways. Number one. It's like a match. It will actually cause the cancer to start. It can alter the DNA. The asbestos fibers are so small they will impale DNA inside a cell. And so it can cause it in that sense as starting it. An initiator is the cancer word.*

Or it can be what they call a promoter. It can make the cancer grow faster. It's pouring gasoline on a fire. And in that way causes the ovarian problems, the cancer problems. And then the third way is it stops the body's defense mechanisms. The fire truck doesn't arrive. So when the body is developing cancer cells, it not only can cause it to develop the cancer cells, it can feed the cancer cells, but it can also stop the body's defenses from attacking the cancer cells.

*So you're not always going to find asbestos in those tissues. **And for Mr. Bicks to suggest otherwise to you to get you to pre-decide this case is not right and not fair**.*

Story: Lanier wants to make sure he addresses this alleged weakness in his case. Some lawyers do this, but Lanier executes the strategy at the highest level by not only showing you why the alleged fact does not weaken his case, but also by killing the messenger (opposing counsel) of the alleged weakness by undermining their credibility when Lanier refers to the attack that has been made by Bicks in voir dire.

We learned in chapter 2 of the importance of listening in order to be a great public speaker. Lanier makes his presentation stronger because he has listened carefully to opposing counsel's statements in voir dire. Another lesson is that the information you gather to win your case continues during a trial. One great source of that information are the statements made by opposing counsel.

It is one thing to tell the jury facts why your case is strong, but if you can prove that opposing counsel is not being candid when they bring up your alleged weakness in voir dire, you can get the added benefit of damaging their credibility. Consequently, Lanier candidly speaks about defense counsel's statements in voir dire that many of the plaintiffs don't even have asbestos in their cancerous tissue. Lanier explains why not and turns the weakness into a strength by declaring that Bicks is untrustworthy for misrepresenting the reason why asbestos won't be found in the cancerous tissue.

Slide: The exposure chart (fig. 16) has the most text of Lanier's 99 slides, but it is still very clear and shows the very high level of Kim's exposure to asbestos. The boy fishing (fig. 17) is one of my favorites because it depicts what we all know, it is hard to catch fish. Lanier uses the picture as an analogy for how hard it is to find asbestos in tissue.

Alibis Don't Hold Up

[1:02:42] *I'm going to go to my last subject area. **Their alibis don't hold up.** Their defenses don't hold up. I want to hear what the company executives have to say.* **[Lanier displays fig. 18.]** *I can't make them show up, we can't force them to go to trial. But I want them to bring one in, and if they will, I'll put them on the stand in my case in chief, him or her, and I'll cross-examine them. I've already taken the deposition of their chief medical officer. I beg her to come in. If she doesn't I'll have to play the deposition, but I want an executive to look at these documents and look you in the eye and testify about them. I just can't force that. [1:03:30] I can show you documents that show Johnson & Johnson's been working on their legal defenses for **50 years**.* **[Lanier uses his tone of voice to emphasize "50 years."]**

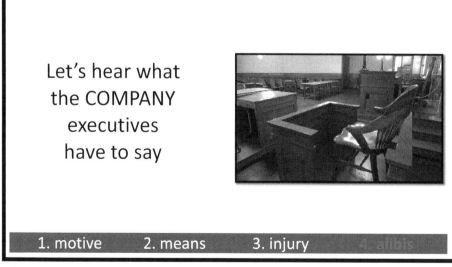

Figure 18. Slide showing missing witnesses.

Their lawyers have been all over this. They've been trying to get this figured out for a long, long time. And as a result, they've worked on it so long they've got shifting stories. They'll tell the government in one breath, asbestos causes ovarian cancer, and then they'll flip-flop and they'll tell the jury, no, asbestos doesn't cause ovarian cancer. [Lanier pauses for a long time to make sure this fact sinks in and displays fig. 19]

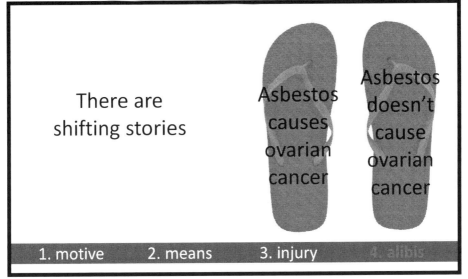

Figure 19. Slide illustrating J&J's shifting explanations.

Slide: Remember, your PowerPoint slide simply needs to enhance what you are saying. The picture of the empty chair (fig. 18) highlights J&J's refusal to bring witnesses to trial. Moreover, the flip-flops perfectly capture the idea of shifting stories. Because it is so creative, long after the opening statements are over, the jury will remember the picture of flip-flops and associate that with Lanier's claim about Johnson & Johnson's defense.

Lanier got the idea of the flip-flops from something he had heard years before. In a presidential debate, George Bush accused Al Gore of being a flip-flopper, saying one thing and then doing another. It really helped him beat Al Gore in the presidential election. Lanier said, "I was watching the debate and then thinking, 'Wow! Powerful, powerful word, powerful word, flip-flopper, flip-flop. Powerful,' then just put the picture with it."

Story: Notice that Lanier does not say, "I anticipate what the defense will say is . . . ." Instead, he refers to it as something more sinister to get the jury emotionally involved. He labels their arguments as alibis.

Well, you know, the truth's the truth the truth, it's not supposed to change. Trust and truth. That was dead right.

[1:04:10] I want you to listen carefully to Mr. Bicks. When he gets up, I don't have a chance to argue about what he said. So you listen carefully, I'm going to be making

notes. And I'm going to come back during this trial, and I'm going to make sure that the truth is out. [**Lanier displays fig. 20.**]

Figure 20. Slide reminding jurors to listen carefully to defense counsel.

This idea that the FDA never found asbestos in J&J talc. [**Lanier points to fig. 20.**] *He said that yesterday [in voir dire]. Have you read the file?* [**Lanier's tone is one of utter disbelief.**]

And the reference that Mr. Bicks is talking about [that the FDA never found asbestos in J&J talc] is a reference that's got a footnote at the bottom that says don't extrapolate these results to all of the products because we didn't have enough to test.

[1:05:07] But I'll show you other places where the FDA has said, yes, we found asbestos in the talc. **So you got to listen real carefully.** [**Lanier motions with his left forearm downward for emphasis**] *Mr. Bicks says there's never been a problem in over a hundred years. I'm sitting there thinking, well, where did you get that from? Your Honor, Plaintiffs' Exhibit Number 10. This is a document from Johnson & Johnson. Todd True. I like that name. . . . He's with the consumer products part of Johnson & Johnson in the U.S. And he's on this e-mail chain talking about it, and here's what he says. "Basically I'm thinking it would be in the brand's best interest to develop a strategy to move out of the baby aisle for our talc product. Either create a direct adult proposition or just replace it with corn starch."*

Corn starch works just as good. It holds the fragrance. In fact, some studies of theirs show it works better. **But when they first started looking at using corn starch they owned a talc mine. They didn't own a corn farm. And, furthermore, they did the math. The corn starch costs 40 percent more than the talc. So they either have to charge more or their profit margin goes down. . . .**

And they keep selling their talc. He says that this would align with our charter of doing the best for the baby to take it out. "I understand this is a $70 million business in the U.S. alone, unsupported. So any changes are risky, but given a number of other *ingredient issues we're facing, this is an easy fix. I know it's going to be controversial. We'll just have to work hard to justify the cost implications."* [**Lanier emphasizes "easy fix" and "cost implications" to make sure the jury understands why Johnson & Johnson did not implement Mr. True's suggestion.**]

Mr. Bicks, there hasn't been a problem in over a hundred years. Yes, Todd True. [**Lanier shows the jury another email from Todd True.**] *"The reality that talc is unsafe for use on or around baby is disturbing. I don't mind selling talc, but we can't continue to call it a Baby Powder and keep it in the baby aisle."*

If you're going to continue to sell it, tell the truth about it. Put a warning on it. Let people make a decision whether or not they want to take that risk and they want to do that. So, I mean, they've been working on this for years.

Your Honor, Plaintiffs' Exhibit 7414. [*Lanier puts letter on ELMO.*] **It's a letter from their mine company to their lawyers at Johnson & Johnson. This is the mine company, Luzenac, that's mining the product in 1994.** *They're talking about how they destroy their samples after two years so that nobody can come back and test them. They've been working at this for a long time.*

They do other things. They go in and they have, you know, when the government was looking at listing talc as a cancer causer, what the company did is the company joined with their mine company and each of them wrote half of a check to these doctors in Pennsylvania to publish a study, but they didn't just go to the doctor and say, hey, here's some money would you publish a study?

Instead, they went through a law firm so nobody would know J&J and the mine company were behind this study. **They hid the money so that they could pretend that the study was independent. And you'll see it. I've got the e-mails.**

[1:08:55] *I'm running out of time. I want to show it to you. What the heck, we're already here.* [**Lanier shows the letter.**] *"Maximize the effectiveness of our use of the attorney work-product privilege for their work. I'll send them a law firm check in that amount to be reimbursed to us by Luzenac and Johnson & Johnson in whatever proportions you choose."* . . . .

Meanwhile, they're writing everybody, the New England Journal of Medicine, telling them there's no asbestos in here. They're telling juries there's no asbestos in here. They're telling the judge, there's no asbestos in here.

You see, what they were doing is they were trying to protect their market. Let me go back to the PowerPoint for a moment. **Ninety-nine percent of the time, the FDA just requires you to self-police.** *You've got to go into the FDA and you've got to say I got to tell you this, we got asbestos in our product. That's kind of like—how many people go to the law and say, you know, this morning I sped through a school zone. There wasn't anybody there to give me a ticket, but I want to self-report, and I'd like you to write me a ticket. It didn't happen that often.* [**Lanier uses an analogy that the jury can relate to that explains why companies don't self-report violations to the FDA.**]

[1:10:16] *And then they're doing all this backroom stuff to secretly distort the science.* [**Lanier displays fig. 21.**] *Where they're getting all these articles written that they*

Figure 21. Slide illustrating J&J's deception.

can use, and their real goal behind all this was protecting their image and their sales. Their goal is not to figure out do we have asbestos in here that's going to kill people.

Do we have mamas sprinkling it on their babies where their babies are going to have ovarian cancer in 30, 40 years, or their mamas from sprinkling it on the babies, or from sprinkling it on themselves. [**Lanier gestures with his hand to imitate sprinkling Baby Powder from a container.**]

Here's Plaintiffs' Exhibit Number 80. Johnson & Johnson Special Talc Study. They're going to do a special study. What's the objective? Is it to figure out if we've got a problem?

No. It's "to monitor and defend against consumerists, against science, against regulatory attitudes and trends that could adversely impact the safety image and the marketability [of cosmetic talcs]." So we've got "to generate and provide the necessary data to support and reinforce safety of our Baby Powder." And they do that.

Story: As we have seen, Lanier uses analogies throughout his opening such as comparing the FDA's requirement of self-policing to the police requiring drivers to self-report speeding in a school zone. But he does more than that to persuade. He backs up his points with hard evidence. He shows the jury preadmitted exhibits that he has highlighted in yellow to prove his points.

Slide: The "Listen carefully" slide is a classic Lanier slide: clean, clear, and crisp. Lanier explained that he thought this slide looks like what you'd see on YouTube video clips, so it would be easy to understand. He also recognizes that he has a jury of different people. He wants his slides to reflect that fact. Here, the slide has the added benefit that there is no ethnicity represented. As a result, "everybody can identify with this type of slide."

Now, this is, of course, at a time where they tested their Baby Powder on the second page and they find asbestos. "Johnson's Baby Powder, .08." They find it. "These results are well below the current two fibers per cc permitted for asbestos." They just say it's not that bad. Hey, let's not quibble about who killed who. And I could keep going, but I'm running out of time. I just will tell you this. [1:12:05] Johnson & Johnson will say one thing now and they'll say one thing later. [**Lanier displays fig. 22.**]

Figure 22. Slide showing J&J's lack of candor.

*They'll say, egads, there's asbestos and then they'll tell everybody there's no asbestos. And all of this time there was a safer alternative. It just didn't make as much money for them. So, he'll tell you it's asbestos-free, when their documents I'll show you later say we can't always tell you it's asbestos-free. I'll show you the documents of them suppressing the truth. **I'll show you how they approved the policy of destroying the samples after two years**.* [**Lanier displays fig. 23.**]

I'll show you that "we didn't know" is not a legitimate excuse. If you do the right test, you'll know. You do the right test, you do it often, and you report it honestly.

So you're going to follow the evidence, I hope to bring the responsible party to justice. It will have a loud, it will—I hope you do this. It's very important because the evidence shows Johnson & Johnson is responsible.

And so if you're the detectives, that's how you'll get there. Thank you very much. Thank you, your Honor, for the time.

Story: Lanier ends his opening very strong. We learned in chapter 4 how devastating a countertheme can be. Lanier takes advantage of this principle with a countertheme to Johnson & Johnson's main point. While Johnson & Johnson will put on testimony that there is no asbestos in its mines or products, Lanier uses the countertheme of talking out of both sides of their mouth to condition

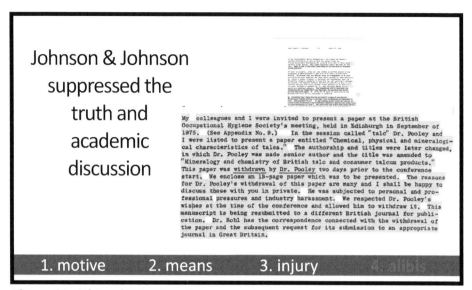

Figure 23. Slide with text and document showing suppression of truth.

the jury to test what Johnson & Johnson's witnesses will say against what J&J's documents will reveal.

   Slide: Most lawyers would simply say that Johnson & Johnson gave inconsistent statements. But Lanier makes it more memorable and creates a visual aid to capture the idea of a company talking out of both sides of its mouth. He also used a slide similar to this on cross-examination in a previous trial where the witness had made several inconsistent statements. He photoshopped the image to put eight mouths on each side, and he left the text boxes blank. Then, he filled them in during the cross-examination. He would write on one side what the company was saying at trial and then show the witness and document that proved the opposite and write that in the text box on the other side.

10.3 OUTLINE OF LANIER'S OPENING STATEMENT AND POWERPOINT

Having analyzed Lanier's opening, let's look at an outline of it to gain a big picture of how he organized his presentation.

1. Thanks the jury.
2. States bottom-line message: Asbestos and Breathed equals Cancer (ABC).
3. Introduces plaintiffs.
4. Tells jurors that they are detectives.
5. Provides structure for the four points of his opening: (1) motive, (2) means, (3) injury, and (4) alibis.
6. Explains why Johnson & Johnson's motive was money.

7. Teaches that Johnson & Johnson had the means to cause injury by explaining how asbestos causes cancer and that Johnson & Johnson used rigged tests to hide the fact its products contained asbestos.

8. Describes the injury of ovarian cancer.

9. Argues why Johnson & Johnson's alibis won't hold up.

10.4 SUMMARY OF THE STORY LANIER TELLS

As we learned in chapter 3, one of the biggest mistakes lawyers make is that they relate the facts of what happened without explaining why it matters. The second big mistake is that they fail to make a connection with the judge or jury. Lanier not only avoids these mistakes but also executes the art of storytelling to perfection. His bottom-line message of what his case is all about uses the Rule of Three: Asbestos, Breathed in, Causes Cancer (A, B, C). He then structures his story using the mystery format. The heroes are the plaintiffs, and the villain is Johnson & Johnson. How does Lanier engage the jurors? He empowers them to write the ending of the story, because he has deputized them as detectives to bring the villain to justice. Wow! But Lanier never forgets that he is in a courtroom where he will have to prove his case. If he said it once, he said it a hundred times in his opening statement: "I'll bring you the documents to prove it."

10.5 SUMMARY OF LANIER'S SLIDES

As for his PowerPoint, Lanier had 99 slides. They were memorable and persuasive for a couple of simple reasons. First, Lanier did not use one bullet point. Not one! Nor did he throw a bunch of text on a slide for the jury to read through. Instead, Lanier's slides averaged seven words. That should be your goal, too. That is proof of how clear and concise his message was. In addition, each slide had a picture that was interesting to look at and precisely conveyed the message that Lanier was talking about.

The test for the success of any PowerPoint is this: Does it persuade you while you are watching it, and does it continue to impact you after you have seen it? Lanier's PowerPoint sets the standard for success. Set aside for a moment how persuasive the slides were when you watched in real time. Long afterwards, whether it is a few days, several weeks, or several months, you will remember the images on those slides and what they stood for. For example, when you think about the picture of flip-flops, the image will instantly remind you that J&J changed its story. Similarly, if I were to ask you what the cockroach image stood for, you would immediately say that asbestos fibers can survive anything.

Moreover, while Lanier used 99 slides in 75 minutes (about one per minute), it does not seem like he used that many slides. It seems more like 30 or so, because each picture seamlessly complimented what Lanier was saying, and each was so interesting that you looked forward to the next slide. The point is, creative and clear slides that support what you are saying instead of distracting from what you are saying can raise your ability to persuade to the highest level. There is no better example of this than Lanier's PowerPoint.

10.6 SUMMARY OF LANIER'S STYLE

I was sadly not surprised when one of the first things Bicks said in his opening statement (see below) was that he was not going to scream and shout like Lanier but instead talk about the evidence. That is a tired cliché defense attorneys use against plaintiff's attorneys. It works well against bad plaintiff's attorneys, who indeed may shout with emotion and bring few facts to the jury. However, it does not work against good plaintiff's attorneys and in particular one as great as Lanier. Moreover, it hurts Bicks's credibility when he says something that is inconsistent with what the jurors observed.

Lanier hardly screamed and shouted but instead was a masterful teacher in the courtroom. His goal is to be the most trustworthy lawyer by being sincere and likeable, and by supporting what he says through documents—many of which he showed the jury during his opening statement—and very credible witnesses. He is always engaged with his audience. As we learned in chapter 2, to be persuasive you must constantly think about WIN, What Is the Need of your audience, the jury. Lanier values their time, their common sense, and is aware if they are able to hear and see what he presents. Moreover, he executes all the principles discussed in chapters 6 and 7 about not using notes and using effective gestures.

However, as great as Lanier is, I would caution you not to try to be just like him, because you cannot, and even if you could, you would not be authentic. Lanier echoes this warning. I asked him in our interview if he was scared that by sharing his secrets with me defense attorneys that he goes up against would imitate him and take away from his success. He explained, "If someone tries to be Mark Lanier, they will seem disingenuous, and that violates rule one, which is to be authentic. My goal is to share with others so that they can do a better job at what they do. I've been told, 'Don't share your secrets.' There's plenty of food to go around. I'm not starving."

Moreover, remember Oscar Wilde's quote from chapter 2, "Be yourself; everyone else is already taken," and Carlos Santana's advice, "We tend to look for greatness always in somebody else rather than yourself. Go inside and get your sound." My hope is that after reading and seeing Lanier's opening statement, you will be inspired to incorporate and adapt what you found effective into your own skillset and personality as you prepare for your next hearing or trial. That is the true pathway to discovering your own greatness that is already within you.

10.7 DEFENDANT'S OPENING STATEMENT

In summary, the main problem with the defendant's opening statement is that it did not match the evidence—at all. After the huge jury verdict, Johnson & Johnson appealed, and an appellate court found that "Plaintiffs proved with convincing clarity that defendants engaged in outrageous conduct because of an evil motive or reckless indifference" and that there was "significant reprehensibility in defendants' conduct."

The appellate court agreed with what Lanier promised to prove in his opening statement and found that Johnson & Johnson "discussed the presence of asbestos in their talc in internal memoranda for several decades; avoided adopting more accurate measures for detecting asbestos and influenced the industry to do the same; attempted to discredit those scientists publishing studies unfavorable to their products; and did not eliminate talc from the products and use cornstarch instead because it would be more costly to do so . . . and knew of the asbestos danger in their products when they were sold to the public."

An excerpt of defendant's opening statement can be found on this book's website. I am not going to analyze the opening statement here because I wanted to devote the space in this chapter to Lanier, who did it right as opposed to someone who did it wrong. If you overpromise in your opening statement as defense counsel did, you will never have a chance to win and lower the damages if the jury finds against you. Nonetheless, to provide you with a framework for viewing the video, what follows is an outline of defendant's opening statement and a brief analysis of it.

As you will see from the outline below, Unlike Lanier, Peter Bicks, who was the lead attorney for Johnson & Johnson, did not have a memorable bottom-line message, and he had no overall structure to his opening statement. Instead, he presented facts—the most important of which Lanier proved to be wrong during the trial—but unlike Lanier, because he presented the facts in a dull manner and without structure, they lost their impact. For example, his first slide declared, "Opening Statement" and listed the names of the trial team. That is no way to capture the jury's attention. He then recaps the most important points of Lanier's opening statement and then responds by simply declaring that what Lanier said was not true. Why would he think it was a good idea to repeat what Lanier had just said? As a result, the jury gets a reminder of what the plaintiff's case is all about without Lanier having to say anything.

Outline of Bicks's Opening Statement

1. Summarizes the main points of Lanier's opening statement.
2. Bicks states that, unlike Lanier, who shouted with scare tactics, "I'm not going to scream, I'm going to talk about the evidence."

3. Discusses plaintiffs' burden of proof.

4. Tells plaintiffs that he is sorry that they have cancer.

5. Reminds jury of its promise in jury selection to set aside sympathy and follow the law.

6. J&J acted responsibly by selling talcum powder products.

7. Studies show that talc does not cause cancer.

8. Gives history of J&J.

9. Explains two types of talc: industrial and cosmetic grade.

10. Gives overview of talc mines and processing.

11. Gives overview of different types of asbestos.

12. Explains that rigorous testing and studies show no asbestos in talc.

13. Plaintiffs' claims are based on false alarm from study in 1972 that found asbestos in talc but was later proven wrong.

14. FDA did not require warning label.

15. Cites study of 181,869 women which found no connection between talc and ovarian cancer.

16. Doctors do not know what causes ovarian cancer, but, most likely, causes are due to genetics and a family history of cancer.

17. Declares that asbestos is everywhere.

18. Thanks the jurors for their promise not to be swayed by sympathy and to follow the law and keep an open mind.

If you found the list of topics less than exciting to read and hard to remember, that would be consistent with one's response to watching the one-hour-and-fifteen-minute video of the opening statement. If the best that Bicks can come up with for a bottom-line message is that J&J acted responsibly in selling its products, he is going to lose every time to Lanier, who deputized the jurors as detectives to solve a crime of cover-up. Although some of Bicks's slides were interesting, the majority of them had the look and feel of having been created by a committee that was trying to explain its points to a group of lawyers seated around a conference table and not a jury in a courtroom.

In addition, Bicks's courtroom advocacy was just too conventional, which is the very style you need to avoid if you want to break away from the pack. He paced too much without any reason, and his tone was a combination of overly dry, feigned exasperation, and condescension. Moreover, as mentioned above, the appellate court found that the evidence did not support Johnson & Johnson's claims. You are going to lose all credibility if you don't admit the bad facts in your case. Although Lanier would have had a response, Bicks's best strategy would have been to admit that there was asbestos in the Baby Powder but to also emphasize that millions of women have used Johnson & Johnson's baby products and have never fallen ill, and that each of the different doctors who diagnosed the plaintiffs with ovarian cancer never suggested to them that the use of those products caused their cancer. But instead of highlighting those facts, they were buried at the bottom of a discussion about the burden of proof.

Finally, when Bicks mentions twice to the jury that they must set their sympathies aside and follow the law as they promised in jury selection, that reminder reveals a sign of weakness that Bicks does not trust the jury. How would you feel if you were on a jury and were sacrificing to be there as an act of public service and a lawyer felt the need to remind you to do your job fairly?

> **Practice Tip**
>
> You need to be authentic, have a conversation with the jury, and tell them a story that interests them and makes them care about why what happened to your client matters.

CHAPTER CHECKLIST

1. Lanier is an outlier. He never had a fear of public speaking. Public speaking thrills and invigorates him. The only thing that scares Lanier at a hearing or trial is not knowing the rules well enough.

2. Lanier's recipe for an opening statement is like a recipe for a cake. He has five ingredients: (1) The first ingredient is a *three-columned list* that he writes, in which he lists all the good facts, the neutral facts, and the bad facts. He then tries to see if there are any arguments that can be made that will move as many bad facts as possible into the neutral column or the good column; (2) the second ingredient is *the story* he will use to tell the facts; (3) the third ingredient is *the themes* that he will use. "I've got to have my themes, I've got to have the defense themes, and I've got to have my counter to those themes figured out to integrate them into the opening as time allows also;" (4) the fourth ingredient is *structure*. "Structure the opening in a way that tells a compelling story, but also features three basic points because I believe in the rule and the power of three;" and (5) the fifth ingredient is *the opening presentation*. Change the "opening from an opening statement into an opening presentation. That's my mentality of how I put together the slides that will accompany the voice over to make it a presentation, visually appealing, as well as linguistically appealing. So, hitting both hemispheres of the brain."

3. Lanier does not feel outside pressure when trying high-stakes cases. The pressure comes from within, whether he represents 22 women dying of cancer or whether it is a fender bender. The only pressure comes from within. That drive is to win.

4. Lanier believes the key to speaking from his heart is that he has an overwhelming drive for the truth. He believes that truth is important. This belief sets his tone when he speaks.

5. Lanier's father instilled in him the importance of winning but also of being a good loser.

6. No matter how heated the battle, whether it is with opposing counsel or a witness on the stand, Lanier is always gracious. There is a kindness that envelopes everything he does.

7. There are three things that help Lanier deal with a loss. First, he knew from his father that it was important to be a good sport. Second, Lanier "believes in the jury system." Third, Lanier is determined to learn from a loss so that it won't happen again.

8. Lanier's faith in God influences how he views winning and losing. "I do believe I'm responsible for doing the very best that I can. God has given me talents and opportunities . . . but the nice part about all of that is it's the lesson of Noah and the ark. God told Noah, 'Build an ark. Here's how I want you to build it. . . . Get all these animals. Noah was not responsible for bringing the rain or the weather. I do my stuff. I get in the ark . . . and God decides how much it's going to rain . . . the results, they're in his hands. When I win, praise the Lord. When I lose, praise the Lord. So, my part is to be the cog I can be, but not to devise the whole machine of how it all works."

9. Lanier's rules for PowerPoint slides: (1) think presentation, your slide is presenting something. One point per picture, no more. Avoid distractions; (2) think persuasion. Your slide needs to be crisp and emotive; and (3) think memorable. The slide needs to be memorable.

10. Lanier believes the worst mistake you can make in opening statement is to overpromise what you will be able to prove at trial. "I'm very careful on how I say those things because I want to acknowledge the truth. I don't want the defendant to ever be able to get up in their opening and say, 'Lanier said this. Let me show you why he's lying.'"

11. For a summary of Lanier's outline of his opening statement, his style, and slides, see sections 10.4–10.6 near the end of this chapter (before the Chapter Checklist).

CHAPTER ELEVEN

The Master Oral Advocate, Allyson Ho

"My passion is to analyze a client's problem and craft that one sentence that explains why we should win. I love to stand up for them and articulate their position as persuasively as it can be articulated."—*Allyson Ho*

11.1 ALLYSON HO

Allyson Ho is widely regarded as one of the nation's most accomplished appellate lawyers. She has presented over 65 oral arguments in federal and state courts nationwide, including multiple high-stakes cases on behalf of businesses before the U.S. Supreme Court.

Among her numerous accolades, Chambers has named her one of the nation's top appellate lawyers every year for the past ten years. In addition, she has been profiled in "Supreme Court Insider" (*National Law Journal*, July 21, 2016). *National Law Journal* called her a "Veteran SCOTUS Advocate" in the "upper echelons of Supreme Court practice." *Law360* named her a "Supreme Court Star" and "one of the nation's preeminent appellate lawyers." EmpiricalSCOTUS.com ranked her among "the most successful attorneys that currently practice before the Court."

Though no stranger to high-pressure Supreme Court appearances, she argued two significant Supreme Court business cases in 21 days. Her win in *M&G Polymers USA LLC v. Tackett* was a "significant ruling for employers across the U.S." (*Law360*, Aug. 10, 2016), overturning longstanding circuit precedent and "pav[ing] a new path for companies paying millions of dollars in retiree health care benefits" (*Law360*, Nov. 23, 2015). That case will be analyzed below.

> **CHAPTER ROAD MAP**
>
> - Get access to how Allyson Ho prepares to argue before the U.S. Supreme Court.
>
> - Examine the transcript of Ho's argument before the Supreme Court to learn how to listen, articulate your points, and win.
>
> - Analyze the audio recording of Ho's oral argument on the book's website to learn how she infuses meaning into the words she speaks.

In addition, Ho has appeared in every federal court of appeals in the country. Ho also has a distinguished record of experience at the highest levels of the federal government. She served as Special Assistant to President George W. Bush, Counselor to Attorney General John Ashcroft, and law clerk to Justice Sandra Day O'Connor of the U.S. Supreme Court and Judge Jacques L. Wiener Jr. of the U.S. Court of Appeals for the Fifth Circuit.

Ho shared with me her sharp insights and nuanced observations on oral advocacy that make her a master oral advocate. After learning her strategies, we will examine one of her Supreme Court oral arguments and see how oral advocacy is practiced at the highest level.

11.2 ALLYSON HO'S INSIGHTS ON PERSUASION AND PUBLIC SPEAKING

Overcoming the Fear of Public Speaking

Ho had to overcome a fear of public speaking. She has a lot of empathy for those who have that fear, and she shared with me how she won her battle. "It's something that I've had to work hard at, and challenge myself to overcome fears about it. I will say, now, having done a lot of arguments, there's just no substitute for practice and just getting your feet wet in a variety of circumstances, including making oral arguments, but also public speaking and the like." She added, "I think once you develop your comfort and your confidence, then that builds on itself. For any of your readers who do not consider themselves natural born speakers, I empathize."

As explained in chapter 1, almost everyone has a fear of public speaking, but that fear can be caused by many different emotions. For Ho, the main cause of her fear is that she is a perfectionist, and she acknowledges having had a fear of losing control when speaking in public. She explained, "I felt like I had a lot more control over written work, that I could sit down and write a brief or a paper or an essay, and hone it and hone it and hone it. Whereas in terms of getting up and speaking, responding to questions, that was more unpredictable. I felt like I didn't have as much control over it. I think that might have been the source of a lot of my anxiety. It was just my perfectionist tendencies and wanting to just get everything exactly right." Her solution was to practice, practice, and practice, which gave her confidence over time.

I asked her how she dealt with the unique fear of appearing on the biggest stage in the country, the United States Supreme Court. She responded, "It's just a higher level of scrutiny. You're just up there in real time, without a safety net." However, because she relentlessly prepared and did so many moot courts, she was very confident when she got to the podium.

The Biggest Mistake Attorneys Make

Based on her experience watching oral arguments as a former clerk at the Supreme Court, and then as a lawyer, here is what she observed as the biggest mistake that attorneys make. It is their failure to listen. In chapter 2, we learned that the third principle of public speaking is determining <u>W</u>hat <u>Is</u> the <u>N</u>eed of the audience (WIN). To do that, you have to listen. Ho said, "I think a lot of advocates, whether it's nerves, they're just so caught up in their points and the arguments they want to make that they don't necessarily listen to the question being asked or attune themselves to the body language and facial expressions of others." I asked Ho to elaborate. She explained,

> Listening is not just about being quiet and waiting to make your point, but really hearing what the judge is saying. I think that's sometimes a hard thing to do in oral argument, because it's natural to be focused on what you want to say next in order to make the points you want to make. I think it is really a conversation. Also, remember you are, as an advocate, you're there for the judges. You're there to answer their questions, to address their concerns.
>
> You can't do that if you're so wrapped up in your own points and your own agenda that you're not able to listen to and really hear what they're asking—both the questions that they're asking and the concern that may be animating the questions. I think not listening is one thing. I think not being attentive to cues about what the judges want to hear, and what they're interested in, is another thing.

Too many times Ho has seen a lawyer say after a judge asks a question, "Well, Your Honor, I'm going to get to that a little later." Ho adds that lawyers make this mistake because they have their outlines and want to make sure they hit their points instead of being flexible and talking about what the judge wants to talk about.

> *You're not there to hear yourself talk. You're there to answer questions, address concerns, shore up weaknesses. You want the hard questions, you want to hear concerns.*
> —Allyson Ho

Follow the Rule of Three

As discussed in chapter 3, the Rule of Three is a very effective way to structure your bottom-line message and your story. It is no surprise that Ho said, "I'm a big believer in the Rule of Three. I just think our brains really relate to it." Ho explained two other benefits (not surprisingly, she had three reasons for why she liked the Rule of Three). A second benefit is that it provides great discipline as you craft your argument to narrow it down to three points. Third, sometimes a judge on the panel will interrupt you before you get to state your three points. When that happens, Ho has found that "usually someone on the panel will ask, 'Didn't you say you had three points? What's your third point? Let's get back to that.'" Particularly on rebuttal, where spontaneous energy is important, "if you get up and say, 'I just want to hit three quick points,' you're much likelier to be able to get that out." In the argument we analyze below, you will notice that Ho used the Rule of Three in her rebuttal argument before the U.S. Supreme Court.

The Importance of a Bottom-Line Message

Ho believes the key to her success—and yours—is having a passion for boiling down all the facts of a case to a winning message. She instructs that when you first get a case, "learn like a sponge" everything about the statutes, regulations, case law, and facts. Then, you need to think through it all to "articulate a problem or a solution or a theme that just breaks it open. It's a product of preparation and experience." She spends more time on this one sentence, what is referred to in this book as the bottom-line message, than everything else. She adds that it takes a lot of trial and error, having to go back to the drawing board, and trying it out in front of different moot courts and others.

But the payoff is worth it. "Every case has that 'aha' moment: here's why we win. Again, just finding that one articulation is key, whether it's a sentence or an idea or a theme or a quote that really simplifies it, boils things down to the nub." This is especially important at the Supreme Court, because "you might only get that one sentence out before you are interrupted."

Structure Your Argument Around a Story

As we learned from chapter 3, research proves that stories are the most persuasive vehicle for presenting information, whether you are before a judge or jury. Ho has seen this play out in her countless oral arguments before judges. She relates, "Judges are people too. Stories are how we learn. That's how we relate to the world, is through stories. I'm a big believer in finding the story at the heart of every case and telling it as authentically and as persuasively as you can."

Ho's Speaking Style

One of the overriding theme's in this book has been the first principle of public speaking discussed in chapter 2, Be True to Yourself, which is embodied in Oscar Wilde's advice, "Be yourself; everyone else is already taken." Ho provides wonderful insight on how to do this. I asked her how she developed her oral advocacy style and what advice she had for others. She replied:

> One of the best things I've ever heard said about oral advocacy is that there are many different types of effective advocates. There's one type of oral

advocate who really fires up the room. Then there are advocates who lower the temperature in a room. They're very measured. They're very reasonable. You find yourself leaning in. By the time they have finished talking, you think, well, that's so reasonable, how could anything else be right?

The question then becomes, how do you find your own style? Ho instructs:

> I think the key is not feeling like you have to fit yourself, as an oral advocate, into any particular mode, and to understand and appreciate if you are more of a raise-the-temperature type of advocate, or if you are more of a lower-the-temperature kind. Then finding what works for you is a process of trial and error. I've found that it's when people have an idea of what they think an oral advocate should look like or sound like that they tend to use mannerisms or gestures that are distracting, rather than helping to emphasize or make the point.

Ho adds that the key is to realize that you are on a journey where you observe others and learn from experience until you get comfortable in your own skin. For example, if you observe an attorney do something you really like, try it yourself, and see if it works for you and if you feel comfortable doing it. It is also important to learn from advocates who are different from you because you might be able to modify something that works for them to your style. "For me, it's really about finding your voice as an advocate and not feeling that your voice needs to sound exactly like everybody else's—or whoever you think of as an advocate—to be effective as an oral advocate."

For Ho, she has found that she wants her inner voice to be telling her that she is the most reasonable person in the room. It comes from her clerking days. "First and foremost, you are an advocate and you are pressing for your clients position to prevail, but doing so in a way that you feel like you are part of the process of the judges getting it right, getting the law right, getting the facts right, and doing the hard work before you even get up to the podium, where you feel like, look, I've surveyed the law, I've surveyed the cases, I know my case inside and out." She added, "Its sounds like a cliché, but you should think about your advocacy in terms of being an officer of the court and trying to work with the court to get to a result that's right on the law, right on the facts, and makes sense in the mine-run of cases."

How to Prepare for Oral Argument

In chapter 8, we looked at how to practice your presentation. I wanted to get Ho's insights. After reading everything about the law and facts at issue, she starts thinking about the questions and answers she could be asked and creates a running list that she continually adds to. "The list will be changed up until the night before oral argument, usually refining answers. I feel that also helps me see themes and connections. I really do write things down. I list the question and the answer. The idea isn't to memorize, but to use that as a tool."

She believes it is important to practice like you play. "Oral argument really is about question and answer, and that give and take that goes on. My preparation is to mirror that as much as possible, and I've found that it's that process of thinking through the questions and answers that helps me get to the themes and the 'must make' points."

For a Supreme Court argument, she prepares by doing four to five moot courts. Then, the week before the argument, she is constantly on her feet with her team. For the M&G argument analyzed below, she constantly practiced making her "must make" points. That can be challenging when justices are constantly interrupting you. During practice sessions, one member of her team had a checklist of points that Ho wanted to make and kept track of her success. Other members of her team would purposefully ask her questions that were not on the list, and Ho would practice answering the questions and pivoting to her "must make" points on the list. At the end of a session, the team would go over which points on the list were made and which ones weren't. Ho would continue to practice pivoting to make sure all her points were made.

Another benefit to moot court is that "By the time you're doing your moots, you've completely lived with the case. It can be hard to see it through new eyes at that point. The huge benefit of moots is that you have people come to them who've just read your brief, and maybe read only a few of the cases, which is how the judges will come to it, and you get to hear their questions and find out what they are thinking. That's invaluable, to me, getting that fresh take on your case." Finally, she continues to refine the bottom-line message that she begins her argument with because she wants to create interest in her argument by presenting something new.

> *Judges don't want you to just stand up at argument and repeat and regurgitate your brief.*
> —Allyson Ho

Insights for Oral Argument

Remember that WIN (the third principle of public speaking) means determining What Is the Need of the Audience), Ho explains how important this is. "Your audience is really smart, but you also have really busy judges with a lot on their plates. In your brief, you want to make it easy for them. You want to make it easy to read, easy to understand. I think an argument really puts a premium on truly doing the work to figure out, okay, what is this case really about? What does the judge really need to know to rule in my clients favor? Then discipline yourself to stick to that message."

One of the challenges of oral argument is trying to steer the conversation with the judges to the points you want to make. It takes discipline to be respectful, because you are eager to make your points, and the judges might interrupt you with questions that will take you away from your focus. Ho advises that you should not interrupt the judge. Also, when you give an answer and you are interrupted, you need to stop talking, "even if you suspect that you're being interrupted because you're just about to say something that would be really, really good. You have to stop and then look for other opportunities to come back and do that."

When opposing counsel speaks, Ho listens intently and watches the body language and facial expressions of the judges. She does not constantly write because she needs to stay focused on listening and observing. She remains disciplined and she only writes down things she may want to address in rebuttal in the form of a list. This discipline continues when she speaks during rebuttal and focuses only on what is most important, because she knows you are almost always going to have to cover more ground than there is time for.

How to Handle a Cold Bench

Appellate attorneys will tell you that there is nothing more troubling than a cold bench, a situation where the judges remain relatively quiet. It is unsettling because you want to get a conversation going and answer questions to persuade the judges why you should win. I asked Ho how she handles it. Her approach is to make a strong opening and then her "must make" points. After that, when the bench is quiet, she has the discipline to say, "I'm happy to answer any questions that you have. If not, I'll give back my time to the court." Ho adds that you have to be willing to sit down. If you don't exercise this discipline, your continued talking may raise concerns with the bench and lead the judges to think your path to victory is more complicated than it really is.

End Your Argument Strongly

We've heard Ho's view about the importance of starting with a strong bottom-line message, but she also believes in ending strong. "I also spend time on the last thing, but I don't want to get to wedded to that in case something happens during argument that requires that I be flexible. I have something in mind of what to say if the argument goes the way that I think it will."

11.3 BACKGROUND OF *M&G POLYMERS USA LLC V. TACKETT*

Now that we have the benefit of Ho's insights, let's look at the highlights of one of her arguments before the Supreme Court. Ho represented M&G Polymers USA, LLC (M&G), which had bought the Point Pleasant Polyester Plant in 2000 and entered a collective bargaining agreement (CBA) with the plant's employees. The CBA included language that retirees "will receive a full Company contribution towards the cost of health benefits." The CBA also included a general durational clause, not a specific one, stating that the employer would provide the "program" of healthcare benefits "for the duration of this Agreement." After the expiration of the CBA, M&G sought to require retirees to contribute to their health benefits.

The retirees sued M&G claiming that the CBA created a right to a lifetime of free healthcare benefits, and M&G had no right to now require them to contribute in order to get those benefits. M&G maintained that the provisions terminated when the CBA expired.

The federal circuits were in disagreement about how to resolve the issue when CBAs had general duration language or were silent about the duration of the vesting of healthcare benefits, as M&G's CBA was. The Sixth Circuit, where this case arose, ruled in favor of the retirees. It based its ruling on its precedent in a case called *Yard-Man*, which used inferences from the context of labor negotiations to determine the outcome of disputes in CBAs. It held that absent *specific* language to the contrary, M&G and the union would have intended that healthcare benefits for retirees in a CBA vest for life. The Sixth Circuit reasoned that retiree healthcare benefits were unlikely to be left up to future negotiations once a CBA expired as it did in this case. Most other circuits, however, rejected the *Yard-Man* inference and instead required some specific contract language to vest union retiree healthcare benefits for life.

Finally, whether you are in a trial court or an appellate court, it is often easier to create a story about a person (usually the plaintiff) than a large company because an individual's problems are more sympathetic than a big corporation's. Here, the retirees had the natural sympathy of the justices because they had been given free healthcare benefits and now were being told that they had to contribute to them when they had likely not set aside savings for such a significant and unexpected cost. Ho, knowing that stories are important no matter who you represent, had the tougher task than her opponent; nevertheless, she won.

As you read the transcript below, focus on Ho's skills in presenting her story and her persuasion skills instead of the intricacies of the legal points that are being made. Remember that the justices had the benefit of reviewing detailed briefs of these complex legal issues submitted by the attorneys—which you do not—and thus rightly assumed the attorneys would understand their questions. For now, just keep in mind that the important legal issue is that the Sixth Circuit—although it claimed to be applying ordinary contract principles—was really making assumptions that favored retirees over the employer when the language in a CBA did not specifically address whether retirees who received free healthcare benefits under one CBA would be entitled to free healthcare benefits under all future CBAs.

11.4 ALLYSON HO'S ARGUMENT

Bottom-Line Message

> **HO:** Thank you, Mr. Chief Justice, and may it please the Court:
>
> **A promise of unalterable, costly healthcare benefits should be negotiated at the bargaining table, not imposed at the courthouse**. In a series of cases, the Sixth Circuit has required courts to infer from contractual silence a promise of vested benefits.
>
> *JUSTICE GINSBURG: But the—we're dealing with a case where there isn't silence.*
>
> . . .

Ho knows that she is likely to get interrupted soon after she begins, as that is the custom of the justices. As a result, she wants to state her bottom-line message so the justices can filter the remainder of her argument through the lens of her bottom-line message. She is taking advantage of confirmation bias discussed in chapter 4.

A closer look at her bottom-line message reveals how powerful it is. As discussed in chapter 3, one requirement of a bottom-line message is that it be no more than one sentence. Also, remember from chapter 3 that the key to having a compelling story is that your bottom-line message must convey a human value so that your audience will care about what you are saying. The human value here is "fairness." Everyone, even a company, deserves to be treated fairly, and that is an important emotional truth that Ho evokes.

Let's look at how each word Ho uses highlights the importance of her theme of fairness. One of the most important things she does is to elevate a rather bland issue about a contract provision into one of a promise. Ever since we were children, we were taught the importance of not breaking a promise. But the promise Ho talks about is not just an ordinary promise, it is one that is "unalterable" and "costly." Ho has raised the stakes in the first five words she speaks to the court. Ho does not stop there. Not only are the terms of the promise very unforgiving, but the promise deals with one of the most serious issues in life, healthcare.

Notice also that Ho uses her bottom-line message to structure her story by using a comparison: the courthouse versus the bargaining table. She emphasizes to the Court that when the stakes of a promise are this high, the meaning of the promise should be understood by the two sides who made it and not by an impersonal distant courthouse with its own views.

Finally, Ho told me that she incorporates into her bottom-line message a principle that one of her mentors taught her: every word should push your argument and your point forward.

Be the Expert in the Room

JUSTICE SOTOMAYOR: Assume—assume that I find those words ["receiving a full company contribution"] ambiguous, you had a hearing. The district court had a hearing, and it didn't—I don't think the district court relied on a presumption. It relied on a bevy of evidence, including the fact that your company bought the predecessor company, assessing the health contributions at full value for retirees. Why wouldn't ordinary contract principles permit the district court to do exactly what it did here?

HO: Justice Sotomayor, I want to go back to—to the first part of your question which said, well, wasn't—wasn't there a trial here? And our position is that it never—it never should have gotten to that because the district judge initially, as a matter of law, looked at the contract language here, declined to apply *Yard-Man*, and said, I don't find a promise of vesting. On appeal, the Sixth Circuit said, we disagree. Under *Yard-Man*, there is at least an inference of vesting here and instructed the district judge to apply *Yard-Man* on remand, which the district judge did, and on page 20 of Petitioner's appendix, in the opinion on remand, the district judge says, "Those directives," meaning the Sixth Circuit's directions in *Yard-Man*, "require this court to reach the conclusion that the part that the plaintiffs here obtained vested benefits."

Here, Ho's knowledge of the facts wins the argument for her with the justice. She is so well prepared that she can cite the exact page of an appendix to support her position. Because of her preparation, she convinces the justice that that district court really did not apply ordinary contract principles, but was bound by the principles of *Yard-Man*. Your goal is to be the most knowledgeable person in the room on the case you are arguing. Here, Ho succeeds.

What Is the Need of Your Audience?

A little later in the argument, Justice Elena Kagan jumps in to discuss ordinary principles of contract interpretation.

JUSTICE KAGAN: Ms. Ho, I'm wondering if you would agree with this. . . . I think, [you] just agreed that we would use ordinary contract principles; is that right?

HO: Correct.

When one word is all that Ho needs to answer a question, she is not afraid to use it. However, when she senses that a justice might be misinterpreting her position, she politely but quickly explains her answer, just as she does in the next exchange. Remember from chapter 2 that one of the principles of public speaking is WIN (<u>W</u>hat <u>I</u>s the <u>N</u>eed of your audience)? Ho is always listening carefully so that she can fulfill the needs of the justices.

> *JUSTICE KAGAN: And if the agreement was ambiguous, we could take extrinsic evidence to clarify the terms of the agreement; is that correct?*
>
> **HO:** Objective extrinsic evidence, yes, that's correct.
>
> *JUSTICE KAGAN: Okay, so—*
>
> *JUSTICE SCALIA: You acknowledge that? See, I wouldn't acknowledge that if I were you.*
>
> **HO:** Well, Your Honor, I'm —
>
> *JUSTICE SCALIA: You don't believe in the parol evidence rule?*
>
> **HO:** Objective—objective extrinsic evidence, Your Honor, would be—in other words, admissible—admissible on a finding of ambiguity.
>
> *JUSTICE KAGAN: Custom, practice.*
>
> **HO:** But I—but I think it's important, Justice Kagan, if I may, to point out that in the Sixth Circuit, and I think this is one way in which what happened here departs from ordinary contract interpretation, is that in the Sixth Circuit, the inference applies of vesting based either on text or—
>
> *JUSTICE KAGAN: Yes, I hear you.*
>
> **HO:** —or extrinsic evidence.
>
> *JUSTICE KAGAN: Yes, I hear you. I was not getting you to agree with YardMan and I was not getting you to agree to the Sixth Circuit.*
>
> **HO:** Certainly, Your Honor.

Have a Conversation, Not an Argument, with the Court

The fourth principle of public speaking discussed in chapter 2 is to think in terms of having a conversation and not an argument during your hearing. Let's look at how Ho responds to Justice Kennedy's question and then the challenge from Justice Scalia.

> *JUSTICE KENNEDY: And the question—the principal question here is whether the YardMan presumption should have a—play a significant part in the interpretation of this contract, and you say no.*
>
> **HO:** Correct.
>
> *JUSTICE KENNEDY: And there would be—and presumably there would be—we could make that decision in remand so that we don't interpret this contract initially without— without the benefit of what the district court and—and the court of appeals would say without the YardMan presumption if you prevail.*

HO: Certainly, Your Honor.

JUSTICE SCALIA: Unless, of course, the YardMan presumption is normal contract interpretation. That is, you know, the court of appeals could be saying that when you look at the totality of the contract where the benefits are being given for, as payment for work, you get them if you've worked so many years, they increase when you've worked more years. Where that is the case, it is a reasonable assumption, call it a presumption if you like, that any promise to pay those benefits continues after the termination of the—of the union contract. In other words, I'm not sure that the court of appeals would agree that—that this presumption is contrary to normal contractual interpretation. I think the court of appeals would say that is normal contractual interpretation.

HO: Justice Scalia, I think there's—I think you're right that the Sixth Circuit would and has said that all it's doing in these cases is applying ordinary contract interpretation. **I think as Judge Sutton and others have pointed out, saying doesn't make it so**. And I think there can be no question when you look at the—when you look at the cases, and I think this case is a good example of the work that *Yard-Man* is doing. And *Yard-Man* itself, Justice Scalia, in a footnote in its opinion, acknowledges that ordinary contract interpretation rules apply with respect to interpreting the contract generally.

But with respect to the issue here, which is the duration of the contract, the Sixth Circuit itself in *Yard-Man* said that the normal "strictures," was the word used, doesn't apply. So I think at least as an initial matter, the Sixth Circuit did not conceive of this as ordinary contract interpretation and that it's really its own policybased rationales for why it's appropriate, in a sense, **to put a thumb on the scales here in favor of retiree**. But I think if you look at the rules, maybe that's the most clear way to see that it's not ordinary, is saying to courts you can look at text or extrinsic evidence.

That's not normal contract interpretation. To say to courts you can ignore a contract duration clause if it doesn't specifically refer to retiree healthcare benefits.

Notice that Ho is not arguing with Scalia, but having a conversation with him. She starts out by acknowledging the point he is making but then counters with a succinct theme: "saying doesn't make it so." She builds on her theme of fairness stated in her bottom-line message by pointing out that the Sixth Circuit's application of *Yard-Man* does not appear to be what it claims to be.

She then concludes her response with a wonderful metaphor to make her point. In chapter 3 we learned the importance of using descriptive language and comparisons to make your story come alive. Here, Ho states that the Sixth Circuit has "put a thumb on the scales" to favor retirees. It dove-tails with her bottom-line message of fairness. The scales of justice should treat everyone fairly, and here, the Sixth Circuit is unfairly favoring one side over the other. Notably, the Court used Ho's imagery in its written decision.

Finally, she employs the principle of WIN again. She knows the importance of the audience's needs and realizes she must give them persuasive facts and the correct legal reasoning to win. Ho is so well prepared that she quickly cites a footnote from the *Yard-Man* opinion that supports her legal argument.

Anticipating Your Opponent's Best Argument

Next, Justice Alito challenges Ho's bottom-line message.

> **JUSTICE ALITO:** *This is an **important** benefit and an **expensive** one. Why is it that in this collective bargaining agreement and apparently many others—I don't know whether the figure is 40 percent or whatever it is—there isn't anything explicit [language] one way or the other?*

> **HO:** I think—

> **JUSTICE ALITO:** *This certainly can't be something that didn't occur to the employer or to the union. **Why did they choose to leave it silent?** Why did they choose not to address it expressly?*

> **HO:** I think there—one could consider that they didn't express it directly or one could read the contract as saying there simply is no—**silence says there is no promise of vesting here, because that is an extraordinary obligation for a company to take on**.

Ho's bottom-line message at the beginning of her argument stated that the alleged promise was "unalterable" and "costly." Justice Alito confronts her directly and in essence asks, "Why would the parties not address such an expensive and important benefit?"

In chapter 3, we learned that your story has to tell the good, the bad, and the ugly. In that regard, you must see the weaknesses in your case and be prepared with a credible response. Here, Ho offers a simple response that supports her bottom-line message: the silence means that the promise was never made.

Listening Instead of Arguing

> **JUSTICE SCALIA:** *You know, the nice thing about a contract case of this sort is you can't feel bad about it. Whoever loses deserves to lose.*

(Laughter.)

> **JUSTICE SCALIA:** *I mean, this thing is obviously an important feature. Both sides knew it was left unaddressed, so, you know, whoever loses deserves to lose for casting this upon us when it could have been said very clearly in the contract. Such an important feature. So I hope we'll get it right, but, you know, I can't feel bad about it.*

(Laughter.)

JUSTICE BREYER: Well, you know, the workers who don't discover [until] they've been retired for five years and don't have any health benefits might feel a little bad about it.

HO: And—and Your Honor, I—I agree.

JUSTICE BREYER: I'm taking sides, but I want to—

(Laughter.)

JUSTICE BREYER: I mean, what I've listened to sort of drives me to the conclusion where you started, decide these things without any presumption, period. Ordinary contract. Go read the contract. Where it's ambiguous, Judge, ask them for extrinsic evidence if they want to present it. Decide it like any other case. I started there. Maybe I've heard something that should change my mind. I often do change it in oral argument, but I haven't yet.

HO: And—and—

JUSTICE SCALIA: He agrees with you, doesn't he? I mean, you're not going to argue that, are you?

HO: No, Your Honor.

JUSTICE BREYER: So you say just have us decide it, and in this case, I've read an awful lot that you may well lose.

HO: Well, your Honor. There's no disagreement that ordinary contract interpretation principles apply. I think the—the dispute is over, number one, how the Sixth Circuit applied them in this case, and it used the *Yard-Man* presumption, which we disagree with. But I think under—under either sort of—however much clarity is required in these contracts, I think in this case you only get to a promise of vested benefits by reverse engineering language elsewhere in the agreement that only highlights the lack of it where you would most expect to find it, and that ignores the contract expiration clause here, which makes clear it's a full company contribution during the term of the agreement. And if I may reserve the rest of my time for rebuttal.

CHIEF JUSTICE ROBERTS: Thank you, counsel.

Ho knows that to tell an effective story, you must accept the good, the bad and the ugly facts about your case. Here, Justice Scalia drives to the heart of the problem in the case. The parties are before the Court because their understanding of the vesting of healthcare benefits was not clearly drafted. Ho does not get defensive when Scalia says he doesn't feel sorry for either side. She listens carefully, correctly reads the temperament of the justices, and decides to let Scalia's admonition stand without a response.

She then decides to conclude with a forceful argument that the Sixth Circuit wrongly applied *Yard-Man*.

I asked Ho if she thought of responding to the laughter in the courtroom in response to the exchange between Justice Scalia and Breyer with a humorous comment of her own. Ho explained that what was going through her mind was that Justice Scalia does not have any equal in terms of his ability in oral argument to deliver a zinger or to make a point. "I thought any attempt on my part to respond or whatever, I just thought this is just a moment and it's a priceless Justice Scalia moment. I'm just going to let that moment be." Knowing your limitations is important. "I'm sure there are other advocates who would have been able to come up with a good zinger. That's just not my style. I knew I wouldn't be able to parry in that fight. Let it be."

11.5 BOTTOM-LINE MESSAGE OF OPPOSING COUNSEL

Julia Clark argued on behalf of the respondent retirees. She is an excellent attorney, but her bottom-line message was not nearly as persuasive as Ho's. Here is how she began her argument.

> **CLARK:** Mr. Chief Justice, and may it please the Court: As the Court has so aptly noted, this is a contract dispute, and our argument is simply that contract disputes relating to retiree health benefits should be decided like every other dispute under a collective bargaining agreement. To determine what the parties intended without applying any presumptions—
>
> *JUSTICE BREYER: Isn't that what Justice Scalia believes? . . .*

Unlike Ho's bottom-line message that emphasizes fairness, Clark's bottom-line message does not convey a human value that makes you care about her case. She really had the factual advantage over Ho in that she represented everyday people (whereas Ho represented a large company) who were expecting the continuation of free healthcare benefits that had already been given to them and suddenly found that their expectation did not meet reality.

Instead of evoking a human value, Clark matter-of-factly stated that the case was about contract interpretation.

11.6 REBUTTAL ARGUMENT

The Rule of Three

> **HO:** Thank you, Mr. Chief Justice. **Three points**: First, I think at a minimum we're not hearing a lot here today defending YardMan. I think there can be little serious question that *Yard-Man* infected every aspect of the proceedings below. Indeed, it was dispositive. So I think at—at a minimum we're entitled to—to a vacatur and remand for ordinary contract principles to be applied. We think that requiring

clarity is consistent with those principles, but even as a matter of sort of what—what Respondent has suggested in terms of reasonably susceptible, the standard that Justice Sotomayor mentions, I think it will be important if this Court remands for consideration of ordinary contract interpretation, that it's clear that what the Sixth Circuit has been doing under that banner is anything but; that looking at putting text on a par with extrinsic evidence is not ordinary contract interpretation; that ignoring contract expiration clauses, unless they specifically reference healthcare benefits, is not ordinary.

Ho believes in the Rule of Three discussed throughout this book. She wanted to open her rebuttal argument with a forceful argument, and she sums her entire presentation up into three points. Notice that she explicitly tells the justices that she is going to make three points at the outset. This gives her some breathing room to make the points because most panels out of deference are going to allow you to make three quick points. If she had said she had five points or started rambling, she would have been quickly interrupted.

Ho Ends Strong

HO: So at a minimum we believe that we're entitled to a vacatur and remand for the Court of Appeals to apply proper principles of contract interpretation in the first instance. If there are no further questions?

CHIEF JUSTICE ROBERTS: *Thank you, counsel. The case is submitted.*

As we learned in chapter 3, you need a story that ends strong. Ho forcefully argues her best point. It is such a good argument that when the court made its decision, it did exactly what she wanted and ruled in her favor 9-0.

11.7 COURT'S RULING

The court remanded the case to the Sixth Circuit and instructed it to apply ordinary contract principles to resolve the dispute. In its ruling, the Court echoed Ho's point in oral argument that *Yard-Man* violates ordinary contract principles "by placing a thumb on the scale in favor of vested retiree benefits in all collective bargaining agreements." The Court went on to say, "that rule has no basis in ordinary principles of contract law." The Court further explained that the Sixth Circuit "failed even to consider the traditional principle that courts should not construe ambiguous writings to create lifetime promises." Again, this echoed the bottom-line message that Ho set forth at the outset of her argument: "A promise of unalterable, costly healthcare benefits should be negotiated at the bargaining table, not imposed at the courthouse."

11.8 SPEAKING STYLE AT ORAL ARGUMENT

The audio of Ho's oral argument can be found on this book's website (www .winningatpersuasion.com). Below are comments that reference the time stamps of the audio.

> [0:03] Ho begins by speaking with a confident and calm voice, which she maintains throughout the argument. This tone strikes the perfect balance for persuasion. In short, Ho exudes reasonableness. She begins by delivering her bottom-line message. Notice how she emphasizes the key words in her message. Instead of speaking too quickly, she speaks in measured tones. Like all great public speakers, she is ready to persuade as soon as she begins. She doesn't spend the first minute stumbling over her words or trying to speak slower because she has started off too fast due to nervous energy. Even if you listen really carefully, you cannot detect any nervousness. She projects complete confidence.

> [0:33] Ho has WIN in mind. As soon as a justice interrupts her, she immediately stops speaking and starts listening intently. She knows the argument is not about her but about answering the justices' questions.

On top of this, she emphasizes key words in her sentences, varies the pace and volume of her voice, and pauses for dramatic effect before an important word or phrase. All of this provides variety and indicates to the listener what is important. Likewise, listen to the justices. They have mastered these skills also. They make their questions interesting and provide gravitas for them by the way they emphasize important words and pause for dramatic effect.

> [2:11] Even when she gets a very tough and pointed question, there is no fear in her voice or hesitation in her response. She quickly and thoughtfully responds with an answer to Justice Sotomayor's question.

As you listen to the entire argument, it is clear that Ho is having a conversation with the Court and not an argument. When you are having a conversation, there is always the chance you can convince the person with whom you are speaking. When it devolves into an argument, your chances are over. It is abundantly clear from the tone of voice in the justices' questions that they respect Ho's presentation and the conversation they are having.

> [4:10] This is one of the only times Ho interrupts a justice, and she asserts herself to tell Justice Kagan that the Sixth Circuit departed from ordinary contract interpretation. But notice that Ho does it very respectfully, even asking, "If I may," and then gives a very short explanation. Her decision was perfect because Justice Kagan responds appreciatively, "Yes, I hear you."

Just as important, you will notice that Ho listens intently to the justices' questions. Not only does she directly answer each question, she resists the urge that most people would have to interrupt the justice so that they can argue a point more forcefully. Likewise, whenever a justice interrupts her, she quickly stops and lets the justice make their point.

[7:05] Ho gets asked a very pointed question suggesting that her opponent's position is correct. Listen to how well Ho delivers her response. She employs all the techniques of CPRs discussed in chapter 7. She changes the pace, pitch, and volume of her voice. She pauses for effect and repeats key words for emphasis. Finally, she stresses important words for emphasis.

[11:40] Ho maintains her conversational style by responding to a question from Justice Sotomayor, not with an emotional response, but by saying "I respectfully disagree for two principle reasons." Everyone has time to listen to a couple of good reasons for a disagreement. Ho's tone and words are the perfect signal to encourage the justice to be engaged during her short response.

Summary of Ho's Oral Argument and Style

1. Ho started strong with a powerful bottom-line message.
2. Her tone of voice exuded reasonableness.
3. She conveyed a human value in her bottom-line message: fairness.
4. Through preparation, Ho was the expert in the room on her case.
5. Ho followed the principle of WIN.
6. Ho had conversations with the court, not arguments.
7. Ho anticipated her opponent's best argument and had a credible response.
8. Ho listened intently.
9. Ho began her rebuttal argument using the Rule of Three.
10. She ended strong.
11. Her pace was deliberate and easy to follow.
12. She employed the techniques of CPRs from chapter 7: changing the pace, pitch, and volume of her voice; pausing for effect; repeating important words for emphasis; and stressing key words.

SUGGESTED ADDITIONAL READING

1. *Making Your Case: The Art of Persuading Judges*, Bryan Garner and Antonin Scalia (Thomson/West, 2008). Ho is a fan of all of Garner and Scalia's books. I believe this is one of their best.

CHAPTER CHECKLIST

Ho's Insights for Oral Advocacy

1. Ho had to battle to overcome her fear of public speaking. She believes there is no substitute for practice and getting your feet wet in a variety of circumstances, whether they are arguments or public speaking events.

2. If you have an upcoming hearing, relentless practice will go a long way toward building your confidence. Also, there is no substitute for the experience gained from doing several moot courts.

3. The biggest mistake that attorneys make at oral argument is that they don't listen. That is, attorneys get too caught up in their points and the arguments they want to make, and they don't listen to the questions being asked or observe the body language or facial expressions of the judge.

4. Remember that you are an advocate; you're there for the judges. You're there to answer their questions, to address their concerns. You can't do that if you're just so wrapped up in your own points and your own agenda.

5. Ho is a big believer in the Rule of Three. She thinks it is something our brains really relate to. Also, "If you get up and say, 'I just want to hit three quick points,' you're much likelier to be able to get that out."

6. The key to her success—and yours—is her passion for boiling down all the facts of a case to a winning message. She instructs that when you first get a case, learn "like a sponge" everything about the statutes, regulations, case law, and facts. Then, you need to think through it to "articulate a problem or a solution or a theme that just breaks it open."

7. Ho strives to find the story at the heart of every case and to tell it as authentically and as persuasively possible.

8. The key to finding your oral advocacy style is not feeling like you have to fit yourself into any particular mode. Be who you are and find out what works through trial and error and by observing others and deciding what might work for you.

9. "You should think about your advocacy in terms of being an officer of the court and trying to work with the court to get to a result that's right on the law, right on the facts, and makes sense in the mine-run of cases."

10. To prepare for an oral argument, Ho does the following: (1) reads everything about the law and facts of the case; (2) creates a running list of questions that she thinks the judges will ask and the answers she will give; (3) thinks about a bottom-line message; (4) has a moot court (four or five if her argument is

before the Supreme Court); and (5) practices her pivot phrases so she can transition to her "must make" points.

11. At oral argument, Ho relates that the key is to listen. Your audience is really smart, but judges are very busy. Make it easy for them. Put a premium on helping them figure out your case and telling them what they need to know to rule in your favor.

12. When opposing counsel speaks at oral argument, Ho listens intently and watches the body language and facial expressions of the judges. She does not constantly write because she needs to stay focused on listening and observing.

13. If you have a cold bench where the judges are not asking questions, make your points and have the discipline to sit down.

14. End your argument strongly.

15. For a summary of Ho's oral argument and style, see the text box at the end of this chapter, right before the Chapter Checklist.

CHAPTER TWELVE

Analysis of Great Speeches on Video

"Cancer can take away all my physical abilities, it cannot touch my mind, it cannot touch my heart, and it cannot touch my soul."—*Jim Valvano,* college basketball coach and broadcaster

As discussed in previous chapters, you need to watch as many lawyers as you can in court, as well as other public speakers in other settings. Videos are also another great way to learn. The best place to watch videos of trials is Courtroom View Network, and you can watch many oral arguments on YouTube (e.g., search "California Supreme Court oral arguments" on YouTube).

As our journey ends, I hope the preceding chapters have inspired you to become a better public speaker and given you the tools for how to do it. I want to conclude with brief examinations of some outstanding speeches from three non-lawyers who execute the techniques discussed in this book at a very high level. The speeches are by Bill Gates, David Christian, and Jim Valvano.

As I said at the beginning of this book and as I remind you once again near its conclusion, always be true to yourself. Observe public speakers and decide what you like and don't like. Through trial and error, incorporate what works well for you so that you can develop the greatness within you that already exists.

12.1 BILL GATES — "THE NEXT OUTBREAK: WE ARE NOT READY"

In 2015, Bill Gates gave an eight-minute TED Talk, "The Next Outbreak: We Are Not Ready." [www.winningatpersuasion.com.] Not only has it become very popular since early 2020, when the Coronavirus surprised America, but it also provides a wonderful study for public speaking. Let's focus on his use of visual aids, his bottom-line message, the Rule of Three, and eye contact.

> **CHAPTER ROAD MAP**
>
> - Learn why Bill Gates's visual aids were so persuasive and memorable.
> - Recognize how to make the complicated simple through the use of visual aids and the right metaphors.
> - Learn by watching and learning from the best speech I have ever seen.

First, he does not rely just on a PowerPoint for visual aids. In fact, he makes a dramatic entrance to his speech as he walks on stage with a hand truck loaded with metal cylinder cannisters. He immediately captures everyone's attention, because the audience wants to know why he brought the cannisters out and, more importantly, what's in them. He quickly tells us.

When he was a child, the disaster his family worried about most was a nuclear attack. If it came, people were supposed to go into their basements and live there while surviving off the food and water contained in the barrels that were stored there. As he talks about the barrels, he shows a picture of one of them on the projection screen so that everyone in the audience can see one up close. He then warns that the greatest global catastrophe risk we face today is "not this"—as he shows a picture of a nuclear explosion—"but this"—as he shows a picture of a 3-D model of the influenza virus. He is actually using the pictures to speak for him, rather than using them to supplement what he is saying.

Also, notice that in the first 39 seconds of his talk, he has used actual barrels, a picture of a barrel, a picture of a nuclear explosion, and a picture of a virus. They are not slides filled with statistics and text: they are powerful images that complement what he is saying, and in two instances they are a substitute for his words. He then states his bottom-line message: "If anything kills over 10 million people in the next few decades, it's most likely to be a highly infectious virus rather than a war. Not missiles, but microbes." Notice the simplicity and use of alliteration within "Not missiles, but microbes." He then follows this with a slide with text in large font that says, "We Are Not Ready for the Next Epidemic." He uses a minimum number of words on the remainder of his slides—often three or less. When he does use more than three words, he highlights the most important ones in a different color. In the following example, I have bolded where Gates used a different color: "The fact these elements are missing is a **Global failure**."

He then uses the Rule of Three to explain the three reasons—not the four, six, or nine—for why Ebola did not spread more. Gates explained that (1) there were heroic health workers, (2) Ebola is not spread through the air, and (3) by the time you are contagious, you are bedridden.

Gates continues to use the Rule of Three to group ideas throughout his speech. He explains that it would not be too hard to build a good response system to a future epidemic because (1) we have the benefit of cell phones to get information to and from people, (2) we have satellite maps so that we can track where people are moving, and (3) we have advances in biology to create a vaccine to combat the virus. He further explains that we need to prepare for this like the military does for war by having (1) a full-time response team, (2) a reserve response team, and (3) war games that are run.

At the end of his talk he breaks the Rule of Three and summarizes five steps that need to be taken. If you are going to break the Rule of Three—which is fine on occasion—using five as the number of your ideas is not a bad number at all.

The one criticism of the eight-minute talk I have is that Gates does not make very good eye contact with the audience; instead, he spends a lot of time looking up at a monitor in front of him. It appears that the monitor has his current slide and a preview of his next slide on it like PowerPoint would in presenter mode. If he knew his presentation better and made better eye contact, he could have connected with his audience even more.

12.2 DAVID CHRISTIAN — "THE HISTORY OF OUR WORLD IN 18 MINUTES"

David Christian is a historian. The topic of his TED Talk in 2011 was "The History of Our World in 18 Minutes." [www.winningatpersuasion.com.]

This video shows how to make the complicated simple. It is not easy to explain the history of the universe. But Christian does so by using a very powerful visual aid. He starts his speech with a video that shows, in reverse, the process of breaking an egg and scrambling it. Billy Collins, the former poet laureate of the United States, said that when poets tackle a large topic, they use an image as a point of entry to explain that topic. Likewise, Christian uses the egg video and hopes that the audience will "feel slightly uneasy" as they watch it.

This video is a springboard for his explanation of the second law of thermodynamics: "the general tendency of the universe is to move from order and structure to lack of order, lack of structure—in fact, to mush." Christian explains that the puzzle that he wants to solve for the remainder of his speech is how can the universe create something as special and complex as Earth in spite of the second law of thermodynamics. The answer is the "Goldilocks conditions." Human life on Earth was created because the universe can occasionally create complexity with great difficulty when the conditions are just right. He takes the audience back 13.7 billion years and then whisks them to the present to explain the history of human life, its complexity, and its fragility.

Many of the slides and animations are more sophisticated than we would need for most of our cases in a courtroom, and they are the result of complicated graphics design, but they can inspire you to make slides that will make the complicated simple, even with the tools that you have. Moreover, his simple slides are easy to duplicate. He uses a slide that is totally black to symbolize the void at the beginning of the universe. At the 7:38 time-remaining mark, he uses a simple slide with very large font for the title and three large numbers for his list to explain the Goldilocks conditions for life.

In addition, notice Christian's very effective gestures. His hands are never in the fig leaf position or behind his back. Christian makes full use of the gesture strike zone. At the 10:50 time-remaining mark, he talks about stars forming and he uses both of his arms to demonstrate how elements swirl around to form them. At the 10:14 mark he snaps his fingers to show the energy needed to generate further complexity by the universe. At the 7:13 time-remaining mark he uses both arms in an expanding gesture as he talks about the "huge oceans." His speech would have been much more reserved and less interesting if both hands had been behind his back or in any of the other unacceptable positions that were examined in chapter 7.

Did you notice what position his hands were in between gestures? Most likely not, because very few people ever notice where a speaker's hands are when they are not gesturing. However, if your focus were to see what he was doing, you would notice that occasionally he has his left hand on his hip [7:38 time-remaining mark], oftentimes he has both hands extended forward as if he were going to catch a basketball [7:24], and sometimes he has his hands above his waist with the fingertips touching the fingertips of the other hand [7:15]. All of these positions look comfortable for Christian and allow him to be ready for his next gesture.

Finally, look at the simple language he uses ("stuff," "things," "bam," and "Goldilocks") to explain very complicated ideas. Whenever he gets the chance, he simplifies language. He refers to the second law of thermodynamics as the "general tendency of the universe to move from order and structure . . . to mush." If you research the second law of thermodynamics, you will find so many multi-syllabic words in its definition that you won't even be able to begin to understand it.

The next time you are in court, make an effort to use words that anyone can understand. You will find that your effort to make the complicated simple will force you to know your presentation better and explain it more persuasively.

12.3 JIM VALVANO — ACCEPTANCE SPEECH FOR THE ARTHUR ASHE COURAGE AWARD

Jim Valvano was a point guard for Rutgers University from 1964-1967 and head coach of the men's basketball team at North Carolina State University from 1980–1990. He is best remembered for taking the team on one of the most improbable runs in NCAA tournament history when his team won the 1983 NCAA Championship. It was one of the greatest upsets in sports. As seen on live television, one of the most iconic moments of the win was when the exuberant Valvano ran around the court desperately looking for someone to hug in order to celebrate.

Not long after he ended his coaching career, he was struck with terminal cancer and gave an acceptance speech for winning the Arthur Ashe Courage Award, on March 3, 1993 [www.winningatpersuasion.com].

Imagine if you had only 10 minutes to summarize what your life is about. Could you do it? Where would you start? Would you use notes? In 10 minutes, Valvano gives one of the best public speeches. He speaks from the heart to persuade, he uses the Rule of Three, and he does not use notes.

As an exercise, watch the speech and write down every time Valvano uses the Rule of Three, and then look for the answers in the next paragraphs as we analyze his speech.

First, he tells the audience that he doesn't have any cue cards to speak from. Now, the audience knows that he is going to speak from his heart. Then he says, "Time is very precious to me, I don't know how much I have left." That is a powerful lightning bolt (as was discussed in chapter 3) with which to capture your audience's attention. He then foreshadows that at the end of the speech he will have something important to announce.

The first time he uses the Rule of Three is when he shares that he is an emotional person because he was raised in a family where "We hug, we kiss, we love." [2:15]. He then says that there are three things we should do every day: (1) laugh, (2) think, spend some time in thought, and (3) have your emotions bring yourself to tears, whether it is happiness or joy [2:25]. He then pivots to talk about his basketball career as both a player and a coach. He says that there are three things that are important to keep in mind as you live your life. You need to think about "where you started, where you are, and where you are going to be" [3:23]. Notice Valvano's eye contact. He is looking from left to right in a wide area to make sure everyone is included. For this particular segment, he uses the chop gesture with both hands as he moves from his right side to his left to emphasize the three different points he is making.

He then shows his vulnerability by laughing at himself as he recalls how he once tried to imitate Vince Lombardi by giving one of Lombardi's speeches to the Rutgers' basketball team in the locker room before the first game he ever coached. By showing vulnerability, and because we have all been embarrassed, he connects with his audience and draws them further into his story.

Valvano wanted to imitate Lombardi, who had motivated his team when he burst into the locker room of the then hapless Green Bay Packers and told them that they would win if they kept only three things in mind: (1) their religion, (2) their family, and (3) the Green Bay Packers.

Valvano was going to give this same speech to his team, except he was going to substitute Rutgers basketball for the Green Bay Packers. When it came time for him to give his speech, he burst into the locker room just moments before the game but fell down as he opened the doors. Then, he forgot to adjust Lombardi's speech, and told the team that all they needed to do was to think about their family, their religion, and the Green Bay Packers.

Valvano then returns to his main themes and explains how you get from where you are to where you want to be [6:41]: "You have to have an enthusiasm for life, you have to have a dream, and you have to be willing to work for it."

One of the best examples I have ever seen of speaking from the heart to persuade comes at 7:05, where he is talking about the support of his family members who are in the audience, when a message flashes on a screen to warn him that he has 30 seconds left. Most people would hurry up and end their speech. But Valvano knows that he has something important to say, that he owns the moment, and that no one is going to take it away from him. He gets a huge laugh when he tells the video person, "*A Finabla*," which means "Go to Hell."

He then signals to the audience that he is going to wrap up his speech. But before he does, he circles back to the three important things we should do each day. He urges his audience to enjoy their lives and the precious moments that they have. Valvano knows that he's giving an oral speech and not a written handout. So, he wants to remind the audience of the three things they should do each day so they will stick with them. He reminds them to laugh, think, and cry, but then he adds credibility to what he is saying by reciting a quote from a famous person, Ralph Waldo Emerson: "Nothing great can be accomplished without enthusiasm." He adds to that by advising "keep your dreams alive in spite of whatever problems you have."

He then concludes by talking about his third important thing to keep in mind as you live your life, which is to think about where you are going. He uses a transition by saying that he knows where he is now, and wants to talk about what he wants for the future [8:18]. He brings in facts to support what he wants to do next. He instructs that 500,000 people will die from cancer this year, but that the funding has been neglected. He says that the money may not save his life, but it may save his children's lives or someone that you love. He then announces what he foreshadowed at the beginning of his speech, that ESPN is going to partner with him to start the Jimmy V Foundation for cancer research. He uses the Rule of Three again to urge people to donate so that others "might survive, might prosper, and might actually be cured" [9:50]. Again, Valvano shows his vulnerability by acknowledging that the money won't come in time to help him, but that it will help others.

He then ends strong by using one last Rule of Three [10:34]. He proclaims that "cancer can take away all my physical abilities, it cannot touch my mind, it

---

Valvano's use of the Rule of Three

1. He comes from a family where "We hug, we kiss, we love."

2. Each day you should laugh, think, and cry for joy.

3. In your life, think about "where you started, where you are, and where you are going to be."

4. To achieve a goal, "You have to have an enthusiasm for life, you have to have a dream, and you have to be willing to work for it."

5. Donate to Jimmy V Foundation so that others "might survive, might prosper, and might actually be cured."

6. "Cancer can take away all my physical abilities, it cannot touch my mind, it cannot touch my heart, and it cannot touch my soul."

---

cannot touch my heart, and it cannot touch my soul." Notice also that he uses anaphora, the repetition of the same word or phrase.

Valvano is also inspiring because of how he spoke from his heart to persuade. He was so ill during and leading up to when he gave the speech that he was constantly vomiting on the flight he took there that day. You will also notice that he was so weak that he had to be helped on and off the stage.

He also did not give a memorized speech. He spoke about ideas and he used the Rule of Three to frame them. At your next hearing, you could frame your story by telling the judge, "Your honor, let me tell you where we began, where we are now, and where we will be."

Valvano also told a story, one that included his upbringing, his career, and what he was going through in his battle with cancer. His gestures added to his speech. He did not grab the podium, but instead freely used his hands in the gesture strike zone (discussed in chapter 7).

He varied his voice. He used pauses for important points and emphasized key words in phrases. Finally, he started strong to capture the audience's attention and he ended the same way.

The one thing his speech did not have was visual aids. He did not need them, because he spoke so powerfully from his heart that the audience held onto his every word. However, think for a moment about what you have learned from this book and decide what images you would suggest for Valvano to use if he had asked for your advice. There are many great possibilities.

If Valvano had wanted to use photos, here is what I would have suggested: a family photo when he was a child; a picture of him coaching the Rutgers' team as a 21-year-old; a photo of him running and looking for someone to hug after winning the NCAA tournament; a slide with the words "Think, Laugh, and Cry"; and, as he talked about the Jimmy V foundation, a picture of a doctor helping treat someone with cancer with the caption "Don't give up."

Whenever someone asks me "What is the best speech you have ever seen?", I always think of Valvano's speech. I think it is the perfect way to end this book, and I hope you found it as moving and as instructive as I did.

APPENDIX A

Basic Skills for Creating PowerPoint Slides

This section will explain some basic PowerPoint skills. Trying to teach computer software in a book is challenging and requires many pages with screenshots to take you through all of the necessary steps to master various skills. I have found that the best way to learn PowerPoint is at www.Lynda.com. Courses on it are now a part of Linkedin.com/learning, which can overwhelm you with its many offerings. Since Lynda.com has the best videos on how to learn PowerPoint, go instead to www.Lynda.com, where you can more easily access those videos. For a $30 monthly fee, you can join and have access to a wide variety of videos. You won't need to join for more than a month or two to learn all you need. Below are some basic tips to get you started.

Background and Text Color

The first thing you need to decide when creating a PowerPoint presentation is what will be the color of your background and the color of your text. When you open PowerPoint and click on "New" in the left-hand column, you are given several templates to choose from. None of them are very good. Plus, everyone is already using them. The good news is that it is easy to create one that will work and make your presentation stand out. Select Blank Presentation (see fig. 1).

Once you open Blank Presentation, there will be an interface that allows you to select a design template for all of your slides by clicking on the "Design" tab at the top. Once again, PowerPoint's template choices are not very good. Instead, let's create a better one.

Click on the Design tab at the top left of your screen (see fig. 2). Then, click on Format Background on the right side of your screen. Once you have done that, a side panel will open that will have several options (see fig. 3).

Once the side panel is open, you will see that the circle in front of Solid Fill is highlighted. Below it and to the right is an icon to select a background color. Once you click on that icon, a drop-down panel will open that allows you to select from a wide variety of colors. Hover your cursor over a box and then click to select a background color that will have a high contrast to the text color you will select next. Here are some examples: (1) a dark grey background with white text, (2) a white background with black or dark colored text, (3) a dark blue background with light blue text, and (4) a black background with white text.

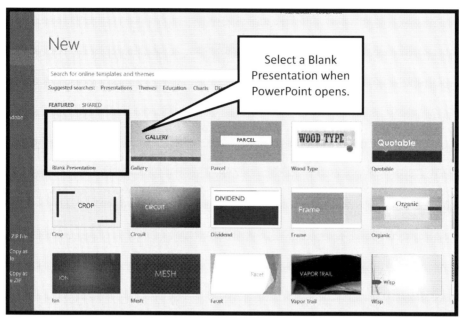

Figure 1. Select Blank Presentation.

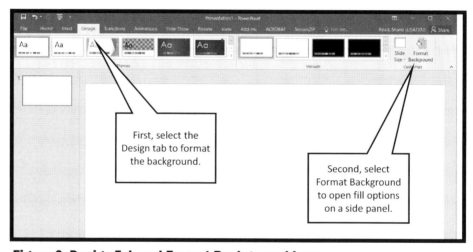

Figure 2. Design Tab and Format Background Icon.

Because this book is printed in black and white, color versions of these slides are available for you to see at www.winningatpersuasion.com. Some people like to use a black background with white text. I'm not a fan of that because the contrast is too much, but try one until you find one you like.

I often use a grey background with white, bolded text. However, my current favorite is a little more complicated: a dark grey background with a light orange text. It has a nice contrast and is different from what you see in most other PowerPoints, which makes my presentations unique. You can find a sample on

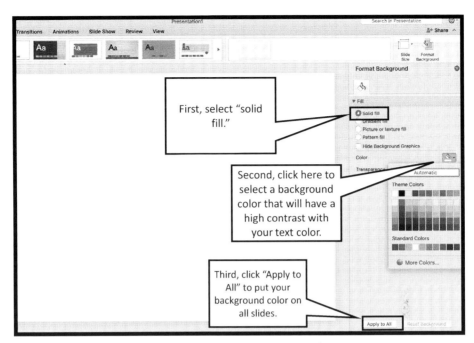

Figure 3. Side panel with Format Background Options.

this book's website, too. To match everything exactly, here are the details. The text is Calibri (Heading), font size 48, with a color model for the orange text of red(255), green(147) and blue(0) (see fig. 4). The color model of the grey background is red(51), green(50), and blue(56). To create a custom background color, when you select your color, there will be an option at the bottom of the box to select "More Colors." After you click "More Colors" you will be given the chance to enter the color properties you want as mentioned above in this paragraph.

Whether you use a PC or a Mac, the steps to select the background color are the same as shown above. However, to select the text color, PowerPoint has a different process for PCs and Macs. To match my text color for your text when using a PC, highlight your text, click on the font color from the tool bar at the top of the screen (see fig. 4), and click on More Colors. Once you select More Colors, a drop-down box will appear. Select Custom at the top of that box and the RGB Color Model will appear for you to input your color numbers (see fig. 5.). If you are using a Mac, you need to click on More Colors, then select the slider icon (see fig. 6). Once you have selected the slider icon, select RGB slider. Then, once the colors appear, input the numerical figures above for each color (see fig. 6).

Once you have selected your background and text colors, make sure your slides will look their best on the projection screen. Without going into the details, you are always better off using widescreen slides rather than the default size that

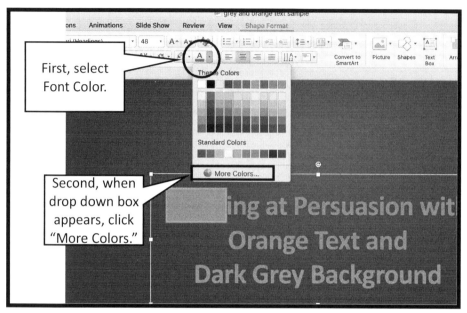

Figure 4. Selecting Text Color on a PC.

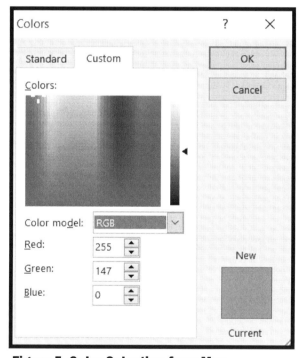

Figure 5. Color Selection for a Mac.

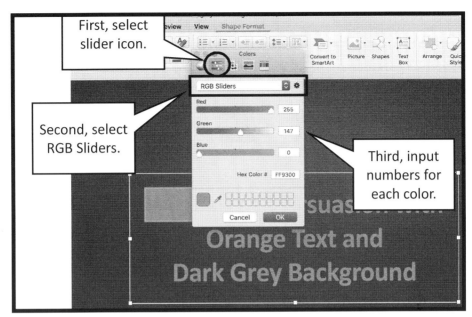

Figure 6. Selecting Text Color on a Mac.

PowerPoint selects. To fix this problem, click on the Design tab (see fig. 7) from the top menu bar, then look for "Slide Size" on the far right of the tool bar. Click on it and select "widescreen" from the drop-down choices (see fig. 8). This will make your slides look their best on almost all projection screens.

Font Size and Style

The next step is to decide on your font size and style. For the size, there is not much choice. For your text to be seen by a jury or judge in most courtrooms, the font size must be at least 32 points. However, I find that 44-point size works best. Not only is it the perfect size for a courtroom audience, but it is also large enough that it prevents you from cramming too much text on a slide. Depending on your slide, you should even use a larger font size than 44 points, if it looks good.

Then, select a font style (see fig. 9). Microsoft provides an overwhelming number of choices. Let me narrow them down and then give you my favorites, which are entirely subjective. Use whichever one you like best. Some popular and excellent choices are Arial Black, Book Antiqua, Calibri (Body), Franklin Gothic Demi, Gil Sans MT, Segoe UI Semi-bold, Tahoma, and Verdana. My favorite is Calibri (Body). While some come in boldface, I would boldface any font that you choose. The samples below have been bolded (see fig. 9). Use the same or at most two font styles throughout your PowerPoint.

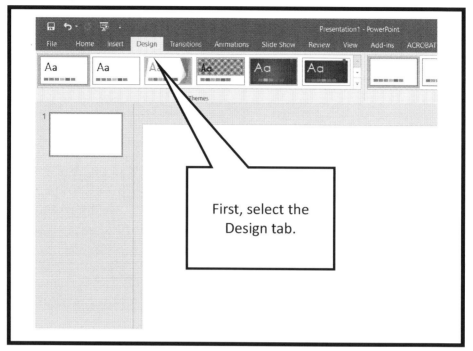

Figure 7. First Step for Creating Widescreen Slides.

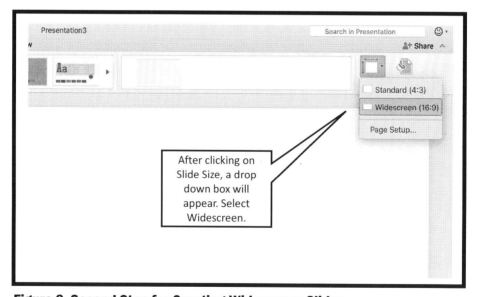

Figure 8. Second Step for Creating Widescreen Slides.

1. **Arial Black**
2. Book Antiqua
3. Calibri (Body).
4. **Franklin Gothic Demi**
5. **Gil Sans MT**
6. Segoe UI Semi-bold
7. **Tahoma**
8. **Verdana**

Figure 9. Selection of Font Styles.

WORKS CONSULTED

Chapter 1

1. Gilovich, T., V. H. Medvec, and K. Savitsky (2000). "The spotlight effect in social judgment: An egocentric bias in estimates of the salience of one's own actions and appearance" (PDF). *Journal of Personality and Social Psychology.* 78 (2): 211–222.

2. Kick (gokick.com). "Can Beta Blockers Really Reduce Performance Anxiety? We spoke with Yale Physician Dr. Robert Attaran to Find Out." https://www .gokick.com/blog/beta-blocker-tales/can-beta-blockers-really-reduce-performance-anxiety-spoke-yale-physician-dr-robert-attaran-find/.

3. Thaler, Richard, and Cass Sunstein. *Nudge: Improving Decisions About Health, and Happiness.* New York: Penguin, 2009.

4. Woods, Tiger. Quote from "Never say never: An oral history of Tiger Woods' magical fifth Masters' victory." Golfdigest.com. March 24, 2020.

Chapter 2

1. Spence, Gerry. *How to Argue and Win Every Time.* New York: St. Martin's, 1995. 47-48.

Chapter 3

1. Gottschall, Jonathan. *The Storytelling Animal: How Stories Make Us Human.* Boston: Mariner Books, 2013. 104-108.

2. Haven, Kendall. *Story Proof: The Science Behind the Startling Power of Story.* Westport, CT: Libraries Unlimited, 2007.

Chapter 4

1. Cialdini, Robert. *Pre-Suasion: A Revolutionary Way to Influence and Persuade.* New York: Simon and Schuster, 2018.

2. Kahneman, Daniel. *Thinking Fast and Slow.* New York: Farrar, Straus and Giroux, 2013.

3. Thaler, Richard and Cass Sunstein. *Nudge: Improving Decisions About Health, and Happiness.* New York: Penguin, 2009.

Chapter 6

1. Anderson, Chris. *TED Talks: The Official TED Guide to Public Speaking.* Boston: Mariner Books, 2017.

2. White, Ronald C. A. *Lincoln: A Biography.* New York: Random House, 2010.

3. For non-verbal communication studies, see Vrij, Aldert, Lucy Akehurst, Stavroula Soukara, and Ray Bull, "Detecting Deceit Via Analyses of Verbal and Nonverbal Behavior in Children and Adults," *Human Communication Research*, 30 (2004); Chesebro, Joseph L., "Effects of Teacher Clarity and Nonverbal Immediacy on Student Learning, Receiver Apprehension, and Affect," *Communication Education*, 52 (2003); and Riggio, Ronald E. and Robert S. Feldman (eds.), *Applications of Nonverbal Communication.* Mahwah, NJ: Erlbaum, 2005.

Chapter 7

1. "60 Hand Gestures and Their Meaning," scienceofpeople.com (last visited April 2021).

2. Holler, Judith and Geoffrey Beattie. *Gesture use in social interaction: how speakers' gestures can reflect listeners' thinking.* Second conference of the International Society of Gestures Study, 2007.

3. Humes, James C. *Speak Like Churchill, Stand Like Lincoln.* New York: Random House, 2002.

4. Lucas, Stephen E. *The Art of Public Speaking*, 9th ed. New York: McGraw Hill, 2007. 305-307.

5. Marsha Hunter, Brian K. Johnson, and Jami McKeon. *The Articulate Advocate: Persuasive Skills for Lawyers in Trials, Appeals, Arbitrations, and Motions*, New York: Crown King Books, 2016.

6. Mehrabian, A. *Silent messages: Implicit communication of emotions and attitudes.* Belmont, CA: Wadsworth, 1981. http://www.kaaj.com/psych/smorder .html.

7. Petrocelli, Daniel and Peter Knobler. *Triumph of Justice: The Final Judgment on the Simpson Saga.* New York: Crown Publishers, 1998.

8. The study on pointing was done by Allan Pease and discussed in his TEDtalk, which can be found here: https://www.youtube.com/watch?v=ZZZ 7k8cMA-4.

Chapter 8

1. Hunter, Marsha, Brian K. Johnson, and Jami McKeon. *The Articulate Advocate: Persuasive Skills for Lawyers in Trials, Appeals, Arbitrations, and Motions.* New York: Crown King Books, 2016.

Chapter 9

1. Aristotle. *On Rhetoric: A Theory of Civic Discourse.* Oxford: Oxford Univ. Press, 1991.

2. Humes, James C. *Speak Like Churchill, Stand Like Lincoln.* New York: Random House, 2002.

3. White, Ronald C. A. *Lincoln: A Biography.* New York: Random House, 2010.

ACKNOWLEDGMENTS

There are too many people to thank, but I want to mention a few. I am so grateful to Mark Lanier for literally sharing with me—and you—the very secrets that make him successful. He is unique in that regard. Almost every successful trial lawyer keeps those secrets very guarded. But Lanier has a generous spirit and believes there is plenty of success to go around and wants others to learn from him whatever they find helpful. I hope I have been able to help you through his generosity.

This book would not be complete without Allyson Ho's very generous participation. The truth is that trials are hard to come by and most of our opportunities for persuasion come in the form of hearings or oral arguments. Ho is at the top of a very elite field that practices before the United States Supreme Court. To be able to share her unique insights was a great privilege for me. She donated much time and effort to this book because she believed in helping others like her mentors had helped her, and for that I am very grateful.

In chapter 2, I state that knowing the What Is the Need of your audience (WIN) is a key principle of public speaking. It is also true for writing a book. First, you need a wonderful editor, who I have found in Tim Johnson. I am a decent writer, but he makes me look great and knows what readers want. You also need friends and colleagues to provide candid advice about the strengths and weaknesses of the drafts of the book. Vince Parrett is an outstanding lawyer and provided a wake-up call to me that set in motion a thorough rewriting of the entire book. When I first heard his feedback, it confirmed a nagging feeling that I had but had been unwilling to act on. I am very grateful for his honesty. Allison Schultz is an extremely smart person with tremendous judgment who gave me candid advice on every aspect of the book, and her insights are reflected throughout. It is a much better book thanks to all of her efforts.

Angela Dooley teaches presentation and persuasion skills on a national level and was a very helpful sounding board for many of the ideas in this book. Bryan Danilovich at Courtroom View Network (CVN) made chapter 10 come to life. Next to being in trial, there is no better way to learn persuasion skills than studying trials. Bryan and his team at CVN share my belief and produced the videos that make chapter 10 a truly unique learning experience.

I also want to thank two outstanding lawyers, Sarah Delaney and Braden Civins, who gave me the inspiration to write this book.

My adult daughter, Caroline, who truly has the writing talent in the family, provided expert advice and encouragement that only a daughter can when I needed it most. Finally, none of my books, and particularly this one, could have been written without the patience, support, and expertise of my wife, Linda. I am sure there were many times when she dreaded me saying, "What do you think about this idea in chapter __?" or "Does this make any sense to you?" But she never lost patience. Her feedback on everything from the original idea to write the book, its structure, and much more made this book far better than it would have been otherwise. But most of all she believed in me and this book. I don't feel right sharing the details of the moments of doubt I had and how she got me through them, but it is safe to say, it could not have been written without her loving support.

I always feel certain that each book I write will be my last but that never seems to happen. Not sure why. I only intended to write one book, *Winning at Trial*. What I do know is that I cannot help but be inspired by others who have excelled at whatever their skill is. It makes me think that I should do more. I don't want to get stuck on the OK plateau. We will see what comes next.

ABOUT THE AUTHOR[1]

Shane Read is the author of bestselling litigation textbooks such as *Turning Points at Trial* and *Winning at Deposition*. Two of his textbooks have won the Association of Continuing Legal Education's top honor for Professional Excellence. He is the only author to win this award twice. His textbooks have been adopted in law schools across the country and critically acclaimed by publications such as Bar Journals and Kirkus Reviews. In addition, his textbooks have been endorsed by judges, professors, a former U.S. Attorney General, a former U.S. Solicitor General, and past presidents of city, state and national trial lawyers' organizations such as IATL and ABOTA.

He has been an adjunct professor in trial advocacy since 1999 at Southern Methodist University's Dedman School of Law. He is also a faculty member of the National Institute of Trial Advocacy. He has also taught new and experienced lawyers throughout the United States, including training programs at the National Institute of Trial Advocacy's headquarters, the Department of Justice's National Advocacy Center, and state bars around the country.

He is a graduate of Yale University and the University of Texas School of Law. He began his legal career in 1989 at Akin Gump in Dallas, before joining the U.S. Attorney's Office in Washington, D.C., from 1992 to 1998. Since 1998, he has worked at the U.S. Attorney's Office in Dallas in both the civil and criminal sections. He has tried over 100 trials to verdict over the past 30 years and has served as lead counsel for 22 oral arguments before appellate courts.

For more information about the author or his books, go to www.shaneread.com.

---

[1]The views expressed in this book are solely those of the author and do not reflect the views of the Department of Justice.

INDEX

A

adrenaline, 8, 20–22, 123

Ali, Muhammad, 17

A. Lincoln (White), 166

alliteration, 49, 51, 170–171, 244

"Alumnus Football" (Rice), 9

analogies, 62–63, 210, 213

anaphora, 51, 170–171, 190, 204

Anderson, Chris, 114–115

Angelou, Maya, 32

apologies and eye contact, 112–113

arguments *versus* conversations, 36–37, 169, 233–234, 239–240

Aristotle, 163–166

Arthur Ashe Courage Award acceptance speech, 246–250

artists, stealing like, 27–28

art of memory, 116–119

asbestos. *See* talc powder trial

associative stage of learning, 38

assonance, 51, 168

assumptions. *See* confirmation bias

athletes' fear of failure, overcoming, 10–14, 15

attention span, 58, 80–81, 169

Atwood, Margaret, 45, 70

audience, 14–15, 82–83, 245

    See also emotional connection; judges; jurors; What Is the Need of the audience
        (WIN) question

authenticity of self, 12, 26–28, 31, 177–178, 218

autonomous stage of learning, 38–39

B

Baby Boomers, 82

baby powder trial. *See* talc powder trial

Bach, Richard, 40

Bacon, Francis, 73–74

Band on the Run (album), 172

Beattie, Geoffrey, 131

Beck, David, 62

judges
  being respectful to, 229
  eye contact with, 110–111
  feedback from, 39
  forgiving mistakes, 14–15
  needs of (WIN), 33–36
  remaining quiet, 229
  thanking, 57
  "Why should I care?" question, 43–44
  See also Ho, Allyson
jurors
  forgiving mistakes, 14–15
  generational differences in, 82–83
  inviting to solve mysteries, 81
  needs of (WIN), 33, 34
  thanking, 57
  visual aids for connecting with, 37
  See also emotional connection
Just Mercy, 29

K

Kendon, Adam, 132
key words, 140
Kiernan, David, 61, 62
Kim, Krystal, 95, 96
King, B. B., 154
Kleon, Austin, 27–28

L

Landry, Tom, 10
language. *See* descriptive language; metaphors
Lanier, Mark
  building trust, 80
  changing bad facts into good facts, 47–48, 179–180, 193
  checklist, 221–222
  courtroom style, 218
  on hearings *versus* trials, 43–44
  interview with, 175–181
  journals used by, 25
  jurors solving mystery with, 81
  as master trial lawyer, 175
  Vioxx trial, 61
  visual aids, 91–96
  See also DePuy hip implant case; talc powder trial

N

P

S

Made in the USA
Middletown, DE
24 March 2023

27033806R00170